Good Day!

Good Day!

THE PAUL HARVEY STORY

By Paul J. Batura

Since 1947
REGNERY
PUBLISHING, INC.
An Eagle Publishing Company • Washington, DC

ISBN 978-1-59698-156-0

The Library of Congress has catalogued the hardcover edition as follows:
Batura, Paul J.
  Good day! Paul Harvey's story / by Paul Batura.
    p. cm.
  ISBN 978-1-59698-101-0
  1. Harvey, Paul, 1918-2009. 2. Radio broadcasters—United States—Biography.
I. Title. II. Title: Paul Harvey's story.
  PN1991.4.H34B37 2009
  791.4402'8092—dc22
  [B]
  2009014422

Published in the United States by
Regnery Publishing, Inc.
One Massachusetts Avenue, NW
Washington, DC 20001
www.regnery.com

Manufactured in the United States of America
10 9 8 7 6 5 4 3 2 1

Books are available in quantity for promotional or premium use. Write to Director of Special Sales, Regnery Publishing, Inc., One Massachusetts Avenue NW, Washington, DC 20001, for information on discounts and terms or call (202) 216-0600.

Distributed to the trade by:
Perseus Distribution
387 Park Avenue South
New York, NY 10016

To Julie, whose love and beauty
light up our home.
She has turned one "good day" after another
into many wonderful years of life together.

Larry King: *Who is Paul Harvey? Is he a newsman? Is he a personality? Is he a raconteur? Is he a storyteller? Is he a pundit? Is he a commercial? Is he a salesman?*

Paul Harvey: *He's all of those things, and kind of a professional parade-watcher, who just can't wait to get up every morning...*

Larry King: *And why does he like so much telling us?*

Paul Harvey: *Probably, he's something of an exhibitionist. But, also, when we pray for guidance, and doors continue to open instead of close, a person comes to think of his job as an obligation, to enlighten and inform.*

Larry King: *So you're all of the above.*

Paul Harvey: *Probably some of each.*

—*Larry King Live*, CNN, January 30, 2003

Contents

Foreword

As a boy in a little town in Arkansas, if you had told me I would someday substitute for THE Paul Harvey on *Paul Harvey News and Comment*, I wouldn't have believed you. If you'd then said I'd write the introduction for the first biography ever written of Paul Harvey's life, I would've thought you were really pushing the edges of truth. I grew up listening to Paul Harvey—and never quit. When Paul Harvey came on, my fireman father would say, "Y'all be quiet. I want to hear Paul Harvey." Gee, he never told everyone in the room to be quiet so they could hear me! Tuning into Harvey's show became a life-long ritual. As a fledgling disc-jockey and radio announcer at age fourteen, I dreamed about meeting this gentle giant of the airwaves. Beyond the story of a life well-lived, *Good Day!* captures the essence of this late radio pioneer. Mr. Harvey embodied our common American ideals. He worked hard to achieve his dreams and encouraged us to do the same. He was not just the VOICE of America—he embodied the VIRTUES of America. He was a patriot, even when it was unpopular to love our country. He always looked for the best in his fellow man, confident we would live up to his belief in us. He loved his Creator, his family, and his country, and sought to serve them with his utmost—which he did until the day he went to be with his Lord. Radio has lost the voice of one of her founding fathers, but America bears his imprint in the essential decency he promoted and the legacy he left for us all, following the admonishment of a much earlier Paul in the Scriptures he so revered: "Finally, brothers, whatever is true, whatever is noble, whatever is right, whatever is pure, whatever is lovely, whatever is admirable—if anything is excellent or praisewor- thy—think about such things." Preserving the memory of the hope- ful broadcaster who shared the news of the day in a fresh, honest, and entertaining manner is even more important as our culture moves far- ther away from the virtues Paul Harvey held dear. In the years to come, our struggle will be figuring out how to explain the importance of Harvey's sunny, indomitable outlook to future generations. Paul J. Batura's *Good Day!* gives us an excellent place to start.

Mike Huckabee
April 2009

Taps at Reveille

In the warmth and fading light of the late winter Saturday afternoon, America's longest running and most popular broadcaster slowly and softly slipped away. Paul Harvey, a sunny man of Middle America who chased and reported stories from all over the world, was ninety years of age.

Though February 28, 2009 was a "good day" for the inhabitants of heaven, it was a sad day for those still on earth. Everybody knew it would happen; his passing was ultimately inevitable; but somehow, it was still startling. Maybe we were beginning to believe him when he said he'd go on forever.[1]

"We earn the sweet by-and-by, by how we deal with the messy here-and-now,"[2] Paul Harvey was fond of saying. Yet at the end, the ABC Radio commentator shielded his listeners from the unrelenting realities of his own life. Struggling with the consequences of chronic pneumonia along with a host of other ailments exacerbated by age, he still took to the air, broadcasting only days before his death at the Mayo Clinic in the Phoenix desert.[3]

His life was as deep and as wide as it was long.

To the millions of his listeners spanning seventy years of broadcasting, Paul Harvey's words were akin to a balm on a burn. His voice was settling and reassuring, with a laconic cadence as distinctive and intoxicating as it was soothing. "You can almost hear the amber waves of grain,"[4] as his longtime friend, actor, and comedian Danny Thomas once said about Paul's voice. Turning the dial during one of his programs was nearly impossible. He always left his listeners wanting a little more. Maybe that's how we all feel now that the golden voice has fallen silent.

To have met Paul Harvey was to have witnessed the walk and talk of a gentle and gracious spirit. Simple, sincere, and humble, there was no measure of braggadocio or posturing for position. He was comfortable in his own skin and unconcerned with labels, but very interested in truth—wherever it might lead.

He and his late wife Lynne were the closest thing to royalty the broadcasting business had. "My father and mother created from thin air what one day became radio and television news," Paul Harvey Aurandt Jr. said, hours after his father's passing. "So in the past year, an industry has lost its godparents and today millions have lost a friend."[5] As the writer Stephen Vincent Benet, on the occasion of F. Scott Fitzgerald's death, said, "You can take off your hats now, gentlemen, and I think perhaps you'd better."[6]

Chapter One

A Boy of Tulsa

Forty-four-year-old Harry Harrison Aurandt stepped out onto his front porch at 1014 East Fosteria Street[1] in Tulsa, Oklahoma. The light of the late summer morning was beginning to brighten the eastern sky. Clouds were scattered. Temperatures would soar to nearly 90 degrees by the day's end. The clatter of a car from the Tulsa Street Railway Company rolled by, ferrying area residents into the downtown business corridor. Bending down to pick up his copy of the *Tulsa Daily World*, Aurandt saw a two-tiered headline bringing news from across the Atlantic, "British Sweep Continues With Enemy in Hurried Retreat as Line Crumbles."[2] Just above the fold, news out of El Paso, Texas reported the death of 200 Mexicans at Pilar de Concho in a clash between the federal command of General Ernesto Garcia and Francisco Villa. In lighter news, Tulsa county roads expert E. B. Guthrey had grabbed headlines that morning for being the first person to drive a locally manufactured automobile up to the summit of Pike's Peak out west in Colorado Springs, Colorado. A local high-profile murder trial was ending, a conviction likely. Coverdale's, "The Popular Price Store," on Main Street, was advertising dress shirts for

50 cents, cotton blankets for $3.45, and women's fall suits ranging in price between $27.50 and $49.75. A car dealership at 316 East 2nd Street was highlighting a 1917 Studebaker for $500. An elegant 1917 Marmon touring car was listed for only $2,500.[3]

Walking back up the steps to the house, past the porch swing, Harry Aurandt was distracted. His adrenaline was high and his excitement was mounting. His beautiful wife of fifteen years, Anna Dagmar Aurandt, was resting inside the gray clapboard residence and would give birth to his only son by the day's end. Nobody knows if Harry took the time to turn the page of the paper on this particular Wednesday morning. If he had done so, he would surely have seen two items with almost prophetic relevance. Just under the heading "Daily Food" were printed the words of the prophet Jeremiah: "Call unto me and I will answer thee and shew thee great and mighty things, which thou knowest not."[4] The daily horoscope was even more prescient, "Children born on this day are likely to be clever and intelligent—but erratic and changeable."[5]

Later that evening, Paul Harvey Aurandt entered the world.

★   ★   ★

If a producer was casting the role of an old-time radio newsman who could hear and identify with the heartbeat of Middle America, care a little about a lot of things, appreciate the value of hard work, marvel at the eccentricities of mankind, admire the scrappy, and respect the wealthy—he probably would have scripted Tulsa, Oklahoma as his boyhood hometown. Established by the Muskogee Native American tribe in 1826, "Tallasi," meaning "old town,"[6] would prosper as a cattle town until the discovery of oil in 1901 transformed it into a "little New York," full of fortune seekers and home to a symphony, ballet, and opera. By the time Oklahoma entered the Union in

1907, the city of Tulsa boasted a population of just over 7,000 people.[7]

Paul Harvey Aurandt's birth in booming Tulsa on September 4, 1918 came at a tumultuous point in world history. The Spanish influenza pandemic was just beginning, destined to claim over 25 million lives in six short months, with well over a half a million of those in the United States.[8] After four years and 116,000 American deaths, World War I was on the verge of ending.[9] The Russian Empire was still reeling from its raucous and deadly revolution a year earlier. The United States Congress voted standard time zones into law,[10] and the House of Representatives passed an amendment allowing women to vote, which would lead to women's suffrage two years later.[11] Of less consequence but no less interest, baseball's Boston Red Sox would defeat Chicago's Cubs, claiming their last World Series title until 2004.[12] In addition to Aurandt, the "birth class of 1918" included such notables as evangelist Billy Graham, broadcasters Howard Cosell and Mike Wallace, future first lady Betty Ford, retail mogul Sam Walton, advice columnist Abigail Van Buren, baseball great Ted Williams, and entertainers Ella Fitzgerald and Art Carney.[13]

Paul's father, Harry H. Aurandt, was born on January 27, 1873 in Martinsburg, Pennsylvania. He was descended from John Aurandt who had arrived in the United States in 1753.[14] John served with George Washington's Army in the Revolutionary War, a fact the family embraced with great pride.[15] Harry was tall, handsome, resourceful, and considered by all accounts to be affable and gregarious—a friend to all. Aurandt would eventually find his way to Tulsa via career stops in Harrisburg City, Pennsylvania and Sedgwick City, Kansas. According to the 1900 U.S. Census records, Aurandt listed his occupation as a "Passenger Breakman" on the railroad.[16] Those same Census records appear to indicate that Harry was married once before, in

1893, to a woman named Elizabeth. They resided in Harrisburg, Pennsylvania and listed a daughter, Susan, six years of age.[17] It's not clear what became of either Elizabeth or Susan—or if Paul Harvey was even aware of his father having a first marriage.

By 1910, Aurandt was employed as a "Yard Master"[18] in Sedgwick City, a town in southern Kansas approximately 135 miles west of the Missouri line and just two counties north of the Oklahoma border.

Anna Dagmar Christensen was born in Denmark in 1883. She and her parents emigrated from Denmark in 1890, enduring a horrific storm at sea that seemed to foreshadow the challenges their strong and resilient Danish daughter would face in the years to come.[19]

She met and married Harry, a man nine years her senior, in Princeton, Missouri, a town along the Iowa border in 1907. By 1910, they had settled in Wichita, Kansas where they had a girl, Frances. Just prior to Paul's birth in 1918, the Aurandts relocated to Tulsa, Oklahoma for a job opportunity. Harry took a position as a secretary, a fairly common male occupation prior to World War II, in one of the hundreds of oil offices in town.[20] They quickly began putting down roots.

The Aurandt home was humble but neat, tidy, and more than adequate for a growing family of four. Two stories high, with an open-air porch and a balcony gracing its front exterior, it was ideally located just a block and a half from red-bricked Longfellow Elementary School that sat at 1249 East Fifth, and a few blocks from downtown Tulsa. The neighborhood was full of working class families; the Aurandts' immediate neighbors were a bookkeeper and a watchman for a local tool shop. Tulsa had grown up along class lines by income, profession, and race—and the neighborhoods reflected it.

Years later Paul would reflect, speaking in the third person, on the modest accommodations of his home as compared to many of his wealthy high school friends whose parents had found success in the oil fields and boardrooms of Tulsa.

"It was in that house that a well-meaning mother arranged a surprise birthday party when he was sixteen; invited his school friends, including delicate Mary Betty French without whom he was sure he could not live. He hated that party for revealing to her and them his house, so much more modest than theirs."[21]

Was the Aurandt family poor? "Anyone who grew up in the terrible Depression still feels a little insecure," he would offer in retrospect. "It left terrible scars. As kids, we cried if we lost a dime in the grass on the way to the store."[22] Taking off the rose-colored glasses, Harvey would eventually shoot straight. "We *were* poor, but we didn't know it," he remembered. "There were no government bureaus in those days presuming to determine where poorness begins and ends, but I don't remember ever being hungry."[23]

When Paul was two years old, Harry Harrison Aurandt transitioned from his position as a secretary in a Tulsa oil office to the more prominent role of Secretary and Purchasing Agent to James Moore Adkison, Tulsa's Commissioner of Police and Fire.[24] By 1921, the 47-year-old father of two had found favor and friendship in his new department and had settled into the rhythm of Commissioner Adkison's busy but predictable routine at the downtown Police Headquarters.

The political and social climate of the city had been heating up for several years by the time Paul's father started his job. Being on the inside, Harry Aurandt would have been aware of rising tensions, overheard unsettling conversations, fielded urgent phone calls, and seen confidential reports. It was a sensitive time, and the simmering dysfunction was becoming obvious. Burglaries, hold-ups, and violent racial disputes between whites and blacks were rising. A general sense of lawlessness and civil disorder began creeping into the daily fabric of life. Tulsa was living up to its billing as a Wild West town. But Harry Aurandt could not have conceived how soon the simmering cauldron of crime would boil over in the most terrifying manner imaginable.

CHAPTER TWO

Riot

The fabric and composition of America's citizenry was changing. The end of the first World War dramatically accelerated the pace and rate of immigration to the shores of the United States. On average, over 2,000 individuals were arriving in the country's ports each day.[1] While the last half of the nineteenth century brought predominantly English, Irish, and Scottish arrivals, the crammed ships were now carrying a much more diverse mix of men, women, and children. The entire world had now warmed to the promise and hope of America. They came in droves. Germans, Italians, Russian Jews, Poles, and Czechoslovakians would clear Customs in record numbers.[2]

For many of those already established in the United States, the infusion of unfamiliar races was unsettling. To a few, it was outright unacceptable. At the time of Paul Aurandt's birth, Madison Grant was a popular and outspoken critic of immigration, publishing a best-selling book entitled, *The Passing of the Great Race*.[3] In his stunningly populist creed, the Yale University graduate advocated for a separation and purifying of the races. It was nothing short of a page from the future playbook of Nazi Germany's Adolf Hitler. Yet he struck a chord. His message was warmly welcomed by supporters of the "nativism" movement that was gaining steam in several sectors, primarily among white-Anglo Protestants. World War I had turned many Americans against those of German descent. There was also opposition to the arrival of low-skilled immigrants from Italy and Poland. Today, Grant's words are chilling, but in the 1920s they were considered by some in the intelligentsia to be enlightened:

> We Americans must realize that the altruistic ideals which have controlled our social development during the past century, and the maudlin sentimentalism that has made America "an asylum for the oppressed," are sweeping the nation toward a racial abyss. If the Melting Pot is allowed to boil without control, and we continue to follow our national motto and deliberately blind ourselves to all "distinctions of race, creed, or color," the type of Native American of Colonial descent will become as extinct as the Athenian of the age of Pericles, and the Viking of the days of Rollo.[4]

Although the sentiments expressed by Grant represented an extreme element who despised the arrival of a new breed of immigrant, suspicion among the races existed in communities across the country. Post-Civil War Reconstruction led to many blacks leaving the south in pursuit of work in the north and midwest; some viewed their arrival with fear and distrust. Meanwhile, newly enfranchised blacks distrusted their access to equal rights in a system that had viewed them as property only a generation previously. Lingering resentment would occasionally manifest itself in cities like Tulsa.

The reemergence of the Ku Klux Klan in Atlanta at the start of 1915 only exacerbated an already volatile environment.[5] More than two dozen racial disturbances and riots broke out across the nation in the year of 1919 alone. The rioting was so rampant between April and October that the six months became known as "Red Summer."[6] Between 1911 and 1921, twenty-three black Oklahomans were lynched in more than a dozen different Oklahoma communities.[7] Verifiable figures are impossible to come by, but some estimates suggest that by 1920, Tulsa boasted nearly 3,000 active members of the Klan.[8]

By 1921, Tulsa was a city of two towns, one white and one black. The black population of 11,000 resided just north of the railroad tracks along Greenwood Avenue in a thirty-four square block area.[9] A prosperous and thriving enclave, it became known at the time as the "Negro Wall Street" of America. Prohibited from shopping in many of the white areas, Tulsa's black population simply set up their own shops and conducted commerce on their own turf and terms. The Greenwood neighborhood consisted of twelve grocery stores, dozens of restaurants, a postal substation, a Y.M.C.A., two schools, four hotels, twenty-three churches (more per capita than white Tulsa), two theaters (the Dreamland and the Dixie), a pharmacy, and even a library. Two newspapers, *The Tulsa Star* and the *Oklahoma Sun*, were published within the confines of the community.[10]

The rapid influx of money into Tulsa, Oklahoma was staggering. Its rate of growth into a business center in not just the southwest region but in all of the United States was nothing short of remarkable. The 1920 Census reported a population of 75,000 people, a spike from just over 7,000 in 1907. By the second decade of the twentieth century, more than 400 oil and gas companies were headquartered in the city. White collar jobs were plentiful. Over 200 attorneys, 150 doctors, and 60 dentists called the town home.[11] The harshness of the once untamed west had been tempered with all the usual characteristics of a cosmopolitan city.

But the relatively easy oil and gas money brought the predictable misery of a smorgasbord of vices. When the United States Congress overrode President Wilson's veto and officially passed the Volstead Act on October 29, 1919, banning the sale and consumption of alcohol, the die had seemingly been cast.[12] In the now bustling metropolis, entire streets were run over by brothels, speakeasies, and drug dealers. As a multiplicity of gangs and outlaws strengthened their grip, law enforcement officials, paralyzed by a combination of ignorance and apathy, would inevitably lose their influence and ultimately, their authority and control. The climate was ripe for trouble.

★ ★ ★

Paul Harvey Aurandt was a few months shy of his third birthday as Memorial Day of 1921 approached. He didn't see very much of his father during the latter days of May. Police Commissioner Adkison had his hands full; as his secretary, Harry Aurandt no doubt longed for his days back at the railroad or his less contentious times in the oil business. A dramatic prison break in the early hours of May 26 down at the county courthouse, the site of many of Aurandt's meetings with his boss, had thrown the city into crisis mode. Twelve prisoners escaped the top floor jail, four stories up.[13] A saw had been smuggled in and was used overnight to cut through the one-inch steel window bars. Using blankets they tied together, the men lowered themselves down to the street level under the cover of darkness. Just four days later, on May 30, six more prisoners took advantage of the poorly repaired window and successfully repeated the daring escape route.[14] Adkison was under fire. Serving in a support capacity, Aurandt could only do so much. The wheels of law and order were coming off.

The *Tulsa Tribune*, the town's afternoon paper, had been turning up the heat on law enforcement officials, heavily criticizing them for steadily losing control of the city. The paper's editor, Richard Lloyd Jones, was at the *Wisconsin State Journal* when he bought the *Tulsa Democrat* in 1919 and renamed it the *Tribune*.[15] Jones had a reputation for stirring the pot. Some people said he liked to antagonize the establishment. Others referred to him as the quintessential gadfly of the news business. More than anything else, he wanted to sell more newspapers than his rival, the more reserved *Tulsa World*. Lloyd was wise to how intolerant the local population had grown of the foibles and follies of the Tulsa Police Department.

Capitalizing on the frustration caused by the crime sprees, Jones launched an investigative series researching the complaints and analyzing the facts and proposed solutions. A string of bombastic editorials accompanied the feature with such headlines as "Catch the Crooks," "Go After Them," "Promoters of Crime," "The City Failure," and "Make Tulsa Decent."[16] The editorial staff, namely Jones, championed an aggressive campaign to once and for all establish order and snuff out crime. On May 14, the *Tribune* editorialized, "The people of Tulsa are becoming awake to conditions that are no longer tolerable."[17] Only days later the paper warned that if the city didn't get on top of the disorder, "an awakened conscience will do it for them."[18] This time around, the words of the predictably inflammatory and hyperbolic prone editorial writer would prove prophetic.

★ ★ ★

On May 30, 1921, little Paul Aurandt would have enjoyed the pomp and pageantry of the Tulsa Memorial Day parade that marched its way down Main Street. At the same time as the parade, a 19-year-old shoe-shiner by the name of Dick Rowland, a former star halfback at Booker T. Washington High from the Greenwood section of town, headed for the Drexel Building in the downtown corridor. Reports suggest he was either delivering polished shoes or was looking for business from the crowds who gathered on the upper floors to watch the parade. What followed would serve as the catalyst for the deadliest race riot in Tulsa's history.[19]

Seventeen-year-old Sarah Page was employed on May 30, 1921 as an elevator operator in the Drexel Building.[20] Somehow, as Rowland stepped into the elevator, he fell into Page, a white girl, and grabbed her arm or stepped on her foot.[21] She screamed that she had been assaulted. Rowland ran. Police caught up with him, and he was brought in for questioning the next day, May 31. Detectives grilled the frightened teen, and Sheriff William M. McCullough considered Rowland's side of the story credible and planned to chalk the incident up to an unfortunate misunderstanding.[22]

Various versions of the incident exist. It's a reasonable assumption, though not verified, that Page was familiar with Rowland and had seen him in the building prior to this particular Memorial Day. Police would later conclude that Rowland's fall was most likely accidental. But the investigation hadn't yet been finalized when the *Tulsa Tribune* released its afternoon edition. Though not the lead story, the headline, "Nab Negro for Attacking Girl in Elevator,"[23] ran on the front page in bold print. In the same paper, an even more inflammatory headline ran on the editorial section with the words "To Lynch Negro Tonight!" emblazoned across the top half.[24]

The threat of a public execution was acute due to a recent and raucous lynching. Just months earlier, a white man by the name of Roy Belton, accused of shooting a taxi cab driver, had been grabbed by a mob before trial and hung high before a loud and boisterous gathering. Though the police objected to the vigilante expression of justice, they nevertheless succumbed to the pressure and allowed their prisoner to be taken to the gallows by blood-thirsty civilians. The police would even wind up directing traffic as crowds flocked to see the lynching in person.[25]

As the sun rose on Tuesday, May 31, tensions flared on both sides of town. E. W. Woods, the principal of Booker T. Washington High School, dismissed his students early and urged them to go home and warn their parents of the *Tribune's* call to lynch one of their own citizens. The sides were drawn. White belligerents began gathering at the County Court House to demand Rowland's execution—preferably by another public lynching. A black contingent also arrived, determined to prevent a repeat of what occurred to Belton, and offered their services to the sheriff, which he declined.

Commissioner Adkison was furious. He had had enough. Determined to hold the line and prevent the reoccurrence of the vigilante barbarism of months earlier, he asked Harry Aurandt, seated at his desk inside Police Headquarters at Second and Main Street, to place a call to Sheriff McCullough at 1:00 p.m. Adkison urged McCullough to move his prisoner to a more secure location, maybe even hustle him out of town. But the Sheriff rebuffed the suggestion and assured Adkison his prisoner was safe and that he had taken special precautions.[26] Still concerned, Commissioner Adkison took matters into his own hands and left his office, meeting a party of between sixty and seventy armed blacks just three blocks north of the courthouse. He asked them to surrender their weapons. They refused. Adkison escorted them back in the direction of their Greenwood neighborhood.[27] It's not known if Paul Harvey's father accompanied Adkison on this risky call, but given his role in the office, and the trust he had earned as his confidant, there is a very good chance he was there. Though serving in a primarily administrative role, Aurandt was still technically considered an officer of the law and enjoyed all the benefits—and burdens—of the professional affiliation.

By 9:00 in the evening, a crowd of approximately 400 white men had assembled outside the jail. Some unconfirmed reports estimated the number as high as 2,000.[28] They were soon joined by nearly seventy-five black men. When a white man attempted to disarm a black, a gun was accidentally discharged and according to Sheriff McCullough, "all hell broke loose."[29] More shots soon rang out. So much for dignified and cosmopolitan culture; the wild west was raging in Tulsa. By midnight, twelve men lay dead—two blacks and ten whites.[30] Traditional and ordered justice failed as a vicious race riot broke out. Overwhelmed by the mayhem, Police Chief John A. Gustafson decided to deputize select individuals to contain the chaos. As Sheriff McCullough later described, "The police gave everyone a gun who came in" to the police station.[31] Police Commissioner Adkison would later testify that "we were unable to limit the commissions to our choices.... Some of those men might have lost their heads."[32] In 1926, the Oklahoma Supreme Court concluded that these very same deputized individuals were responsible for a significant portion of the devastation.[33]

In the early hours of June 1, mobs of white men armed with guns and flaming torches made their way across the railroad tracks. Oklahoma Governor J. B. A. Robertson had declared martial law.[34] Looting and cold-blooded murder ensued. Over 1,000 homes and business—and more than thirteen churches—were burned.[35] By the end of the rampage, the Greenwood section of Tulsa lay in smoldering ruins. The carnage was heartbreaking. The accurate death toll has never been fully verified, but most likely numbered several hundred. There were reports that 184 blacks and 48 whites were hospitalized needing some form of surgery, and over 500 others were treated for various injuries.[36] Over $1,500,000 worth of property was destroyed.[37]

In the aftermath, Oklahoma's governor activated the National Guard. Arriving just as violence dropped, the military forces moved over 6,000 of Greenwood's displaced citizens into makeshift internment camps.[38] The move was as much for their own safety as it was to try to sort out the consequences of the catastrophe. Many of the detained weren't released until their white employers showed up to vouch for them. Now homeless, those released from the camps would live wherever they could find shelter. Tents became a familiar sight in Tulsa in the summer of 1921—and beyond.

Remarkably, Sarah Page never pressed any charges and Dick Rowland was released from prison.[39]

Police Chief John A. Gustafson was suspended and convicted at trial of two separate charges: "for failure to take proper precautions for the protection of life and property during the rioting...and conspiracy to free automobile thieves and collect rewards."[40] He was forced from office. Assistant Chief George H. Blaine would assume the helm on July 24, 1921, only seven weeks later.[41] But Commissioner Adkison and his secretary, Harry Aurandt, stayed on.

The riots had drained everyone and sealed the fate of those left in power. Political watchers began to speculate that the accumulation of scandals and sorrows would likely force the Republican administration out of office in the coming elections in April of 1922.

As the smoke began to clear, and the horror of the riots began to subside, Harry Aurandt was likely thinking about his next career move. Commissioner Adkison was on thin ice. A new mayor would surely clean house and bring in new blood. Although bruised and embarrassed by the violent riots, Tulsa was still a booming and profitable oil town. Aurandt had many employment options. But Harry had at least six months until the election, and he was looking forward to the coming holidays and time with his family.

As a small child, Paul Harvey Aurandt wasn't totally insulated from the horror of the events occuring only a few miles from his quiet, tree-lined neighborhood. One memory remained clear. Paul recalled playing in the front yard when his mother came running over, placed her hand over his eyes, and quickly ushered him inside the house. "I shall recall with repugnance forever the scene which she sought to hide from my eyes: National Guard trucks piled with the bleeding bodies of Negroes who had been caught up in a sudden cataclysm," he wrote in 1965. "A man from across the tracks in the all-Negro Greenwood section of the segregated city was accused of assaulting a white elevator operator. For that one alleged crime, hundreds were caught up in the ghastly two-day purge. 'To teach them a lesson' it was said, innocent Negro men, women and children were dead, their homes burned."[42]

His father had survived the deadliest riot in Tulsa's short but tumultuous history. But the cold winter was on its way.

CHAPTER THREE

An Incalculable Loss

"Doctor, this is awful, isn't it?"[1] The surgeon at Tulsa's Oklahoma Hospital looked down at his patient, an ashen and weakened 48-year-old Harry Aurandt. His question was haunting. It was nearly 9:00 in the evening on Sunday, December 18, 1921.[2] Aurandt was losing blood. He was fading. The doctor on call was devastated. Although no stranger to trauma or tragedy, the exchange nearly choked him up, for there was no easy answer. Only moments earlier, sirens from the arriving ambulance had pierced the relative quiet of the cold Tulsa night. The hospital staff had been hoping for a peaceful and uneventful evening. They would have no such luck. Police and rescue personnel began flooding the hospital hallways. The emergency squad had sprung quickly into action, but the diagnosis for Aurandt was grave.

"Yes, Harry," he replied directly, his voice somber, "this is very serious."[3]

"And only to think," Aurandt responded meekly, "the dirty sons of guns shot me with both hands in the air."[4]

"Do you know who did it?" the doctor replied, leaning forward.

Harry Aurandt silently nodded in the affirmative, but he spoke not a word.[5]

★ ★ ★

Harry had lost his own father when he was just two years old. It was hard to miss a man he never really knew, but he carried internal and intrinsic curiosity about his heritage. To only see a father in faded photographs, or simply hear stories second or third hand, leaves a son with an increased sense of conjecture about what traits he might have inherited or characteristics they might have shared. Aurandt would be blessed with his only son, Paul, much later in life than most of his peers. He was forty-five years old, the age of many grandfathers, when the infant Paul was first placed in his arms. He certainly wouldn't have taken the privilege of parenting for granted.

December 18, a week before Christmas, Harry Aurandt invited his friend and police colleague, Detective Ike Wilkinson, to go rabbit hunting. He offered to drive. After months of dealing with interoffice politics and the stress of life in Tulsa, the men were looking forward to the opportunity to unwind, enjoy the fresh air, and maybe even shoot enough sustenance for a meal or two.

But they almost didn't go. Earlier in the day, Anna urged Harry to attend a revival meeting with her down at the Tulsa Coliseum. The famed British evangelist Rodney "Gypsy" Smith was in town, and Paul's mother was eager to go hear him. Despite a snowy forecast, thousands were anticipated downtown. But Harry decided he would rather go hunting.[6] There would be another opportunity to hear the popular preacher.

The sun had already set when Aurandt pulled up outside Wilkinson's home on South Victor Avenue just before seven o'clock in the evening. The veteran detective carried his shotgun with him, and slipped into the passenger seat of Aurandt's automobile.[7]

The outing had all the markings of an uneventful but enjoyable evening, though in a town the size of Tulsa, something always seemed to be going on—especially in 1921. A wave of crime in the form of stolen automobiles had overtaken the police chatter and captured the attention of its residents. The theft ring appeared to be fairly organized and run by numerous outlaws. They seemed to be brazen, even violent. That very day, a large black Buick touring car had been hijacked in broad daylight. Its owner, Tulsa resident Frank Clayton, was forced off the road by three armed men and had no choice but to turn over his car to the suspects.[8] All Tulsa police officials, even those who were off-duty, were told to be on the lookout for the vehicle along with the three marked men.[9]

Looking for a good field for hunting rabbits, Aurandt and Wilkinson decided to head north on Federal Drive,[10] just east of Tulsa, around eight o'clock that night. Spotting a car parked on the side of the road that closely matched the description of the one the three hijackers had taken, Aurandt slowed down in order to get a better look. Suddenly, another car pulled up alongside them. Curtains masked its occupants, but three revolvers were seen protruding from the windows. His grip on the steering wheel grew tighter. A voice from his inside the car shouted for Aurandt and Wilkinson to pull over. Looking down the barrel of three loaded weapons, they did as they were commanded.[11]

Suddenly, the car that had drawn even with them sped up and around them, and parked approximately twenty feet directly in front of their vehicle. Aurandt's car headlights cut through the blackness of the otherwise dark and deserted road.

According to court-documented testimony, a bandit by the name of Tom Cook got out of the car along with a man named Alvis Fears.[12] They were out for blood, and may have recognized Aurandt and Wilkinson as law enforcement to be silenced. As Harry Aurandt started to get out of the car as well, with his hands in the air, the two bandits suddenly opened fire on the vehicle. Detective Ike Wilkinson groped for his hunting rifle and attempted to fire on the bandits, but the .44 caliber shotgun jammed and the shell failed to explode. "It is a good thing for him that it did snap," he said later that night, "for I would have blown the top of his head off."[13]

In the hail of gunfire, Fears' shot hit the defenseless Aurandt, penetrating his liver, and perforating his stomach, intestines, and spleen. But he was not done. Another bullet struck Aurandt midway up his left leg. Thrown into a sudden state of shock, Aurandt cried out, "Don't shoot me that way!"[14] The desperados paid no attention to his plea.

Meanwhile, Ike Wilkinson was also severely wounded, taking a shot in the thigh and leg.

As quickly as the drama unfolded, the bandits were gone. The smell of fresh gunpowder hung heavily in the cold December air. Slumped in a pool of gathering blood, Wilkinson cleared the chamber of his shotgun and fired five times at the car as it sped away, but without hitting it. He quickly realized that his mobility was extremely limited. He was paralyzed, and Aurandt was critically wounded.

Despite searing pain and significant loss of blood, Harry Aurandt managed to climb back into the shot-up car and drive west towards Tulsa in search of help. The Kennard residence stood about a half a mile from the scene of the ambush. Pulling up to the farmhouse, the men cried out for help. Receiving no response, Aurandt exited the automobile and half stumbled, half crawled his way to the front porch, again pleading for assistance. Wilkinson was unable to move from his seat in the car.[15]

Mr. and Mrs. Kennard had been getting ready for bed when they first heard the shots and were alerted to the possibility of trouble.[16]

Rural Tulsans were accustomed to the sound of a gun, but certainly not a barrage of rapid fire followed by the roar of an engine speeding away down the road. They were startled.

Remaining inside their home, they peered out the windows, looking in the direction of the sound. They saw the bandits' car traveling at a very high speed towards Tulsa. But suddenly, it stopped, reversed course, and headed north toward the town of Skiatook. Ignorant of the facts, not sure of what was happening, the Kennards were at first reluctant to come out of their house despite the wounded men's pleas. Was it a set-up? However, within minutes, other neighbors in the area who had heard the commotion descended upon the property.

The shot-up men were in bad shape and getting worse. A phone call was made from inside the farmhouse. Ambulances were dispatched. Police arrived first, trying desperately to piece together the puzzle. "Who shot you?" an officer asked Wilkinson.[17] "Tom Cook and a short little fellow," he answered.[18] He later would clarify by stating, "Tom Cook's gang did it. Alvis Fears was one of them."[19] When another neighbor, unaware of this conversation, lamented to Aurandt that it was too bad they didn't know who did it, Harry gasped in response, "We saw, we saw; I know."[20] Officials, aware of the two men's critical condition, quickly whisked them away to the hospital. It was approximately 8:45 p.m.

Back on East Fifth Place, Anna Dagmar Aurandt was getting the children ready for bed. They were looking forward to putting up the Christmas tree with their father in the coming days. But then came a knock on the door. A Tulsa police officer shared the news of the night's tragic events with Anna as she stood on the front porch. Harry had been rushed to Oklahoma Hospital. But he was alive.

Meanwhile, the manhunt for the fugitives was on. Word spread quickly; outrage even faster. The police hastily organized forces and deputized approximately 200 citizens that evening. Based upon the tip from Mr. and Mrs. Kennard, a contingent deployed for the town of Skiatook. While on lookout in Skiatook, they spied a car traveling at a high rate of speed. When the driver failed to respond to an order to stop, the police opened fire. A chase ensued. But the police soon discovered they had fired on and wounded a woman and a boy with no connection to the incident on Federal Drive.[21] A police representative escorted them to the hospital. The rest of the posse stayed behind, still searching for the bandits. It turned out to be a wise move. The ambitious and determined officers soon spotted another suspicious car approaching. They set up a road block, and the vehicle halted on command. Offering no resistance, Tom W. Cook, Alvis Fears, O. L. "Bob" Ballard, and Bill Dalton stepped out of the vehicle.[22] The police had found their men. It was 11:00 p.m. Harry Aurandt was still clinging to life.[23]

The next morning, Monday, December 19, 1921, the *Tulsa World* carried the news of the previous night's horror. "Wounded When Four Bandits Open Fusillade" splashed the headline.[24] A year of violence and lawlessness was hurtling toward its bitter end, but it couldn't have ended soon enough. The city's resilient residents had grown weary and disgusted with the repeated, blatant disregard for life and property.

Back at the Oklahoma Hospital, Anne Dagmar Aurandt was seated at her ailing husband's side. His breathing was labored. He was growing weaker by the minute. She held his hand. Her mind wandered back through the years to the sweet memories of their meeting and the times so far away from the stresses of the hour. They had settled in Tulsa together with their daughter Frances, their hopes and lofty dreams as wide and wonderful as the endless western sky. Harry had been given thirteen years with Frances. The arrival of little Paul just three years and three months earlier had been the greatest of gifts, almost a miracle. He couldn't wait to grow old with a son by his side. What plans! But slowly and sadly, Harry Harrison Aurandt slipped away.[25]

The news of Aurandt's death shocked and exacerbated the frustrations of the tired community. Hundreds of agitated Tulsans began to gather outside the courthouse, threatening to charge the jail and exert vigilante justice on the accused killers. In a gathering storm, by day's end, over 1,500 protestors had congregated along the Sixth Street side of the courthouse, evoking the fears and bad memories of the violent riot earlier in the year.[26]

Law enforcement officials had apparently learned their lesson. "These are my prisoners," Sheriff McCullough would tell those assembled, "and I intend to protect them—with force if necessary—but I hardly think it will [be]."[27] The sheriff had actually moved the prisoners out of Tulsa at five o'clock that evening and told the assembled crowd so. He was trying to prevent another public lynching or a riot. But the crowd wasn't convinced and assumed the sheriff was bluffing. To convince them, McCullough allowed a group led by the Reverend William Kerr of Aurandt's church, First Presbyterian, to search the courthouse. Kerr had been praying for a peaceful resolution. He had tried to calm the raucous masses, but they were incensed and wanted quick justice. Reverend Kerr was relieved when his search turned up nothing. He addressed the throng with these stirring words:

"Mr. Aurandt was a member of my own church and a finer man never lived. I want to see justice wrought in this affair as much as you do. But I say let us do nothing that will blacken the reputation of our city. We have searched the building from top to bottom, every cell and cubby hole, and we have found nothing. Let us go back to our homes. Good night."[28] His message resonated, and his prayers were answered. The crowd dispersed.

The funeral was held two days later, on the afternoon of December 21, at First Presbyterian where Harry had been an elder.[29] Hundreds filled the sanctuary and many more stood in reverent vigil in the cold outside. The uniformed members of Harry's police department attended all together, making a sea of solidarity. High ranking city officials joined them, along with Aurandt's brothers from the Knights Templar, the Blue Lodge of the Masonic order. A men's quartet performed.[30]

Reverend Kerr, preaching before Aurandt's closed, flower-laden casket, was bold and pointed. The hour of sorrow and remembrance afforded him a rare opportunity—a chance to speak his mind to many of Tulsa's public officials who he believed were actually contributing to the woes of the city's recent string of violence.

> Human life is being held too lightly in Tulsa and in Tulsa County. No city life can be any better than the sum total of the individual lives of its citizens. We of Tulsa have perhaps not realized the conditions here until they are rudely revealed to us by a shock such as the death of our brother. We have paid too much attention to the material side of our city building and not enough to the moral and spiritual phase of it. Unless we are careful, the surrounding country will be contaminated with our sins.
>
> When Tulsa wants to put a stop to crime and the wave of iniquity in our midst, she can do it. Unless her citizens stand together, regardless of party, for such enforcement of the laws as will stop this lawlessness, it is difficult to tell where it will end. There has been talk of lynching. Lynching is lawlessness, and lawlessness breeds more lawlessness every-

where. Lynch law is no law at all, but only adds to crime. It
is no less a crime because the body of citizens joins it.[31]

At the conclusion of the service, all downtown traffic was stopped in
order to allow the funeral procession to wind its way out to the Rose
Hill Cemetery.[32] Accompanied by an escort of slow-moving police
motorcycles, the body of Harry Aurandt was carried to its final resting place along the same road and past the exact spot of the shooting.

Three hundred mourners were gathered under a large white tent
beside the gravesite for the administration of the Masonic funeral rite.
A stone cold silence met with a chilly breeze as the casket was lowered
into the ground. The chaplain offered a final prayer. Suddenly, a silent
procession of twelve white-robed Ku Klux Klansman, with their distinctive black and red patch known as the "mystic insignia"[33] visible on
their garments, appeared in the entrance of the open-sided tent. Marching inside single file, they encircled the grave. No one had seen them
coming. Audible gasps could be heard from those assembled. A strong
wind had come up, threatening to blow off the Klans' pointed loose fabric hoods. Their leader carried a red cross and each member held a
blood-red rose in one hand while holding down their hoods with the
other. They stood at attention in complete silence as the final portions
of the funeral rite were performed. Then, without fanfare, each man
stepped forward one at a time to drop his rose inside the open grave. As
quickly and as mysteriously as they appeared, they departed, walking
out over the gravel road and down a hill into the fading light.[34]

The next day, December 22, 1921, the *Tulsa Daily World* ran a
photo on the front page that was snapped in haste by staff member
Alvin C. Krupnick. "The Ku-Klux Klan in Action" read the headline,
followed by another story titled, "Robed Klansmen Honor Dead While

Hundreds Stand Agape at Funeral of Harry Aurandt."[35] The two photographs forever froze the bizarre end of a sad good-bye.

The *World* editorialized, "No one in Tulsa has ever witnessed such a ceremony before, nor have they heard of it being performed in any other city. Whether it is part of the Ku-Klux Klan's established rites and ceremonies or if it was inspired locally is a matter of conjecture."[36]

But there is absolutely no evidence that Paul Harvey's father, Harry Aurandt, was a member of the Ku Klux Klan. At the time, the Klan was gathering steam and eager to flex their muscles in public. There would have been no greater spectacle at the time, and they knew the positioned and powerful would be in attendance. The rash of lawlessness also emboldened them—even gave them some credibility. By showing up at Harry Aurandt's funeral, they were making a bold statement. If the Tulsa Police Department couldn't keep order in their town, they would step in and do the job for them.

But the Klansmen would not retain the distinction of giving the final honor to Harry Aurandt. Seventy years later, his name was added to the brand new National Law Enforcement Officers' Memorial in Washington, D.C. as a fallen officer.[37]

On April 22, 1922, Alvin Fears and Tom W. Cook were officially charged with murder.[38] The trial was moved to Pawnee County where a jury deliberated more than fifty hours before finally convicting them. They were sentenced to life in prison,[39] though Cook's conviction was later overturned on appeal based upon several technicalities.[40]

Alvis Fears, however, was released from prison for a ten-day furlough by Oklahoma Governor Jack Walton in the summer of 1923. Unsurprisingly, he never returned and became a hotly pursued fugitive.[41] In November of 1923, the Oklahoma legislature impeached and removed Walton from office after a term of only ten months, for charges ranging from corruption, neglect of duty, moral turpitude, abuse of pardon and parole powers, and general incompetence. Walton's supporters suggested the majority of the charges were trumped up in retribution for the governor's public opposition to the Ku Klux Klan.[42] The convicted murderer, Fears, surfaced again on January 23, 1924 as one of several suspects in a bank heist in Ashbury, Missouri. More than twenty officers and bloodhounds tracked the men in vain. They eventually abandoned the search.[43]

The Tulsa city government had been turned upside down and would soon be turned inside out. In April of 1922 the citizens of Tulsa voted out the incumbents and welcomed in a new mayor, former chief of police and strong advocate for law and order, Herman Newblock. Commissioner Adkison's employment was terminated and he was replaced by Harry Kiskaddo.[44] A new era of relative peace and continued prosperity finally began for the booming town of Tulsa.

But the loss of his father when he was so young cast a long shadow over the course of Paul Aurandt's life. Though he couldn't have fully comprehended the events he saw unfold—the knock on the door, the father who never came home again—he was left with memories resembling an old movie without sound. The pain of it gave him the ability to "recognize scars" in the faces of people similarly traumatized "that others cannot yet see."[45] However, there are some indications he was not privy to the exact details of that fateful night. It is possible the specifics of the tragedy weren't discussed often or in detail. Shortly after President Kennedy was assassinated just one month before Christmas in 1963, Harvey penned a column empathizing with the plight of the late president's son, three-year old John Jr. "I was just his age when just before one Christmastime my own Daddy was cut down by the bullets of assassins."[46] But then Harvey went on to say, "It was Chief Blaine the hijackers were after . . . Chief Blaine's legs were useless thereafter."[47] But it wasn't Blaine at all—it was Ike Wilkinson who accompanied Harry Aurandt on that fateful rabbit hunting trip that forever changed the family he left behind. "My older sister and I were comforted by a grieving mother," Paul later recalled, "but ever after there was to be a sinister shadow dulling the luster of the Christmas season."[48]

CHAPTER FOUR

Stars in His Eyes

On December 21, the Atlas Life Insurance Company, operating out of the third floor of Tulsa's Palace Building, ran a full page advertisement in the *Tulsa World* that would never have run today. The following banner headline bragged: "Atlas Pays Claim in Less Than 24 Hours." A smaller blurb bragged, "Widow of the Late Harry H. Aurandt Received Check in Full Settlement Yesterday."

Following the death of Paul's father, Mrs. Aurandt was forced to make a difficult decision. In addition to coping with the loss of her beloved husband, she was reeling from the reality of suddenly having to provide for two young children. Considering Paul's young age and her inability to pay for outside care, she came up with a plan that would allow her to continue parenting full-time.

With the $1,458.18 she received from the insurance company, Paul's mother extensively renovated the modest home on East Fifth Place. Employing day laborers, Anna had the house expanded and modified in order to accommodate boarders or roomers, a relatively common practice in early, transient Tulsa. Phone directories recorded the official addresses of the apartments as "1014 Rear" and

"1014 1/2."[1] Classified advertisements posted in the *World* regularly drew the attention of temporary workers, often single men, who were seeking a simple and affordable place to live.

Anna Aurandt was industrious and resourceful. She was also a favorite of neighborhood children. A former resident of East Fifth Place, Sam Lee, remembered her as "a nice lady who sometimes had treats for me."[2] But within the family, she was a survivor, Paul's rock, an anchor in times of sunshine and strife. Her stability and predictability "gave substance to my self-confidence," Paul would later say. "Whatever storms, there was always a shelter back home."[3] When put to the test, she did what she needed to do in order to provide for her growing family.

★ ★ ★

Growing up without a father was probably more difficult than Paul could say—because he rarely did. Beyond a few highlights selectively shared on broadcasts, he was relatively silent on many specifics of his childhood. His son, Paul Jr., would crack the window ever so slightly on the innermost feelings of his father, only remarking that little Paul had grown up "lonely" and "self-conscious."[4] But the Tulsan himself once tried to explain the scarcity of detail. "Ever since I made tomorrow my favorite day," he would say whimsically, "I've been uncomfortable looking back."[5] He would be in good company. As Thomas Jefferson once wrote, "I like the dreams of the future better than the history of the past."[6]

But the stories he did share hint at a childhood rich in the overlooked magic of every day experience. Paul would say that it was in Tulsa as a youngster that he "learned the wages of sin, smoking grapevine behind the garage and getting a mouthful of ants." "Tulsa was watermelon picnics in the backyard and a small Paul blowing taps on his Boy Scout bugle over the fresh grave of a dead kitten. . . . " It was where a young boy took a "slingshot made from a forked branch, shot at a living bird, and the bird died and he cried and he is still crying." And "it used to be the fragrance of honeysuckle on the trellis behind the porch swing."[7]

As a 7-year-old boy, Paul suffered his first crush, but like most grade school children, he had a funny way of showing it. Just hoping his new love would notice him, he snapped a rubber band against the neck of poor little Ethel Mae Hazelton. She ran home crying.[8] He continued to carry a torch for Ethel Mae into his teen years, and found more positive ways to express his interest, "where theretofore Ethel Mae had been the sometimes target of my rubberband, two-finger slingshot and had gone home in tears . . . now she was more likely to be invited to share my licorice whip which left our lips black and giggly."[9] He also flirted with two other girls who lived on his street, Frieda and Doris McIntyre, "If [the McIntyre sisters] were not raving beauties as girls, they were obviously different from boys," Paul remembered.[10] As a 13-year-old, Paul would recall sitting in the front lawn of his house with those same girls of the neighborhood. "I'd be on one side, braced on an elbow, chewing a clover blossom and looking at those girls."[11] But his first kiss, he regularly would claim, came from a teacher. "I remember I was 7; she must have been 100," he said. "I forget what I had done thus to be rewarded, because I was so flustered when she kissed me. She kissed me right on top of the head—when there was hair there. Instantly, I was in love forever."[12]

His memories of second grade run deep. "If our work was completed on time," he remembered, "[Miss Harp] would read to us for the last few minutes of each class period. I can't remember much of what she read. But you know how it is when you're seven . . . or you're in love . . . and when you are both . . . it's quite an experience."[13]

That same year, in 1925, Paul was admitted to the Oklahoma Hospital for a routine surgical procedure. The 7-year-old would have both his tonsils and adenoids removed—unremarkable but for the fact that from then till the ailments he battled in his ninetieth year, he had "NEVER!" spent another day in a hospital.[14]

Children with the means—thirty-five cents—would flock to Saturday matinees at the Rialto Theatre on Third Street. Chances are the Aurandts' budget didn't allow for weekly attendance, but when Paul did go, it was often with his best friend of boyhood, Harold Collis. In the winter, a doorman in a Russian Cossack overcoat would greet guests. Rich or poor, kids were made to feel like royalty. To those like Paul with meager resources, it was a rare and delightful taste of the luxury of high society. Harvey's memories were framed by the recollections of high ceilings, velvet ropes, and flowing curtains. The theater was an escape from the mundane. There was also the Majestic, an equally popular movie house which employed girls, much to the delight of its male patrons.

As a boy, Paul Harvey would have his window on the world opened even wider while walking the floors of the newly opened Brown-Dunkin Department store (known as the Hunt Dry Goods Company until 1924 when it was sold to new owners and expanded), located at the southeast corner of Fourth and Main streets in downtown Tulsa.[15] The largest department store in the southwest, it was a magnificent art-deco building of six vast floors. Customers would come to know and love Mrs. Weber, the elevator starter in the building, who would direct customers to the floor and merchandise of their choice. Everybody had their favorite spot. Dr. Ben Henneke, a lifelong Tulsa resident and the former president of the University of Tulsa, would speak warmly of Lewis Meyer's Book Shop located within the building. "He was located on the mezzanine floor, hardly far enough up to make taking an elevator worthwhile, but his books and his conversations were worth the trip."[16] The Brown-Dunkin was sold in 1960, and in 1974, its name was changed to Dillards. Though the franchise continues to exist under that name, the original building has since been demolished.[17]

If Paul could scrape together a few extra dimes, the 46th Star Candy Store just across the alley from Kress's was a popular stop. Ike's Chili Parlor on Main Street and Boulder, sitting right beside the Rialto Theatre, was another hangout. But Ike's was not for the faint of heart. Ike's was well known and loved for its brusque and no-nonsense philosophy of hospitality. When Harvey and his friends congregated there, the establishment employed only male servers, all wearing a uniform of black pants, a white shirt, and an apron.[18] The menu was simple: two types of chili. Baskets of unwrapped crackers were always scattered on the tables. Although they've moved locations since young Paul Harvey was a customer, Ike's survived and still serves the same chili recipe it offered in the 1920s and 1930s.

Paul Aurandt was just nine years old on September 30, 1927 when he joined the throngs of eager town folk at McIntyre Airport to welcome Charles Lindbergh and his plane, *The Spirit of St. Louis*, to Tulsa.[19] Only four months earlier, the famed aviator had successfully flown non-stop across the Atlantic to Paris, France. He was an overnight sensation, an idol and hero to every young girl and boy. Harvey watched Lindbergh step out of the cockpit while "pressing against the restraining ropes daring to foretaste fame—and falling in love with the sky."[20] Harvey would go on to become a licensed pilot, learning to fly in a rebuilt Monocoupe in 1933. His passion for flying also almost got him killed. "My life was so wrapped up in that plane," he recalled, "that the one time I should have jumped, because there was no possible place to set down outside of some trees, I didn't. All that was going through that young brain of mine was 'If anything happens to this airplane,

I don't want to go on living anyway.' So I went ahead and landed it in the trees."[21]

Long before he was on the radio, he built radios. Homemade crystal sets were all the rage during the 1920s. A crystal radio is the simplest of all receivers and requires no battery or conventional power source to operate. As a Boy Scout in Troop Number One, Paul constructed his own receivers by wrapping a homemade tuner conductor coil around a cigar box or a drinking glass.[22] A simple piece of wire served as an antenna, completing the device. With an inexpensive pair of headphones, he could pick up KVOO, the "Voice of Oklahoma," broadcasting right out of Tulsa. (Sometimes the signal from KVOO was so strong that it bled through telephone receivers.)

Ever the enterprising youth, Paul made and sold the sets for extra income. Using the discarded cigar boxes, he constructed them for less than a dollar and easily sold them for double his expenditure. He was always proud to do his share and contributed his modest earnings to his mother. Making the sets was a way for him to manage meager circumstances. As he would later say, "I was never one who sought to make the small man tall by cutting off the legs of a giant. I wanted to drag no man down to my size. Only to preserve a way of life which might make it possible for me, one day, to elevate myself until I at least partly matched his size."[23]

When Paul wasn't mowing lawns for twenty-five cents, making deliveries for neighborhood grocer, Mr. Wright, or a local market called the Colonial Grocery Store, running errands for his mother, or working on his beat-up airplane, he was listening to his radio. While his friends spent their summer evenings outside playing ball, stickball, tag, King of the Mountain, and shooting marbles, he played Lowell Thomas, gentleman, linguist, scholar, and famous radio newsman of the National Broadcasting Company.[24]

The clock struck the top of the hour. Aurandt, lying on the floor, was leaning on his elbows. He edged forward. "Good Evening Every-body!" Thomas began with his familiar resonance.[25] The *Lowell Thomas and the News* fifteen-minute daily feature was underway. Paul was taken with the eclectic mix of news stories. The cadence he heard was steady and clean. Thomas always took a sort of sandwich approach as he weaved his way through the news of the night. Every newscast had its meat, the substantial features, but he never forgot the lettuce, tomato, and mayonnaise—the humorous or lighthearted sto-ries. He wanted to give people time to absorb it all, which they couldn't do if the whole newscast was heavy.

Walter Winchell was another famous radio newsman who caught Paul's ear early in life. He was so popular that trains would stop so passengers wouldn't miss his evening report. Winchill was sometimes considered the "prime minister of the airwaves." If Thomas was the dignified newsman, Winchell was the equivalent of a *National Enquirer* reporter.[26] Though he was considered to be a tireless self-promoter, a commentator in the 1930s once said Winchell enjoyed "the largest continuous audience ever possessed by a man who was neither a politician nor divine."[27] Paul was one of his fans.

As a young man in Tulsa, Aurandt was also listening to Hans Van [H. V.] Kaltenborn, a radio newsman from Wisconsin who first broad-casted on the CBS Radio Network and later on NBC. Kaltenborn, a renaissance man who was known for precise diction and eloquence as well as creative ad libbing, impressed the young Paul. H. V. Kaltenborn was right more than he was wrong, though in 1948 his early predic-tion that Republican Thomas Dewey had likely defeated incumbent Harry Truman was credited to a large degree for instigating the infa-mous "Dewey Defeats Truman" newspaper headline that proved to be incorrect by the next morning.[28]

H. V. Kaltenborn's influence on Paul Aurandt is probably best exemplified by Harvey's penchant for personalizing stories or trying to get into the shoes of his audience during a broadcast. Kaltenborn's boss would grow irritated with this style and once told him, "Just don't be so personal. Use such phrases as 'it is said,' 'there are those who believe,' 'the opinion is held in well-informed quarters,' 'some experts have come to the conclusion . . .' Why keep on saying, 'I think' and 'I believe' when you can put over the same idea more persuasively by quoting someone else?"[29] Kaltenborn wasn't convinced and neither would Paul Aurandt be. Years later, the Oklahoma native would regularly remind critics that his show was, after all, entitled *Paul Harvey News and Comment*.

There were many more influences, though several would come a few years later after Aurandt was already on the air. Gabriel Heatter, the melodious baritone, impressed upon the young broadcaster that a silver lining could be found in the darkest cloud. Heatter would become the voice of World War II, regularly bringing an encouraging perspective of America's progress in battle. His signature phrase, "There's good news tonight!" that kick-started most of his newscasts has long been credited for helping to keep the country's morale up even amidst all of the initial bad news from the front.[30] One fan letter in particular summed up the impact he was having on the public. "Thank God for Gabriel Heatter," wrote the listener, "who makes it possible for us to sleep at night."[31]

Indiana-born and bred Elmer Davis was another inspiration. Along with his command of the English language, Harvey appreciated Davis's style of mixing a wide range of stories into his national program. It was from Davis that Harvey would learn the necessity of balancing topics within the body of a broadcast. From thousands of possible stories, Davis—and later, Harvey—would try diligently to select a mix of stories based upon what they believed people needed and wanted to know.

As a young boy, Paul Aurandt was also influenced by the *Youth's Companion*, a tremendously popular children's magazine that claimed over 500,000 subscribers until it merged with *American Boy* in 1929.[32] (Residents of his boyhood house would report finding copies of both the *Youth's Companion* and *Boys' Life* in his attic, addressed to the young Aurandt, years after he lived there.) Its creators fashioned the periodical much like the *Reader's Digest*, filling its pages with a range of articles that would interest various levels of readers and ages. Some parents would read it aloud in the living room or at the dining room table. Children looked forward to each issue with great anticipation. The magazine's motto, "Nothing But the Best," nicely captured and matched Aurandt's American ideals and his instinctually sunny outlook.[33] When he was only five years old, the editors responded in the magazine's pages to the growing popularity of radio. Parents like Anna Dagmar Aurandt would be encouraged, maybe even relieved, to read what the writers of the magazine had to say about it:

> *There are several engaging thoughts as to what the outcome of the widespread use of radio will be. Not the least pleasing of them is the idea that thousands of boys and girls will listen for an hour or more a day to fair sort of spoken English, clearly enunciated. Youth is quick and imitative, but we hope that on the waves of the ether may come lessons that will enlarge our vocabulary and improve our pronunciation.*[34]

The radio was a natural draw for a boy like Paul, who loved words. It was a comfortable fit and a faithful and reliable partner. It stretched his imagination, challenged his critical thinking, and broadened and expanded his concerns and interests beyond the borders of Tulsa. The new medium of radio also cultivated his curiosity, made him a great listener, and taught him the art of conversation.

Absorbed in what he heard, he spent many hours inside the house on East Fifth Place with his homemade crystal radio set resting atop a table, the headphones pressing against his neatly combed blond hair, or lying on the living room floor in front of the family set. Paul Aurandt began to imagine what it would be like to be on the other side, sitting inside a studio behind a microphone, and talking; painting wonderful pictures with colorfully crafted words. Despite his limited resources, he allowed himself to dream.

★   ★   ★

Paul would grow up during the Great Depression. Though the presence of big oil had insulated some sectors of the community from dire deprivation, it had drastically magnified the chasm between classes. As Paul Harvey tells it, he got down to one pair of wearable trousers. Before long, normal wear and tear took its toll; the seat became completely worn out, and finally worn through. He made the startling discovery while in class and was mercifully excused from school early. Embarrassed, he walked sideways down Main Street and while doing so, spotted a chauffeur driven automobile transporting one of the oil barons of the city. Usually even-keeled, his temper flared. For the first time in life, he began to feel sorry for himself— and jealous of a man he had never met.[35]

When he arrived home, he showed his mother the hole in his pants. She took him by the hand to downtown Bell's clothing store where she purchased a new suit of clothes for him that came with two pairs of pants. It cost eleven dollars and ninety-five cents.[36] Paul would later learn she had taken the money from the account she set aside for paying taxes.

Depressed over the experience and his reaction to it, and needing to process the emotion, he sought out the counsel of a trusted and beloved former teacher, Miss Harp of Longfellow Elementary School. Her response was like a line straight from a Horatio Alger novel. She told him, "Paul, never feel resentment in your heart for those who have more than you. Just do all that you can as long as you live to preserve this last wonderful land in which any man willing to stay on his toes can reach for the stars."[37]

He never forgot her words.

CHAPTER FIVE

Good Advice!

On a sun-drenched September day in 1933, an eager and anxious
Paul Aurandt strode past the tall columns bordering the shaded
sidewalk toward the wide cement stairway of Central High School.
Stepping through the massive glass and wooden double doors for the
first time, he turned in wonder and marveled at the energy and bustle in the crowded halls. Classmate and lifelong Tulsa resident George
Winkert remembers the difficulty he had walking through those hallways. "You were always knocking elbows and running into people. It
was wall to wall kids, hustling between classes, all on those beautiful
hardwood floors. The place was always jammed!"[1]

Tulsa's Central High School, a massive and stately redbrick building at the corner of Sixth and Cincinnati, was an easy half-mile walk
in any weather from the Aurandt's family home. Constructed in 1917
after voters approved $300,000 in bonds, the exploding population of
Tulsa forced an expansion of the building in 1922.[2] Another separate
structure was added to the campus in 1925.[3] The new Manual Arts
Building at the corner of Ninth and Cincinnati helped relieve some of
the overcrowding, but the class sizes continued to grow. By the time

Paul Aurandt arrived from Horace Mann Junior High and entered the
tenth grade in 1933, nearly 5,000 students were enrolled at Central
High School.[4]

Campus facilities felt like a modern-day college. Central's cafeteria
was extremely well organized and was run with the efficiency of a
chow line onboard a naval vessel. School officials paid a great deal of
attention to the arts, commissioning paintings and sculptures from
the pool of its many talented, budding artists for display around campus. Music was another priority. The Board of Education approved the
purchase of a massive pipe organ in 1926, installing and dedicating it
in March of 1927, six years before Paul arrived.[5] He would remember
sitting in assemblies in the South Auditorium, singing the school
hymn, "O, Great Spirit," and participating in other special events, like
the Coliseum frolic, all enhanced by the mighty roar of the $35,817
instrument.[6] Financed by an initial gift from graduates of the class of
1926, and paid off by subsequent classes through 1935, it would cost
approximately $750,000 to replace today.[7] In 2003, the American The-
atre Organ Society oversaw a painstakingly complete restoration of
the organ, which is still played.[8]

Incoming students were assigned a permanent homeroom for the
duration of their tenure at Central. Paul would wind up with Miss
Margaret Coats in room 220.[9] A young woman with a round, cherub-
like face and short, closely combed auburn hair, she would preside
over forty-two students, twenty-three girls and nineteen boys. As the
only white high school in the entire city of Tulsa, Paul's classmates
were boys and girls of varying means.

In addition to the excellent and broad liberal arts curriculum, the
bustling campus of Central had something for everyone. "Man's existence is centered about his activities," stated the opening line in a section of the *Tom Tom*, the school's yearbook. "Without diverting

interests, his life becomes useless and barren."[10] There was the usual smorgasbord of sporting programs—football, baseball, basketball, wrestling, and track and field, among others. Central had its own Olympic-sized indoor swimming pool and swim team. There was a debate club, several service organizations, a band, an orchestra, and numerous choirs and choruses like the *A Cappella* singers and the Orpheus Club.

Students from Central High School would regularly congregate at the Bob Evans Drug Store, located just around the corner from the campus on South Boston Street.[11] In fact, if a door at the school was left unguarded (monitors were posted at each exit to check passes and prevent class cutting), students would often sneak out and grab a Coke at the soda fountain or smoke a cigarette in an act of willful defiance. In addition to selling beverages and prescription medications, Bob Evans carried an assortment of newspapers and magazines. As the winter turned to spring in April of 1934, Paul's sophomore year, there was a buzz around the newsstand. *The Atlantic Monthly*, the popular magazine of news and cultural commentary, was headlining an excerpt from a new best-selling book by the British author James Hilton, entitled *Good-Bye Mr. Chips*.[12] The book quickly became the hottest literary commodity and a must-read for everyone, Paul included. The owners of the drug store couldn't keep it on the shelves. Bookstores everywhere stocked the title.

Locked in the tight grip of the Great Depression, Americans were eager for good news—fiction or nonfiction. In 1934, federal officials were finally cracking down on another crime wave that had occupied the attention of Oklahomans. Outlaws Clyde and Bonnie Parker (a.k.a., "Bonnie and Clyde") met their end in a hail of bullets down in Louisiana. John Dillinger was shot and killed in Chicago. Oklahoman Charles "Pretty Boy" Floyd, a bandit known to rob from banks

to give to the poor, was killed in Ohio (he would later be immortal-
ized by Woody Guthrie in the song "Pretty Boy").[13] George "Baby
Face" Nelson was found facedown, dead in a ditch from a gunshot.[14]
It was quite a year.

So a gentle and sentimental novel like *Good-Bye Mr. Chips* was
warmly welcomed. It raced up the charts. Students wanted to be seen
with the white and blue book tucked under their arm. The novel follows the touching story of a beloved teacher, Arthur Chipping, who is
employed at a boy's boarding school for nearly fifty years. Although it
takes a little while for Chipping to warm up and connect with his
pupils, he finally turns the corner and slowly and steadily grows into
the legend of the campus. All the students know and love "Chips," and
all seek his advice and counsel. His wisdom opens the doors of their
world. His life is ordered and simple, but it is tremendously significant
because of the contribution he makes in the lives of his students.[15] Central High had its own Mr. Chipping, as Paul would discover.

Paul was a member of the T-Club, an invitation-only group based
upon academic excellence. He was also a proud participant and leader
in the HI-Y Club, a team of clean-cut and articulate men whose sole
purpose was to "create, maintain, and extend the high standards of
Christian fellowship throughout the school and community."[16] Paul
served on play committees as well, lending his insight and talents to
various school productions. He was not the life of the campus or the
center of all attention. He never sought the spotlight, seemed hungry
for self-aggrandizement, or craved the adulation of his peers. With
over 1,000 students in his class, Paul Aurandt played his own part in
a few small circles of influence. He kept his focus, narrowed his pur-
suits, and poured himself in to whatever he did. He knew where he
wanted to go—radio—even though he wasn't quite sure how to get

there. Although no success is ever solely attributable to one source, Aurandt would find his way—and the role of a lifetime—thanks to the wonderful advice of a single teacher of speech and drama named Isabelle Ronan.

Miss Isabelle E. Ronan joined the faculty at Tulsa's Central High School in 1920, when Paul was only two.[17] Hired to teach speech and drama, she would preside over the department for thirty-three years until her retirement in 1953.[18] With an undergraduate degree from Michigan State Normal College in 1910 and a Masters from the University of Wisconsin a few years later, Ronan was nearly obsessive in her pursuit of higher education.[19] In her free time, at her own expense, she registered for acting and voice lessons at schools in New York, Chicago, and Texas—all in the hope of passing on a new technique to a promising student. She was a woman of modest means; she would never marry, lived with her sister, and wore the same simple and plain wardrobe year after year. Instead, Isabelle Ronan invested in the things money could never buy.

When Paul Aurandt entered Room B-16 in Central High School back in 1933 and met the exacting, demanding, and lovable Miss Ronan,[20] he was aware of her reputation and eager to witness it firsthand. If every good teacher has a recurring theme in their educational tool box, Ronan's centered on memorization. Students were regularly admonished to remember their lines, the author, their stage presence, their smile, to always stand tall—and to breathe. Remember! Remember! Remember![21] Nearly forty years after graduation, Paul returned to Tulsa to deliver a speech and visited with Miss Ronan prior to going on stage. Minutes before he ascended the stairs of the dais, the retired teacher leaned over and whispered, "Now remember, Paul, stand tall and breathe from the diaphragm."[22]

In her thirty-year career, Ronan would have nearly 3,200 students enrolled in her drama and speech classes.[23] Her students put on a play every two weeks, for she believed that the pressure of performance brought the best out in the actor. Paul would participate each year in one of her most popular stage creations, an all-school variety show called *Central Daze*.[24] Critics suggested it rivaled the complexity and innovation of modern Broadway productions.

Few teachers have seen the fruits of their work become so high profile as Miss Ronan. In addition to Paul Aurandt, dozens of future television and radio stars sat inside room B-16. Some were highly visible, like the late actor Tony Randall, best known for his portrayal of Felix Unger on the television sitcom, *The Odd Couple*.[25] (As someone once cracked, Randall was the finest British actor ever to come out of Tulsa, Oklahoma.)[26] Many other former pupils were heard but not seen, like the late Danny Dark.[27] Best remembered for his commercial work, Dark's deep and resonating voice would be featured in StarKist commercials, telling Charlie Tuna, "Sorry, Charlie," or in Budweiser advertisements, uttering the immortal words, "This Bud's for You." The network brass in New York and California became well familiar with Ronan's name and became impressed with her record, hiring numerous alumni like NBC producer Wade Arnold, film star Noel Warwick, Leonard Rosenberg, star of NBC's *Mr. Peepers*, Cal Tinney, a nationally known humorist, and commentator Lillian Herndon, an actress on the Jack Benny show.[28] Miss Ronan's class also served as a popular springboard for higher education in Tulsa. Former University of Tulsa president Dr. Ben Henneke and TU professor Dr. Ed Dumit also sat under her tutelage.[29]

Her motivational trick was really pretty simple. Paul Aurandt would tell you that his dear teacher had an incredible knack for identifying the unique gift of each student and allowing them the freedom to individually express their talent. She didn't try to force her students to conform to a specific formula for success. Instead, she'd catch her students doing something right—and build upon it. In an interview years after retirement, Ronan said bluntly, "I always found something good in all of them."[30]

Dr. Ed Dumit, a Tulsa gentleman who made his living first in voicing commercial radio spots, making records, and later as a professor of speech at the University of Tulsa, fondly remembers her for something else, too.

"She had an amazing drive for perfection and detail," he said, "and demanded it whenever and wherever possible. But for me, her greatest impact was that she was the first person that told me that I wasn't perfect—and showed me areas where I needed to improve."[31] Dr. Dumit, a child prodigy of sorts, received elocution lessons at age five, and was regularly on *The Kiddies Review*, a program sponsored by the Jenkins Music Company that aired on Saturday morning radio. His parents regularly encouraged and praised him, but never were inclined to critique. Ronan knew how to find the balance between encouragement and correction.

Students would long remember one of Ronan's other popular sayings. "Almost anyone can play Guinevere [the legendary queen in King Arthur]. But it take a great sense of drama to be a convincing Elaine [the damsel in distress], either in life or on the stage."[32]

Students of Isabelle Ronan would be labeled "Ronanites" and identified not only by stories of their accomplishments and credits, but also by their precise and clear diction. For example, if you were a student of hers, the word "either" was to be pronounced "eether"—not "eye-ther"—and the word "neither" was articulated "nee-ther"—not "nyether."[33] Ronan also considered warming up the voice to be an essential component of preparation. As a 14-year-old boy, Aurandt

learned a series of vocal exercises. Variations of the following phrases
would be uttered moments before every one of his on-air appearances
for the next seventy-five years:

   *Me-me-mama-moo . . . Wolf-one-two-three-four. Wolf one-two-three-
   four. . . Diddle-de-diddle-de-dee.*[34]

   Aurandt was instructed to say them quickly, in a sing-song manner. One industry critic would later suggest those words might be the
most important Harvey ever offered, as they would help keep the
golden pipes polished and in working order for so much longer than
his contemporaries.

   Paul Aurandt appreciated and embraced the wisdom of Miss
Ronan, enjoyed participating in the school productions, and always
thrived inside her classroom. He quickly endeared himself to her and
loved the work she demanded. But it was the allure of performing and
announcing on the radio that ignited the flame of his professional passion. He looked forward each year to the Ronan-inspired creation,
"KVOO Day," where Central High speech students took over broadcasting responsibilities of the station in Tulsa.[35] He would also participate in another brainchild of Ronan's, entitled "Experimental Theater
of the Air," broadcast on Saturday mornings at KOME, a radio station
in Tulsa. On both stations, her speech pupils would perform an array
of live music along with drama and comedy shows. Much of the material was written by the students themselves, though looser copyright
laws back in the 1930s allowed them to use a lot of previously created
and broadcast material.[36]

   In April of 1936, three months before Paul would graduate from
Central High School, Miss Ronan launched a six-scene Easter pageant.
Her students, Paul included, participated. The production would grow
in size and scope, morphing to 40 scenes with over 100 actors. To this
day, it remains one of the longest running traditions in Tulsa.[37]

   Miss Ronan's teaching career lasted thirty-three years. She retired from teaching in 1953, after a final curtain call for her directing the play, *The Late Christopher Bean*. Ralph Blane, an Oklahoma-born composer best-known for penning hits for MGM musicals, including "Have Yourself a Merry Little Christmas" and "The Trolley Song" for the 1944 musical, *Meet Me in St. Louis*, was in the audience. He performed a special song he composed in honor of Miss Ronan. Sung to the tune of "Thanks for the Memories,"[38] it began:

> *Thanks for the Memories*
> *The happiness it brings*
> *To think about our friends,*
> *Each time that we forgot our lines*
> *You prompted from the wings.*

Though Paul was unable to attend that evening, sending a congratulatory telegram in his place, he did see her again. In the late 1960s, Paul was making a speech for the Tulsa Boys Home dinner. Miss Ronan surprised him by attending. When he spotted his old teacher, according to Eula Griffin,

> [H]e stopped what he was doing and came to her. He kneeled before her as she was sitting and told her that two women had influenced his life, his mother and her, and then bent to kiss her. It was one of the most touching moments of my life.[39]

She would return to her hometown of Marshall, Michigan in 1973.[40] In 1980, at the age of ninety-two, Isabelle Ronan took her final bow on earth.[41] Chuck Ellis, a Tulsa resident who worked with Miss Ronan for so many years on the Easter Pageant, would say she was the kind of woman "who made things happen."[42] Her students would agree, but with a slight amendment: she was a woman who made things happen—*for other people*—often at her own expense, as Paul Aurandt would come to learn firsthand.

CHAPTER SIX

On the Air

*W*hen Paul Aurandt settled into his desk in Isabelle Ronan's classroom in the fall of 1933, she had been teaching at Central High School for thirteen years. Ronan had heard plenty of promising voices and crossed paths with hundreds of talented thespians. But there was something about Paul Aurandt that was different—something about his inflection and his unique style of elocution. Even back then, she knew his was a voice you didn't want to turn off.

Larry King once said, "It's impossible to have Paul Harvey on your radio and punch the button. You cannot have Paul Harvey on the radio and hit another station!"[1]

Seventy years earlier, Isabelle Ronan had the same opinion. She decided to do something about it, and made an appointment for Paul with the program director of the local radio station in the fall of 1933.[2]

Paul wore his trademark coat and tie. Walking on the outside of the busy city sidewalk, there was an eager bounce in his step. He was excited. Isabelle Ronan walked beside him; she was all business—a woman on a mission. They walked from the main entrance of Central High School, south down Sixth Street, turned right onto Boston, and

finally left to 115 West 3rd Street.[3] They arrived together at the Wright
Building, the headquarters of radio station KVOO—the legendary
"Voice of Oklahoma."

KVOO started out as KFRU (Kind Friends Remember Us) in January of 1925, broadcasting out of Bristow, Oklahoma. KFRU would
enjoy the distinction of being one of the first stations to broadcast
country music. Its owner, an oil magnate named E. H. Rollestone, fell
on some hard financial times and moved the station to Tulsa in 1927,
where it was renamed KVOO. Oilman W. G. Skelly, otherwise known
as "Mr. Tulsa," acquired the station in June of 1928.[4] He had already
become one of the richest men in the world when he bought the
10,000 watt station. A community figure, he had previously invested
in the community by building the Tulsa Airport, the Spartan School
of Aeronautics, and the Spartan Aircraft Company. He also gave to
countless causes and institutions like the University of Tulsa, setting
an example of local investment for the young Paul Harvey.[5]

When Miss Ronan and Paul arrived at KVOO, the program director greeted them warmly. He had known Miss Ronan for years, so she
got right to the point.

"This boy needs to be in radio!" she said matter-of-factly, pointing to
the silent, smiling Paul Aurandt.[6] He sheepishly nodded his head. An
audition was scheduled for the coming Saturday. He'd be there—early.

It was an auspicious beginning. Fourteen-year-old Paul Aurandt
arrived back at KVOO inside the Wright Building shortly before two
o'clock.[7] The autumn weather that Saturday afternoon was crisp, with
clear, open skies. The station was in the middle of a local program but
the announcer was preparing to transition into the weekly airing of
the Metropolitan Opera broadcast.

Aurandt was ushered into the studio, handed a pair of headphones,
and briefed on what they expected of him. He sat down and settled

in, reviewed the script, and tried to remember all the lessons Miss Ronan had taught him. As his time approached, he nervously reread the script.

"2:30 p.m. Metropolitan Opera Tannhäuser (Monitor Fade In)."[8]

The parenthetical reference was a reminder for him to listen to the opera on his headphones as the local program wound down. He was then to say a few words and simultaneously "fade in" the full transmission of the Richard Wagner opera. With his mother and all the members of his world listening, the man who would become the most popular radio personality in the world began his on-air career. He was finally live on the airwaves of KVOO. Though apprehensive, he was in good voice.

"We join the Blue Network to bring you the Metropolitan Opera broadcast now in progress. This afternoon you will hear the immortal opera Tannhauser by Moan-ee-tore Fahd-een."[9]

There were quite a few chuckles out across the miles of the Oklahoma plains. Paul probably fooled quite a few people, confused others, and caused them all to wonder.

In the years since that memorable Saturday afternoon in downtown Tulsa, Paul Harvey grew fond of the following quote, often employing it when attempting to emphasize the brighter side of a dark piece of news: "As Mark Twain is said to have said about the music of Richard Wagner, 'It's not nearly so bad as it sounds.'"[10] Maybe he was always subconsciously trying to get back at the German composer for tripping him up.

Fortunately, the station brass agreed with Miss Ronan that Paul had talent and looked beyond his opening faux pas. It wouldn't be the last time Paul Aurandt mispronounced a word. The boy with such great promise was given a second chance. He would sign on with the station, working mostly for free his first year with some spot announcing, guitar playing, and sweeping up at night. "I was too young to work under the government's child labor laws," he recalled, "but I managed to get a special work permit."[11] His start wasn't glamorous. In those early years, Paul handled a broom as frequently as the microphone.

But he didn't seem to mind it at all. He was just glad to be on the inside of the studio glass. As some psychologists will say, if someone can find a job that he loves, he'll never really work a day in his life.

Paul Aurandt, fourteen years of age, got his start sitting behind a silver-plated microphone, not getting paid a penny. Though without a dime in his britches to show for his effort, he felt like the richest man in town.

CHAPTER SEVEN

Climbing the Ladder

*W*hen you start at the bottom, there is nowhere else to go but up. The KVOO studios were located in the basement of the Wright Building, an eight-story red brick building with interior gray marble walls and stately dark slate floors.[1] Erected in 1922 by Dr. Walter E. Wright at a cost of $680,000, the lower level radio facility was simply furnished yet expansive. In addition to the broadcast studios, there was a rehearsal room, control room, music library, three general offices, a men's smoking room, and a rest area for women. The space was critical; the station employed a thirteen-member orchestra that regularly played live for daily broadcasts.[2]

KVOO's chief engineer, Watt Stinson, literally lived at the station. Living quarters were carved out of a corner of the cellar. Although KVOO didn't broadcast twenty-four hours a day in 1933, there were always complications and problems to resolve in order to keep the fledgling station on the air. W. G. Skelly felt that Stinson's close proximity to the equipment was a tremendous competitive advantage. His presence not only helped keep his station running, it kept them a step ahead of the competition.[3]

By Christmas of 1933, Paul Aurandt was settling into the rhythms of his various responsibilities at KVOO. He eagerly accepted every assignment; though only a rookie, he was usually given local announcing opportunities—news, weather, sports—between both the national and locally produced programs. Those early stints were short and scripted. He wished they were longer, but it was a start. Hours might sometimes pass between the on-air opportunities. He kept himself busy, but he was still holed up in a windowless basement, devoid of glamour and glitz. Truth be told, Aurandt could not care less. To him, the view was just fine. He had arrived. It didn't matter that he couldn't see the sky—he could see hints of his future. The teenager who had started pursuing his dream by making crystal radio sets as a 5-year-old was now a member of the fraternity of broadcasters.

Business was booming. By early 1934, KVOO had outgrown their facilities in the Wright Building. At the time, the station increased its signal strength from 10,000 to 25,000 watts, significantly increasing its reach, and moved from its modest subterranean accommodations over to the gleaming Philtower, a twenty-three-story, gothic-style structure in downtown Tulsa. With a commanding view from their high rise studios, KVOO was moving up in the world—literally and figuratively.[4]

Dubbed the "queen of the skyline" when it opened in 1928, the Philtower was the creation of Tulsa oilman Waite Phillips. After Phillips sold his company in 1925 for $25 million, he poured his resources into the construction of his famed building.[5] A bit of a nonconformist, he spurned the art-deco style architecture that was defining the city and instead pushed for an "old-world symmetry" that included entryway gargoyles, an elegant lobby, and stunning glass chandeliers. There was also a broad and polished staircase connecting the second and third floors and opening up onto a popular shopping plaza. Marble and mahogany were everywhere. The 323-foot tall tower was topped with a red and green shingled pyramid-shaped roof. It could be seen for miles around, especially at night, when its neon lights lit up the downtown sky. More importantly for Paul Aurandt, the strong and "clear channel" signal of KVOO took his voice and the station's eclectic mix of programming straight across the state and all around the southwest region.

The eccentric but philanthropic Phillips was thrilled to count the "Voice of Oklahoma" as one of his tenants. Announcers were actually required to mention their location as a way to help "pay the rent."[6] Few buildings were cited as frequently on the air in those early days as was the Philtower. Presiding over affairs from a penthouse office that boasted twenty-foot ceilings and a huge fireplace, Phillips was a generous man and a supporter of the Boy Scouts of America. In 1949, he would actually deed the building, along with approximately 40,000 acres of his ranch, to the non-profit organization.[7]

By the spring of 1935, 16-year-old Paul Aurandt had emerged as one of the station's more popular announcers. KVOO listeners loved his distinctive voice and crisp elocution, along with his dramatic use of the pause. Unlike so many other broadcasters, Aurandt wasn't afraid of silence. Every announcement was made with a dramatic flair. He could make a sunny weather report sound fascinating or spice up a routine account from City Hall with carefully selected words. His age was no secret. It likely added to his allure. Few people had heard someone so young sound so darn good. To accommodate his school schedule, the teenager's on-air shifts were usually in the evening hours or on weekends.

Station manager William B. May was able to build a wide and loyal audience by sending his on-air talent to "remote" locations throughout the city and state. By 1934, KVOO had twenty-one different sites for various remote broadcasts within its listening area.[8] Some were high-energy gigs in hotel ballrooms around the city and others were from more sedate settings like the campus of A&M College at Stillwater. Wherever the setting, Paul loved the thrill of connecting personally with his audience

A teenage prodigy, Paul benefited from being the youngest on the staff; he could get the seasoning he needed without too much pressure or expectation of performance. He impressed his colleagues with his work ethic and enthusiastic and tireless ambition. Paul earned the nickname of "Moonglow" amongst the engineers, a sign that he was accepted as one of their own.[9] Its meaning and origins have been lost. Harvey was probably content to let it die.

★ ★ ★

It was Thursday, February 8, 1934. A thin layer of ice coated the roads. Paul Aurandt was still in school at Central High School when a four-door 1932 Buick drove up outside the front doors of the KVOO studios. Two gentlemen emerged from the front seat. The driver, O. W. Mayo, carried a black briefcase. His passenger, toting a fiddle case, was a musician by the name of Bob Mills. Though nobody realized it at the time, a future legend had just arrived in Tulsa.[10]

It is a purely American story of brilliance, persistence, hard work, fame, ego, and resilience. In 1931, a talented group of mostly Texas-born musicians managed to land a fifteen-minute daily radio gig sponsored by the Burrus Mill and Elevator Company. Their job was to help sell the company's flour by performing clever and memorable music, including composing silly jingles touting the superiority of the products. Led by Bob Wills and dubbed the "Light Crust Doughboys," the group struck a chord with audiences. At the time, their music, which later became known as "western swing," was known as "hot hillbilly music" or "hot string-band music"—a mixture of fiddles with a hint of blues and jazz, all pulled together by a toe-tapping rhythm.

The Burris Mills Company was managed by W. Lee "Pappy" O'Daniel, a reportedly ruthless and hard driving businessman with a substantial ego.[11] He positioned himself as the spokesman for the group and insisted on being the program's announcer. Not content with their musical prowess or performance, O'Daniel almost made the men haul sacks of flour when they weren't playing. Disgusted, Wills and his boys quit. When they tried to promote themselves on a flyer as being "formerly the Light Crust Doughboys," O'Daniel sued them for $10,000. Wills eventually won the case.[12] When they attempted to switch to another station, O'Daniel tried to bribe or blackmail the station management, offering to buy time so long as they didn't hire Wills. Finally, the group made their way from Texas to Oklahoma and eventually to Tulsa to request an audition with KVOO. By the time they arrived in town, they had changed their name to "Bob Wills and the Texas Playboys."[13]

Sitting across from Wills and Mayo, William May was skeptical. He had just lost Orvon Gene Autry, "Oklahoma's Singing Cowboy," to Sears and Roebuck's WLS (World's Largest Station) in Chicago. Autry had been recommended by Will Rogers. What did this group have to offer? Reflecting on the meeting in a 1939 letter to the group, May wrote, "Selling me on the idea that our public was interested in a group of Texas kids with no particular claim to glory was not easy. When I finally relented, due entirely to your superlative ability to sell yourselves, there was still considerable doubt in my mind. Now I am convinced that you knew exactly what you were talking about when you said you'd prove a success."[14]

The group would eventually settle on a daily 12:00 p.m. time slot, playing six days a week over the airwaves of KVOO, including

Thursday and Saturday nights at the Cain Ballroom in downtown Tulsa. On Sundays, they were often called on to play at funerals. As their guitarist, the late Eldon Shamblin, once said, "I can remember doing seventy-two one-nighters without getting a night off."[15] Although they were busy, they were by no means wealthy artists. Holding it all together by a shoe string, Wills and his men lived in a basement apartment of the Philtower, just a few floors below the radio studios. Their popularity soared with each performance. The music of Bob Wills and the Texas Playboys was a pleasant reprieve for listeners still muddling their way through the drudgery of the Great Depression. Forced to conserve energy and cut costs, many Tulsans would limit their daily radio usage to just one hour a day in an effort to save battery power.[16] More often than not, they would use it to listen to Bob Wills and his boys.

Much to his delight, Paul Aurandt was often called on to serve as the station's on-site announcer for Wills's performances at the Cain Ballroom. It was one of the hottest tickets in town, and the young Aurandt was in his element standing before a thousand whipped up fans. Although his voice may have been years ahead of his age, Aurandt was soon stricken by a typical ailment of burgeoning youth: acne. Though faceless to the listeners at home, radio announcers assigned to remotes in those early days were expected to maintain a sharp visible appearance.

William B. May was forced to break the news to the disappointed Aurandt that until his skin cleared, he was going to have to pull him off the plum, live on-air announcing assignments and back into the studios. May expected him to be devastated, but instead Aurandt took the news like a professional.[17] Relieved that he could still serve at the station and confident that the blemishes would pass, Paul was content to look ahead at what might be coming next. Always a man of measured emotion, he would say he was taught to stay in his seat come times of trouble, for "it's only people who jump off the roller coaster who get hurt."[18]

Paul Aurandt would not only develop an affinity for Wills's music, but also a deep respect for the integrity and character of the man himself. In his early days at KVOO, the Tulsan saw Wills strike up friendships with loyal listeners, even small children. One in particular was with a very young boy named Earl Edward Basse who had contracted polio. Five-year-old Earl would often come with his parents to hear Bob's performances at the Cain. With each visit their friendship grew deeper, and Bob always made time to visit with the little lad. But at the age of six, the blond-haired Earl succumbed to the ravages of the disease. Bob and the boys of his band attended the funeral, KVOO staff in tow, and played the emotional tune, "Mother, Put My Little Shoes Away." Among the six hundred people in attendance, there wasn't a dry eye to be found.[19] But Paul Aurandt was learning from what he saw; themes of kindness, for instance, that even the smallest person was important, or the humble always deserved exultation. There would be many more examples for Paul Aurandt, but none quite like the life of Bob Wills.

At the time of his graduation from Tulsa's Central High School in June of 1936, Aurandt was employed full-time at KVOO as a station announcer and earning $29.50 a week for his efforts.[20] Still living at home, the compensation was adequate enough to allow him the freedom to register as a freshman for classes at the University of Tulsa in the fall. Ever the curious and competent academic, school came fairly easily for Aurandt. Yet increasingly pulled by the allure of the radio, he decided to pull up stakes to pursue an offer he couldn't refuse. With a twinge of sadness but a sense of excitement, anticipation, and adventure, the 19-year-old packed up and headed north to Salina, Kansas for a job with KFBI (Kansas Farmer Bankers Insurance) radio.

Formerly KFKB (Kansas First, Kansas Best), the radio station had been owned by John R. Brinkley, nicknamed the "goat gland doctor" by friends and foes.[21] Shortly after going on the air, Brinkley was accused of using his station as a front for a bizarre medical business designed to promote his theory that a man's sexual potency could be restored by receiving the transplanted prostate of a goat. His radio show was called the *Medical Question Box*. Vulnerable or just plain gullible listeners would call or write to the station to receive Brinkley's counsel.[22] As his audience of victims grew, he became tremendously wealthy. Patients were charged $750 for the prostate transplant procedure.[23] It didn't work, of course, but that wasn't the worst of it. Many suffered debilitating side effects and countless victims died from infection. Ever the unscrupulous "medicine man," Brinkley cut a deal with a local pharmacy and received a kickback from all medications that he prescribed to listeners. When law enforcement officials finally moved in, Brinkley bolted for the Mexican border.[24]

When Farmers and Bankers Life Insurance Company bought and renamed the station, they counted on relocating it to Wichita, where they were based. When the new owners petitioned the FCC for permission to move its base of operations out of Salina back to Wichita, however, the agency stubbornly refused to grant their request. Management was told that the only way they'd be permitted to move was to show they couldn't turn a profit where they were currently licensed.

"So what they did," Paul Aurandt later explained, "was to hire the least experienced teenage applicant they could possibly find to help them lose money and that was me!"[25] And so in 1937, at the tender age of nineteen, Paul Aurandt was named KFBI's Station Manager.[26] Financially, it was a lateral move; his salary remained $29.50 per week. But he had a title and the authority to call his own shots and claim as much airtime as he wanted.

The 7-year-old theater was an art-deco design punctuated by gold leaf paint, gleaming chandeliers, and a wide staircase. Constructed at a cost of $400,000, the studios of Paul's new station were situated on the second floor mezzanine just behind the balcony.[27] Though it was a nice location, Paul wouldn't be spending much time inside. He wanted to get out and meet the few listeners his station enjoyed and, just as importantly, build an audience of new friends.

The Duckwall's Five and Dime in downtown Salina became a favorite host location of Paul's for a regular slate of remote broadcasts over the airwaves of KFBI.[28] Established in 1906, the variety store was an ideal place for taking the pulse of the town's population. Although their founder, A. L. Duckwall, passed away the year Aurandt arrived in town, the store remained true to his belief in the power of repetition and grassroots marketing. The five and dime store convinced farmers to allow them to paint advertising slogans on the sides of their barns. Phrases like, "There are others, but none like Duckwall Brothers" and "Meet your friends at Duckwall's" became engrained in the minds of Salina shoppers. Duckwall's promised "A Little of Everything" to its customers. Paul Aurandt would do the same for his audience by delivering, in an entertaining fashion, a colorful mix of news, sports, and weather.[29]

At Duckwalls, Paul Aurandt's listeners got their first taste of the emerging radio newsman. The typical scene was Paul surrounded by wires, equipment, and inexpensive and practical merchandise in a hard chair behind a small table. He would hold a thick stack of paper, each page containing just one news item a few lines long—more than enough to tell him what he needed to know. When he was through reading it, he tossed it onto the floor to avoid losing track of where he was in the broadcast. Customers watched as he announced the news. He enjoyed the audience and was always glad for the crowd that gathered. He winked and waved while on the air, and stayed as long as he could to visit when his shift was over. By the conclusion of his broadcast, he'd be surrounded by an avalanche of paper on the floor.[30] Customers didn't seem to mind. Some were amused by the spectacle. They'd never really seen anything quite like it.

On top of delivering the news, Paul Aurandt would conduct a series of "man on the street" type interviews from his broadcaster's perch in Duckwall's. The feature was a big hit. He was always interested in people and their thoughts, so the segment was a natural fit for Aurandt's style and personal demeanor.[31] His audience began to grow. Management counting on him to fail began to get nervous.

Paul Aurandt bonded with Kansas through the people he met during his time as the station manager. One of his first close affiliations was the Norse Gospel Trio, in its fourth year of performing on KFBI.[32] A popular family singing group based out of Salina that consisted of Bob, Ken, and Bill Peterson, they had struggled desperately to make ends meet after the death of their father, Ephraim. Mrs. Peterson found work cleaning the houses of the wealthy in Salina and assumed the role of janitor at the Covenant Church of Salina.[33]

There was an instant connection between the new station manager and the mission-minded singers. Paul admired the fervency of their faith and the overall resiliency of their spirit, while he appreciated the power of their music. Having also lost his father at a young age and grown up with a mother who never gave up, he shared a common bond with the men.

It wasn't long before Paul Aurandt was traveling with the Trio to engagements all around the state and announcing for them. "Traveling to Kansas corners with the Norse Gospel Trio from our radio station to many Mennonite churches in the state, I learned to love God and country and Kansas. Before you were born I was born again in Kansas," he later told an auditorium full of Kansans.[34]

By the early months of 1939, Paul Aurandt had turned KFBI from a fledgling station on the brink of collapse to a proud, profitable, and popular radio station. The brass at Farmers and Bankers Life Insurance Company were conflicted. They couldn't really regret a success. But Paul Aurandt had foiled their plan to sway the FCC toward granting permission to move their station out of Salina to Wichita. "When I made the station profitable I became disposable," Paul reflected, "but not before I had become a flag-waving Kansan."[35]

In his five years at KVOO in Tulsa and three years at KFBI in Salina, the 21-year-old had done a little bit of everything in the broadcasting business. After announcing, managing personnel, navigating the politics of a small town, overseeing programming for the station, and dabbling in the news, Aurandt realized that he felt most drawn to pure newscasting. When a news job opened up at KOMA back in Oklahoma City, he jumped at the chance, though leaving Kansas was much harder than he first imagined it would be.

The return home to the state of Oklahoma would be brief. Radio was changing and expanding quickly. It was a nomadic business; talent was expected to follow the opportunities. A young man would be foolish to do otherwise. At 50,000 watts, KOMA was considered the mighty blowtorch of the Midwest. Paul's voice was reaching more listeners more frequently than ever before.

For Oklahoma, 1939 was a watershed year. *The Grapes of Wrath*, John Steinbeck's novel chronicling the plight of fictional Okies Jim Casey and the Joad family, was published to great acclaim.[36] Although it was sympathetic to Oklahoma, residents were outraged, believing it portrayed its people as ignorant and uneducated and the state as an unattractive place to live. With his deep roots and charm, Aurandt was an authentic and enthusiastic booster for the area—the right man at the right time to counter the negativity. Aurandt found himself covering the ascendancy of the University of Oklahoma athletic programs in Oklahoma City. The Sooners enjoyed their first appearance at a football bowl game and advanced to the semifinals of Final Four in basketball.[37] No matter the subject, he was a natural. The emotion in the voice was genuine. He was happy to be home, and assumed he would never leave again.

But then came the call that changed everything.

Aurandt's boss in Oklahoma City, Allen Franklin, had just left KOMA to take the top job at a new station in St. Louis, KXOK. Franklin had grown fond of Paul's captivating style and broad abilities. He wanted Paul to join his team as the number two announcer on staff.[38] A dialogue was initiated, followed by some good-natured negotiations. By the middle of 1939, Paul Harvey Aurandt had moved again, assuming the position of Special Events and Newsman at 630 KXOK. Financially, it was yet another lateral move, but there was someone waiting for him in St. Louis that all the money in the world couldn't buy.

CHAPTER EIGHT

Meet Me in St. Louis

The 5,000 watt KXOK, whose signal could reach eastern Missouri and southern Illinois during the daytime, was owned and managed by the *St. Louis Star-Times* newspaper. As the 1930s rolled to a close, so did the so-called "press-radio war" that had been raging since the late 1920s when radio began to compete seriously with print journalism.[1] The merging of the two entities into a single building and cohesive operation heralded a new and exciting cooperation between rivals. In announcing the partnership, the publisher proclaimed, "As edition after edition rolls off the presses the news will be rushed to the radio newsroom on the second floor of the Star-Times Building, there to be edited and put into the fast, clear bulletins the air requires."[2]

When Paul arrived at the station's headquarters at 800 North 12th Boulevard, he discovered a most unusual set-up. The three studios (A, B, and C) were located on the fourth floor; its offices were on the second. The third floor housed the newspaper's giant linotype machines. "I'd step out of the studio and feel the rumble under my feet," remembered Bob Hille, one of the station's first employees. "All three studios were mounted on springs, which was fairly innovative at the time. We had a disc recording set-up that was designed to escape the vibration from the linotypes. They mounted a Presto recorder on legs that ran down about three feet to a huge concrete block. The block was set on top of a large, inflated truck inner tube that kept the vibrations out."[3]

Though housed in fairly tight quarters, the studios were modern and well furnished. Days before they made their on-air debut on September 18, 1938, the *St. Louis Star-Times* bragged about the accommodations of its new radio station:

> The studios, three in number, are located on the fourth floor....The reception room will be decorated with a chocolate brown floor trimmed in white, with buff walls and ceiling. Opening from the reception room will be an observation alcove where programs originating in studio "C" may be observed. The studio will be decorated with a jade green floor, sea green walls and a buff ceiling. Studio "A," the largest of the three, will be furnished with varying tones of terra cotta, ranging through three shades from the dark floor to a lighter ceiling....[The] observation room for this studio will have theater seats arranged in tiers for the accommodation of visitors.[4]

"KXOK went on the air with a really impressive staff," wrote Bob Hille. "We had a full studio orchestra. We had a classical quartet which included a man who played first cello with the Symphony. We had Skeets Yaney and the hillbillies in the morning. Eddie Arnold was a young kid who played with them. I went on as a studio announcer, which meant I was literally working for nothing."[5] Bob had started at KXOK while he was still in high school, just prior to Paul Aurandt's arrival. Bob commuted on a trolley car and would normally step back into his house just a few minutes before one in the morning.[6] Like his colleague Paul Aurandt, the young man was hungry and grateful for the mere opportunity to be on the air.

As the designated number two on-air talent behind Allen Franklin, Aurandt carried a little weight around the station and enjoyed the privilege of having his own desk, located on the second floor. He didn't have an office; those were reserved for the big bosses around the floor's perimeter. His desk was in the middle of a large open area,[7] which kept him on his toes. There he would plot and plan, work the phones, and cultivate his sources from all over the country. Given his designation as the special events director, Paul was always trying to gin up a new broadcasting idea to further promote the visibility of his station. Few people thought as creatively or executed their ideas as successfully as Paul Aurandt.

In the early days of February 1940, Paul personally and successfully cobbled together dozens of stations to carry his live-on-site Mardi Gras reports from New Orleans via an arrangement with the Mutual Network.[8] It was a significant coup for a reporter his age, at a station the size of KXOK, to enjoy the flagship status of such coverage. There he was on Bourbon Street, in the middle of the French Quarter, a character talking to the characters of a crazy city in a celebratory mood. His knack for asking the right questions by getting inside the shoes of his subjects was on full display. Life on the road agreed with him.

Firsthand reporting became his specialty at KXOK. The more dramatic the event was, the greater his energy and enthusiasm. Paul learned how to deftly match emotion for emotion. He reserved the use of superlatives for extraordinary moments, but because he enjoyed chasing the story, he seemed to find more than most. When the Red

River began to rise and cause flooding along the Texas and Oklahoma borders, Paul Aurandt was there with a microphone in his hand.[9] A masterful talker, he could negotiate his way almost anywhere. When he caught wind of a United States Navy mock bombing exercise over Missouri, he cajoled a pilot into letting him ride along. While the plane was barreling along at 500 mph and dropping explosives on a bridge below, Paul provided color commentary for KXOK listeners.[10]

Just as he did back at KVOO in Tulsa, Aurandt broadcasted from countless dances and band remotes. Headliners like Tommy Dorsey, Glenn Miller, and even Frank Sinatra would cross Aurandt's path during his tenure in St. Louis. He liked them all.

One of the many remote broadcasts Paul covered was a debutante cotillion entitled "The Veiled Prophet Ball," an event that continues to this day. Similar to a traditional beauty pageant, five debutantes were selected to join the "Veiled Prophet's Court of Honor." It would culminate in one woman who was crowned the "Queen of Love and Beauty."[11]

It was a big deal for the society folks in St. Louis and KXOK's main competition, KSD, also covered it as a remote broadcast. Paul's arch rival at KSD was a gentleman named Frank Esehen, widely considered by those with KXOK and elsewhere to be a pompous and stuffy personality. For a laugh, Aurandt decided during his coverage of the event in December of 1939 to mimic Esehen's style in both tone and voice. Anyone who had ever listened to KSD got the joke. Some were offended but most took it in the spirit in which it was offered. Wrapping up coverage, KXOK's gadfly voice signed off with a great and fancy flourish by saying, "This is your obedient servant, Paul Aurandt . . . good night!"[12] It was obvious he loved his job.

His high jinks at the ball were typical. Paul Aurandt had a reputation around the station as a bit of a prankster and practical joke artist.

As a way to test the mettle and concentration of his announcers, he would sometimes bribe a pretty girl to sneak into the studio and crawl up into the lap of the announcer as he broadcasted live on the air. The 21-year-old Aurandt thought the gag was hilarious.

The staff at his new station enjoyed Paul's upbeat and outgoing personality. He liked to have fun; he used to joke with his colleagues that he freelanced in women, and was always interested in a date and a night on the town. The frivolity was always wholesome; he knew how to live it up without tearing himself or others down. He didn't need alcohol to get a buzz. Life was exciting enough on its own. As Bob Hille, who double-dated with Paul, remembered, "He was a bubbly and enthusiastic fellow." "He was different than most guys his age, a true character. He lived the high life, was the man about town. The girls loved him. He always kind of acted like he knew he was going to achieve something. But Paul wasn't cocky; he was confident and competent."[13]

Nicknamed "The Fun Spot," KXOK was a good place for the happy young man. Paul was happy to be climbing the ladder and happy to be receiving pats on the back from listeners down at the local drug store. He was no stranger to success but still never tired of the applause. But there were lots of happy and generally successful broadcasters operating at stations across the country. Mere happiness wasn't going to make Paul a star.

Although still rising, Aurandt was starting to drift ever so slightly as he chased the big dream. He didn't notice it. He assumed the circuitous career path was normal, but down deep he knew there was something missing from the mix. Setting up shop in his fourth city and fourth station in four years, he had yet to find his niche. Still, the most significant job for Aurandt was always the one he had, and he took his responsibilities seriously. He enjoyed the variety and the unpredictable nature of news and humanity.

There was nothing extraordinary on the horizon for Paul when Thursday April 4, 1940 dawned. Spring had fallen upon St. Louis. Skies were crystal clear; the sun warmed the air to a seasonal high of 56 degrees. The trees were finally in bloom. He wore no overcoat, just a suit jacket. Life was good, but it was about to get better. Over the airwaves of KXOK, Paul noted the coming of the baseball season. The hometown Cardinals were wrapping up their training camp with an exhibition game in Pensacola, Florida. They would win 8–4 and prepare to head north for opening day.[14]

It was a pretty ordinary day, but later that morning, everything changed forever. There would be no going back. An era was passing. They met on an elevator.[15] He was going down to chase after a story; she was going up to meet with station management. For Paul, it was love at first sight.

It all started when the striking 26-year-old Evelyn "Lynne" Cooper, also known as the "Blond Blizzard," was hired at KXOK to develop an educational program for the station.[16] "I sent them a list of ideas," she remembered, "and to my surprise, they asked me to do the program on the air. I decided to take on the challenge."[17] At the time, Miss Cooper was also serving as a substitute teacher in the St. Louis County Schools. Her area of interest was English literature. She was only drawn to the station because the position would help her qualify for a coveted "Life Certificate" in teaching.[18] On the day they met, she was supposed to be interviewing the St. Louis Superintendent of Schools but schedules had changed, and she was going to be unable to fulfill the assignment. (As the Special Events Director, Paul would be assigned to fill in for her and conduct the interview.)[19]

"Is that your pretty car out front?" he asked her, pointing to the six-cylinder ivory 1938 Nash Lafayette Coup parked in the lot beside the building.[20] She smiled and nodded.

Thinking quickly, he contrived a story about needing a ride to the airport. "If you'll take me to the airport, I'll take you to dinner," he said.[21] She agreed.

"So we went to dinner, and he proposed to me," she would later say. "I'm sure he must have done that to a lot of people, and I still tease him about it. 'Boy,' I thought, 'these radio people are fast.' But I looked at him, heard that voice, and I thought: *This fellow is going places. I wonder what makes him tick.*"[22] She originally didn't take his marriage proposal very seriously and unceremoniously turned him down flat.[23]

Ever the skillful interviewer, he learned from her at their first dinner that she was nicknamed "Angel" as a young girl. He thought she fit the part perfectly. He started calling her "Angel"—and so would everyone else.

★ ★ ★

Evelyn Cooper was born October 4, 1913, the youngest in a family of five girls and a boy.[24] A review of the official records presents some curious, seemingly inexplicable findings. According to the United States Census of 1920, Evelyn is listed as an "Evelyn Buergler," a step-daughter of William and Mattie Cooper of Independent City, Missouri.[25] Oddly, two of her older sisters, Stella and Mattie, were also listed with a last name of Buergler on the 1920 record and deemed "stepdaughters" in the Cooper clan. Yet, in the 1910 census, both Stella and Mattie were listed as "Coopers"—with the same mother and father (William and Mattie) as they had in 1920.[26] The incongruity has never been explained. Does it come as a result of a clerical error? Or were Evelyn, Mattie, and Stella adopted by one or both parents? The privacy of such sensitive matters, especially given the closed nature of family affairs nearly a hundred years ago, leaves much to speculation. What is known is that Cooper's mother died on February 16, 1924[27] when she was just ten, a devastating blow that would haunt her for years to come. But her siblings stepped into the gap. "I learned something different from each one of them," she said of her older siblings. "The one closest to me was still 17 years older."[28] Lynne's closest sister, June, was a role model for the orphaned young girl.

Through the years, the Cooper clan would instill in their little Angel a love of learning and an appreciation and passion for education. Like her future husband, she loved the wonder and majesty of the written and spoken word. A local Missouri publication described the young Cooper as a "child prodigy."[29] She wrote a novel when she was just eleven. "I wanted to be a writer," she once said, "I was introduced to a professional novelist who discouraged me from trying to make a living in the arts, but my parents always felt there should be no limits on what women could do. That is one of the great benefits of education— it gives each of us the opportunity to choose our own path in life."[30]

An honors graduate of Washington University in St. Louis, she received a bachelor's degree in Language Arts in 1934 and a Master's degree in English in 1935.[31] As she later remembered, her parents "introduced us to the value of a liberal arts education as the basis for a lifetime of learning. My graduate adviser was Richard Foster Jones, who emphasized writing and the importance of research. I don't think many people understand how much research goes into the news business, which is about getting it first—and getting it right."[32] Upon completion of her undergraduate degree, she was elected to four national honorary societies: Phi Beta Kappa, Kappa Delta Pi, Phi Sigma Iota, and Eta Sigma Phi.[33]

Evelyn was a prolific writer, scripting plays for school and church productions.[34] But as creative and imaginative as she was, she would have deemed her coming years to be an implausibly contrived, spectacular plot.

Paul and Lynne's whirlwind romance would culminate in marriage during the summer of 1940. Though Paul always said they were married on June 4, the marriage license on file with the state of Missouri lists their wedding date as August 5.[35] Additional discrepancies are also puzzling. Both Paul and Evelyn listed their hometown as "San Francisco" on the license—even though they clearly lived in St. Louis and worked together at KXOK. Though known to her friends and family as "Evelyn Cooper," the new Mrs. Aurandt wrote her name as "Evelyn Betts." Capping off the mystery is a written request, noted on the official record, not to publish notice of their union. It appears that the young couple was trying to hide something—but it's not clear what—or from whom.

Paul and Evelyn didn't have much, but they had each other, and that was just enough to get by on a combined salary of just over $60 per week.[36] Paul always had sweet memories of his bride and those early days in St. Louis. "I remember her a gentle warrior," he wrote. "Tears over trifles, and yet such courage in crisis as would have awed King Arthur...in the beginning, soup. Sometimes three days straight....Hard work, in a world so small we had to squeeze into it....Happy partnership, each too busy rowing to rock the boat."[37]

A world war was coming, but the love Paul had been praying and looking for had finally arrived. She would come to nurture and shape, corral his seemingly endless pool of energy, help to narrow and exploit the razor-sharp focus, and shape the free-wheeling will without breaking the spirit. From the scope, arc, and influence of a single life he would come to discover how one woman could change the trajectory of a man's days on earth.

CHAPTER NINE

Aloha

From his desk on the second floor of the Star-Times Building, Paul Aurandt had grown accustomed to quickly scanning the relentless flood of wire reports. They were his lifeline, and provided a window on the world well beyond his limited view. Intrigued by a developing pattern, he had made a habit of paying close attention to one particular story. (His colleagues would later recall that Paul always seemed to have a sixth sense for anticipating the magnitude of a story still in the embryonic stage.)[1] He began noticing an increase in reports of the naval maneuvers in the south Pacific. With his nose for news, the trends were subtle and alarming to the young rookie reporter. Like a kettle on a hot stove, he could see things were heating up. He predicted they might soon boil over.

Three days after Christmas in 1939, Aurandt noted that a division of American battleships, along with an aircraft carrier, several destroyers, two heavy cruisers, and a contingent of submarines had been reassigned to Pearl Harbor, Hawaii. Sailors and airmen from the USS *Arizona*, *Oklahoma*, *Tennessee*, *Nevada*, *Chester*, *Vincennes*, and *Saratoga* began to flood the beaches of Waikiki along the Oahu shore.[2]

When pressed, White House officials were dismissive of the move, discounting its significance and suggesting there was no ulterior motive to the decision and that its forces only represented a "good-will squandron."[3] Paul Aurandt didn't buy it. He smelled smoke.

In reality, the tactical shift had been in the works for some time. When the Hawaiian Islands came under the sovereignty of the United States in 1898, military leaders were ecstatic. Considered to be the "crossroads of the Pacific," it was an ideal defensive location. Sitting 2,400 miles from the mainland, 2,289 miles from the Aleutian Islands, 4,050 miles from Japan, and 2,611 miles from U.S. Samoa, American strategists considered it a domestic firewall of sorts.[4] Officially declared a Naval Station by an act of Congress in 1908, the harbor at Pearl was dredged and deepened in order to accommodate large ships.[5] A series of "war games" commenced in the mid-1930s and would occur regularly each year thereafter. Tens of thousands of men and over 150 ships and 500 airplanes would descend upon the outpost per exercise. Bombers conducted mock raids of the military facilities. The roar of blank shells and anti-aircraft ammunition became as common as the sound of the rolling surf. The exercises were fairly routine as preventative measures to prepare the troops. But beyond mere training, they were conducted to deter any country—namely Japan—who might consider the islands to be a soft and easy target.[6]

It wasn't until late 1938 and early 1939 that the United States agreed to divide their fleet between the Pacific and the Atlantic Oceans. At the urging of Rear Admiral J. K. Taussig, forces were dispersed, with the majority of the Pacific presence home-based in the port cities of San Pedro and San Diego, California. Previously, the entire fleet traveled together en masse, under a theory of "strength in numbers." Still, President Roosevelt was not satisfied with only a section of the fleet along the West Coast. He was eager for a strong showing of force at Pearl Harbor, a position he considered to be the heart of the "strategic triangle" in the Pacific Ocean.[7]

As the Commander in Chief, Roosevelt got his wish. Over the objection of Admiral James O. Richardson, the head of the Naval Fleet, the United States officially moved its headquarters to Pearl Harbor on May 7, 1940.[8] It would prove to be a fateful decision, but one that many historians believe might very well have averted a direct assault on the mainland.

Meanwhile, back in St. Louis, Paul Aurandt began to lobby his boss, Allen Franklin, to send him on a special assignment to Hawaii. Aurandt didn't have to sell the general manager on the merits of the move, but practically speaking, it had major logistical challenges to it. In 1940, there were only two commercial radio stations operating on the Hawaiian Islands, KGMB, a CBS affiliate, and KGU, a sister station to Paul's KXOK.[9] Paul might be able to work as a stringer at KGU. However, there was no way to know whether he would be able to transmit reports over shaky phone lines, or what state their equipment was in. There was also the seven-hour time difference between Hawaii and St. Louis to take into account.

Never one to walk away from an enterprising prospect, Aurandt came up with another idea. KXOK was affiliated with the *St. Louis Star-Times*; perhaps he could be sent on a special assignment under the auspice and authority of the newspaper. Elzey Roberts, the paper's publisher, had been favorably impressed with Paul's journalistic prowess and easily warmed to the idea. Other journalists, beginning to perceive what Aurandt saw, were making a beeline for the islands. Roberts didn't like the idea of his paper being scooped by all the big boys—it was time to go on the offensive. For months, Hanson W. Baldwin of the *New York Times* had been filing a stream of interesting and insightful reports from Pearl Harbor. In Roberts's mind, any one of his St. Louis-based journalists, especially someone like Paul, could match wits with any sophisticated East Coast writer. The new assignment was approved. His official title was "Special Events Representative."[10] Once again, Paul Aurandt was on the move, but this time he wasn't alone. The newlyweds scrambled to get things in order, closing up their small apartment, and trying to minimize and bring with them only the necessities for a simple existence. They were excited. Who wouldn't be?

The cold winds of the winter of 1941 were coming to St. Louis, but the Aurandts were headed west. Dressed in their Sunday best, they piled as much as they could manage into Lynne's 1938 Nash coupe and headed west for the Port of Los Angeles. It was a long drive— 1,800 miles—but they didn't mind it a bit. Upon arriving in California, they arranged to have their beloved car shipped over to Hawaii.[11] There are no clear records indicating what specific steamship they sailed on to Hawaii, or whether the car came along at the same time. Longtime friend Carl Lee only remembers they used to give Paul a hard time about his near obsessive attachment to that automobile and the fact that he would have bothered to ship it across the Pacific.[12]

With the first leg of their exciting adventure complete, the newlyweds strolled aboard, feeling as though they were on top of the world.

The journey was pleasant. In 1940, the sail across the Pacific to Honolulu Harbor took approximately four and a half days. These were the pre-jet days, a time when "getting there" was considered by many to be half the fun. Life aboard most steamships was a grand affair, though most passengers were divided into two categories—the majority being in "first class" and a couple hundred designated as "coach." Paul and his bride fell into the latter category. If the Aurandts were aboard a Matson line ship, the dominant company serving the route from California to Hawaii at the time, they would have gotten a chuckle seeing a menu from the "Hard Times Dinner" held one night on board its vessels. Noting its availability, the restaurant assured guests that "our coffee is like the stock market—good until the last drop."[13]

As their steamship pulled gracefully into Honolulu Harbor, Paul and Evelyn Aurandt stood along the metal railing. From their vantage point, they could see crowds gathered at the pier. The arrival of passenger ships from the mainland was a big event. Deemed "Boat Days" or "Steamer Days," the locals turned out in large numbers to welcome the arriving guests. Though the tradition originated with tourism officials, it was charming.

Stepping down the gang plank, the Aurandts were greeted by the regally attired musicians of the Royal Hawaiian Band. Laden with their bags, and glad to be back on dry land, they were welcomed with a serenade. An intoxicating fragrance of native flowers filled the warm and humid air. Hula dancers were lined up and down the docks. Garlands were placed around their necks, and a gentle kiss on the cheek completed the welcome. It was magnificent.

There was a radio reporter at the end of the long line, with a tape recorder strung around his neck and a microphone in his hand. He greeted the Aurandts, and before they knew it, Paul and Evelyn were being interviewed for a radio broadcast in downtown Honolulu, practically in the shadow of the Aloha tower. They were asked about their trip and the reason for their stay. But before long, Paul had turned the tables on the enterprising journalist and ended up asking more questions than he answered. Like a drunk with an open bottle, he couldn't help himself. The boss back at the station liked what he heard. Days later, Aurandt was standing in the same place, conducting his familiar "man on the street" interviews with newly arriving passengers.[14]

When the Aurandts unpacked their bags in Honolulu in late 1940, they saw two different worlds in Hawaii that somehow managed to coexist. As colleagues suffered in the snow and ice back home in St. Louis, the newlyweds walked barefoot along the beaches of Waikiki. Muscled, tan men with names like Rabbit, Chickie, and Squeeze would try to sell them and thousands of other tourists surfing lessons. The water and the sand were like a sedative, protecting them from the cares of the world. "Angel and I were in Hawaii when it looked like the travel folders prior to the big war," Paul would later say nostalgically.[15]

But beyond the hula, the pineapples, and the sugar cane was a subtle but massive military build-up that had been unfolding incrementally since the early 1930s.

Shaking the sand from his shoes, Aurandt went to work. In addition to conducting interviews down at the Aloha Tower, he dug around for stories of interest to readers back home. He continued to cover the military build-up in addition to the first blackout of the Hawaiian Islands ever orchestrated.[16] Still, most people didn't seem to worry. Halfway around the world, the Germans were advancing on Europe, and Great Britain was hanging on by a thread. It was apparently too easy to brush aside the terrors and threats of totalitarian regimes when living in the middle of a tropical paradise. As Aurandt poked around and worked his sources, speculation was running rampant back on the mainland that Roosevelt might send the entire Pacific fleet to the Atlantic. And so, if there was any worry, it was not the Japanese, but instead the threat of losing the money of America's military men.

Touring the facilities and interviewing the brass at Hickam, Wheeler, and Luke Fields, Aurandt wouldn't have gotten the impression the fleet was going anywhere. By 1941, 70,000 naval personnel were stationed around the Islands. Aurandt noted its significant coastal defenses. Guns with a range of 30,000 yards were generously positioned along with numerous mobile artillery units. But he was also aware that though the military seemed on the alert, the natives were ever calm and unsuspecting.[17]

The work wasn't easy. He still chased leads and lived by the clock, but Paul enjoyed the change of pace. The Aurandts fell in love with the Hawaiian Islands and its people. They knew they weren't staying long, but they enjoyed every minute.

Living in Hawaii shaped his perspective on the challenge of finding a balance between responsible development and the preservation of land:

> After the Civil War, carpetbaggers were Northerners pillaging the South for personal profit. Today, intruders, from other states, even from other countries, are paving our horizon with rooftops. Today's carpetbaggers can buy a farm, they can pave it over, they can build whatever, they can turn a profit and run, having destroyed forever the fertile fields from which cometh our strength...
>
> I know. No drunk likes to be reminded of the hangover especially when somebody else is buying the drinks. And I know, these carpetbaggers are offering you a lot of money for your green acres.
>
> But Angel and I lived in Hawaii before the outsiders came and bought up the cane fields, and the pineapple fields and the taro fields and the vegetable crop land and used it up and spit it out. And now, like a locust plague, they move across our mainland, across whatever is left of our green pastures.[18]

Aurandt's free market ideals are were not inconsistent with his romantic point of view. For the rest of his life, he preached the gospel of moderation. "Nothing too much," he would say. "We need water, but too much and we drown, too little and we die of thirst."[19] As his worldview further broadened, the frolicking freelancer celebrated his twenty-third birthday in Honolulu on September 4, 1941. They savored their assignment, but he and Lynne were beginning to suffer from "Rock Fever"—feeling trapped in the middle of the Pacific on the volcanic rocks. It was time to think about the next assignment, the next move. It was time to turn to Evelyn and ask for invaluable advice and counsel, and step off America's Gibraltar in the Pacific.

After prayer, counsel, and conversation, the young couple booked their return to the mainland for the first Friday morning of the month, December 5, 1941. Paul may have had a nose for news, but it was clear he didn't enjoy any gift of prophesy, for he missed out on covering one of America's most tragic and shocking events ever by two days. He later said missing out on experiencing the attack and getting the story was something he would never get over.[20]

"In 110 minutes, 8 big battleships and 3 light cruisers had been sunk or damaged, 188 planes had been destroyed, and 2400 men had been killed," Aurandt would later write. "The blow not only paralyzed us in the Pacific for the greater part of a year, it also exposed our inexcusable optimism and our unbelievable unreadiness for battle." Paul would eventually turn several of his memories of the moment into a script for his popular radio feature, *The Rest of the Story*:

> The Japanese plan of attack was more than theory: it had been proved effective. For in 1932 United States Admiral Harry Yarnell decided to demonstrate the vulnerability of Pearl Harbor by slipping two aircraft carriers in close from the northeast. He launched 152 aircraft that theoretically could have obliterated all airplanes on the ground and

sunk most of the ships at anchor. Japanese naval attaches in Honolulu who read about the exercise were so impressed that they filed voluminous dispatches to Tokyo.

Their report ultimately manifested itself as the Japanese Master Plan. That's right. Almost a decade before the surprise attack on Pearl Harbor, we showed the Japanese how to do it![21]

The SS *Lurline* was steaming for San Francisco, still two days out when the bombs began to fall at Pearl Harbor. It would be years before the public would learn that the ship's radiomen had intercepted a series of Japanese messages during its initial trip to Hawaii from San Francisco between November 30 and December 3. Its personnel turned over all of the data to Navy intelligence upon docking at Honolulu Harbor. While the transfer is noted in the National Archives, the tapes of the "Kana" code have disappeared. In fact, 67 of the 74 intercepted messages that were cracked in the two weeks leading up to the attacks—messages that were delivered to President Roosevelt at the White House—are now missing from the official archives.[22] No explanation has ever been given for their disappearance. And they don't seem likely to materialize.

Speculation about events concerning the missing tapes has run the gamut. Some suggest President Roosevelt deliberately withheld critical intercepted intelligence from Admiral Kimmel in order to justify America's entry into World War II. Still others chalk it up to incompetence and sloppy management.

All Paul and Evelyn Aurandt knew when they stepped off the ship and into the streets of a sunny and crisp San Francisco on December 10 was that America was at war, and thousands of the young men with whom they had crossed paths during their time in the Hawaiian sunshine were now dead, savagely murdered by a ruthless enemy. It was a somber time, but they were eager to lend their hands—and their voices—to the war effort. Constrained from the draft by a medical defer-ment, Paul—and Evelyn—would find a way to join the millions of Americans resolved to offer their contribution on the home front.

CHAPTER TEN

Moving On

*I*n the deep darkness of a late December day, Paul and Evelyn Aurandt arrived at the mouth of the Bitterroot Valley. Nestled in the southwestern corner of Montana, the snowcapped peaks and canyons of the surrounding mountains were breathtaking. Fresh from Hawaii, Bitterroot Valley starkly contrasted with the balmy eighty degree weather they had left. The temperature was now near zero and the wind made it feel even colder. There was snow and ice everywhere. But it was beautiful. As radio nomads, they had grown accustomed to moving and found it fairly easy to fit into new and initially strange environments. They felt right at home under the wide blue skies of Montana.

Looking back on their arrival, Paul described the area as "snuggled in a protective valley with just enough culture imported by the state university and anything you really needed for sale at Missoula Mercantile."[1] They had few demands and were content to live a simple and quiet life in their small apartment, number four on University Avenue.

The decision to settle in the small town of Missoula, Montana came about much like all of the other moves in Aurandt's short broadcasting career. Paul and Evelyn simply went where there was work. Arthur James Mosby of KGVO (Great Valley of Ours), a CBS affiliate, had heard great things about Paul and hired him for various broadcast responsibilities. Initially, he was told he would be covering forest fires, which he thought sounded exciting. He was also assigned to host a "man on the street" type of radio program in and around downtown Missoula.

Arthur James Mosby was a self-made man of stubborn Danish ancestry who launched KGVO on January 18, 1931 in the small college town of Missoula.[2] When the Northern Pacific Railroad arrived in 1883, Missoula was reborn.[3] There was an explosion of growth and construction. Lumber and manufacturing businesses went, and gangbusters, and millionaires emerged from the cozy mountain towns. By the time Paul and Evelyn arrived, the stock market crash of 1929 had long since cooled the growth, but much of the culture and the neoclassical architecture they saw in 1941 was a product of those heady and profitable times.

A. J. Mosby owned Montana's first radio station, made even more remarkable by the circumstances surrounding its creation. Enterprising but brash, the adventurous Mosby got things going when he built a homemade radio transmitter in his small workshop. By consulting a rudimentary diagram he found inside the pages of an amateur radio magazine and, comparing it to an old parts list, he was able to cobble together a functional unit sufficient for broadcast use. Eventually it grew into a 5,000 watt radio facility.[4]

Aurandt dove headfirst into the new role and became somewhat of a regular figure in downtown Missoula. It was easy to spot him with his microphone along Higgens Avenue and Main Street, bundled up against the winter cold in an overcoat, or resplendent in his suit in the summertime sunshine.

Interview subjects were plentiful, and Aurandt could count on meeting all types of interesting people outside the Missoula Mercantile's cast iron deep red storefront. Across the street was the newly opened Florence Hotel, a modern lodge with over seventy indoor parking spaces. Other popular locations for interviews included The Headquarters Building at 113 West Front Street and the Studebaker Building at 216 Main Street.[5] In this role he further cultivated a sunny and upbeat persona. Listeners grew familiar with his opening line, spoken regardless of dour circumstance or brutal weather. In a booming and lyrical tone he would shout, "It's a beautiful day in Missoula today!"[6] The mayor and Chamber of Commerce loved him.

An impressionable and enthusiastic Paul Aurandt began to familiarize himself with the pulse and quirks of the city of Missoula. He liked what he discovered on jaunts and jags around the region. Though reared in a city, he loved the splendor of the mountains and felt at home in the pristine wilderness. "I'd rather go fishing," he would always say, ". . . to find fish which had never seen a man, and let them see me."[7] And so, Missoula was an easy fit, like a glove on a Little Leaguers hand. "We hill folks are not very intellectual about some things," he would later suggest, "but one gets mighty close to the truth with his hands in the soil of these foothills of Heaven."[8]

When he wasn't roaming the streets of downtown Missoula, Aurandt was hosting another show that featured his adventurous exploits in a small plane all around the exciting state of Montana. There was always something fascinating going on, or a moment of drama that Paul seemed to capture eloquently. The verbal pictures he painted were exquisite. The listeners from the small towns he visited would come out of their homes to try to catch a glimpse of the broadcaster and his plane.

The faithful audience envied the traveling role, many considering Paul a modern-day Meriwether Lewis or William Clark.

But in reality, there was no plane. He was never where he said he was—it was all a ruse, a magical creation of the young man. Paul's onsite travelogue was produced and performed from inside the KGVO studies at 132 West Front Street in Missoula, just up the stairs from the Top Hat Night Club. With the use of some sound effects and marvelous writing, he pulled it off without a hitch. "He had quite an imagination," Mary Jane Mosby, A. J. Mosby's daughter, remembers. "He was really something. We always got calls on the Paul [Aurandt] shows because listeners were always wondering where that plane was."[9]

Still struggling to pay the bills and run his business, he became intrigued by the local Missoula story of Thomas Greenough. An Iowa native who settled in Missoula in 1882, Greenough had muddled through a career in railroad construction, enjoying some limited success while refusing to settle for mediocrity. Anticipating the coming expansion of the railroad and sensing an opportunity for a great demand for building materials, the persistent Greenough expanded his interests and opened a lumber business. When he landed a contract to supply wooden ties for the Northern Pacific Railroad's line from North and South Dakota to the Idaho/Washington State line, he was ecstatic. He invested the substantial profits in gold mining and became famously wealthy. By the time the Aurandts arrived in town, both Thomas and his wife, Tennessee, were deceased. But their stunning mansion remained and became a point of great interest to the fledgling announcer.[10]

Aurandt remembers visiting the property. In a detailed recollection he described it as a "handsome 22-room house with ... six baths and marble fixtures and several fireplaces and crystal chandeliers. [It was] a monument to his success and as a reward for the family which had suffered with him through the long, lean years."[11] And then hearkening back to a theme from his conversation with Miss Harp in Tulsa nearly two decades earlier, he concluded, "To me, in those very modest years of early marriage, the Greenough Mansion of tarmac wood with a ballroom on its third floor was tangible evidence that Horatio Alger[12] lives on."[13]

Paul Aurandt's boss at KGVO, A. J. Mosby, would later assume ownership of the property when state officials threatened to tear it down to make room for a highway. Mosby bought the mansion, but had to cut it up into three pieces to allow it to pass safely over the Madison Street Bridge. It was eventually reassembled and restored on a prominent hilltop southeast of downtown Missoula.

Paul loved the symbolism of the move and the tenacity it took in order for it all to happen just as it did. "There, all Missoula, looking up, can see the mansion . . . not to resent those who have more, but to emulate, imitate and outdo them if we can."[14]

★   ★   ★

It was in Missoula that Paul began to really carve out his unique reporting niche that would be both his downfall at KGVO and the secret to his future success elsewhere. Content to leave the "big news" to the network announcers, Paul saw the value of highlighting the softer side of a story. He refused to turn up his nose at angles and anecdotes that so many of his contemporaries would have tossed in the trash or completely ignore. Like he did in Tulsa, Salina, and St. Louis, he was again cultivating and deepening a wide array of simple sources from all across the west.

One in particular was a woman out of Seeley Lake by the name of Jessie Perro Dombey. She was a colorful character. Ms. Dombey was a mail carrier who also ran a gas station—and wrote poetry on the side, which Paul would often read on the air. Thanks to Paul, her pieces were regularly published in journals and some would even find their way around the world. When she penned "More Than a Throne" to celebrate the marriage of the abdicating King Edward to the American divorcee Wallis Simpson, Dombey received a note of thanks from the royal couple.[15] Even at a young age, Aurandt knew that the most important news isn't always printed on page one.

As the summer began, the Aurandts were grateful to see all the green emerging from the piles of melting snow. There was a sense of excitement in the air, a spirit of relief and release from the grip of the long winter.

Paul never would have guessed what was coming next. Early one morning, he was summoned to A. J. Mosby's executive suite in the offices of KGVO-AM.

"Have a seat," Mr. Mosby told him cheerfully. "Have I got something to tell you!"[16]

Aurandt sat up a little straighter, leaning forward ever so slightly. The radio talker was silent, a look of great anticipation across his cleanly scrubbed face.

"I'm going to offer you a big job, Paul," he said. "And in the process, I'm going to give you the best advice you've ever received. I'm going to shoot you straight here."[17]

Paul was all ears, a wide smile and raised eyebrows reflecting his interest.

Mosby began. "You have a silly and funny sounding voice," he told him. "You'd make a great salesman—you can sell anything, but Paul, honestly, you're never going to make it in the news business. You don't have a believable sound for news. It's distracting. People won't trust it. Why don't you join our sales team? The job is yours—but I'm sorry, you're done on the air here at KGVO."[18]

It was bad enough to be fired, but even worse to be told that a lifelong dream is built upon a fraudulent premise and destined for a dead end.

Collecting his wits, Aurandt retreated to the comfort and counsel of his wife, Evelyn. His confidence bruised and battered, she alone still believed in him and that was all that mattered—and all he needed to keep his hope alive.

Veterans of the broadcasting business will suggest that a true star hasn't earned his or her stripes until they've been fired. In fact, the National Radio Hall of Fame is full of people who were told at some point in their careers that they had no chance, no future, no talent, and no right to hold a microphone in their hands. At some point in their careers, luminaries like Rush Limbaugh, Ernie Harwell, Larry King, Mel Allen, Red Barber, and Larry Lujack were shown the door.

Ever the gentleman, Paul Aurandt felt no bitterness towards his old boss. He most certainly disagreed with A. J. Mosby's judgment, but he again saw the hand of Providence moving in his young life. A student of Benjamin Franklin and a man of abiding faith, he believed that, indeed, "God governs in the affairs of men."[19] He would come to credit Mosby with pushing him up by kicking him out.

In any other light, Paul's words upon A. J. Mosby's death on November 30, 1970 would be inexplicable. The gracious man gently and softly announced,

A death in the family. Art Mosby of Missoula, Montana. Pioneer broadcaster and land developer, for more than thirty-years a personal friend. The boss was vigorous through his eighty-second birthday. He will be buried in the shelter of the white-fanged Rockies, in the valley which he watered with his sweat and fertilized with his footprints through a fruitful lifetime. If there is any room for improvement in heaven, they sent for the right man.[20]

This of the man who once told him he had a silly voice and had no future in radio news.

CHAPTER ELEVEN

Leaning into the Winds of War

By the start of World War II, WKZO was arguably the most prominent and polished radio station in the country, if not the world.

Only announcers and talent who had paid their dues and learned their lessons elsewhere were given on-air roles and broadcast responsibilities. The station's owner, John Earl Fetzer, was an engineer by trade when he purchased the fledgling station he had been hired to manage, then WEMC, located on the campus of Emmanuel Missionary College in Berrien Springs (now Andrews University). The college was in need of money and asked for $10,000. Fetzer negotiated them down to $2,500, renamed the station WKZO (Kalama**ZO**o), and moved it to Kalamazoo, Michigan.[1]

If there is an emerging theme revolving around the early pioneers of radio, it would be that they often stood alone and against the prevailing wisdom of the age. To each and every one one of them, failure was never final, and strain along with struggle almost always preceded and accompanied success.

In 1931, the Indiana-born Fetzer arrived in Kalamazoo with only $156 and some used radio equipment in the trunk of his beat up old car. When he approached a bank to inquire about the possibility of a loan, he was denied and even scolded. "Young man," the bank official told him, "find something else to do. There is no way that somebody can make an honest living from the air."[2] To further compound his troubles, Fetzer fell victim to the press-radio wars of the 1930s. Newspaper officials warned advertisers not to spend money on WKZO or lose their place of prominence in the paper.[3] It was to be an uphill battle. Fetzer welcomed the challenge.

Persistent, John Fetzer pushed ahead. He traded airtime for meal tickets, groceries, and even a room and some office space at the Burdick Hotel. Makeshift studios within the property were barely sufficient and by no means elaborate. Not content to play by old rules, the innovative Fetzer also wanted to expand his station from just a daytime facility. In order to do so, he developed a directional antenna, which increased output power and cut down on unwanted interference, allowing WKZO to broadcast till midnight. When the signal began to interfere with a Nebraska station, WOW, on the same frequency, Fetzer was sued.[4] A lengthy court battle culminated in 1938 when the mogul was vindicated and his station received the first license to operate a directional antenna. Thousands of stations followed and embraced the new technology, transforming the radio world almost overnight.[5]

Stepping inside the lobby of the Burdick Hotel at 100 North Michigan Avenue in 1942, Paul Aurandt was excited to make his pitch for the advertised announcer position. Aware of WKZO's sterling reputation and demand for excellence, he was confident he was the right man for the job. The interview with Mr. Fetzer was going well, with Paul answering each question thoroughly and convincingly. Fetzer could tell the young man was capable and that he was a talent with a strong ego by his sharp and snappy responses. He immediately liked the kid, but he was also a businessman and always played his cards deftly and carefully.

"O.K., Paul," he said at the conclusion of the interview. "If you think you're so good, why don't you work for free for one week? If I like what I hear and see after the duration of the audition, we can do business together. Is it a deal?"[6]

"Yes, sir!" came the enthusiastic and immediate reply, as the lanky upstart stretched his open hand across the table. "It's a deal!"[7]

He was hired one week later. Acknowledging the talents of Paul's wife, Evelyn, Mr. Fetzer hired her, too. She would eventually write, produce, and even host her own show from time to time on home-making. Engineers would cart equipment out to the couple's home and capture Evelyn in the kitchen in a live remote broadcast that would serve as a precursor to the cooking and home shows now popular on such networks as the Food Channel and HGTV.[8]

It was a short and direct three-mile drive from Paul and Evelyn's apartment near Nazareth College at 3625 Gull Road into the studios of WKZO.[9] Though small in size, John Fetzer's station enjoyed a prime downtown location. A favorite pastime for the young couple was a stroll through the marble-walled corridor of the Burdick Arcade. Located within the confines of the 150-room hotel, it gave them an opportunity to window shop or stop by the Western Union Office to send a note home to Tulsa or St. Louis. Still operating on a limited income, they looked more than they bought, but they still had fun dreaming.

The Aurandts were a great team. Evelyn always seemed to be at Paul's side. Mary Jane Mosby, the boss's daughter at KGVO, hardly ever remembered seeing one without the other. "Paul and his Angel," she said warmly. "They were newlyweds and they came together and she was up there all day. They were smooching all over the place all the time."[10] A passionate lover to be sure, Evelyn was also an advisor and a trusted counselor to her husband. However, the dynamic duo would witness in Paul's new boss and his wife, John and Rhea Fetzer, a grand example of just how much a married tandem can accomplish together. John and Rhea's lives had a profound influence on the newlyweds. Mrs. Fetzer worked beside her husband, serving at one time as WKZO's program director, producer, and secretary. John headed up the sales efforts and kept the station on the air. The Fetzers modeled both professional and personal success and the Aurandts were their prime pupils. They ended up celebrating over six decades of marriage—something Evelyn and Paul would emulate.[11]

It would be an overstatement to say that Paul was a star from the moment he walked through the doors of WKZO. At the time of his hire, he was just another announcer, though he was truly part of an all-star ensemble. Laboring alongside Paul at the time was the future Hall of Fame baseball announcer, Harry Caray. When Paul was doing the news, Harry was doing the sports. From time to time, Paul was forced to fill in for Carey, an occurrence that invariably led to gripes and groans from the cantankerous baseball aficionado. "He teased him all the time," recalled Carl E. Lee, former engineer and eventual president of the Fetzer radio empire. "Paul did a sufficient job, but sports just weren't his specialty."[12]

There were plenty of opportunities for Paul to poke back and reciprocate Harry's good-natured ribbing. In fact, in some cases, all Aurandt needed to do was watch and laugh at Carey's own personal foibles. Both Paul and Harry were regularly tasked with conducting "man on the street" interviews. Paul had long ago mastered the dynamics of the feature, but young Harry still struggled with the need for quick ad-libbing on subjects beyond sports. It also didn't help that Harry had an unfortunate habit of perspiring profusely on even a relatively mild day. "He used to sweat all over the equipment," remembered his chief engineer. "One day out on the street, at the corner of Main and Burdick, I plugged his microphone into the amplifier and because his hands were all sweaty and slobbery, it sent a huge jolt up his arm and knocked him off his feet."[13]

It might be more legend than fact, but Harry was rumored to have first uttered his famous exclamation, "Holy Cow!" while rolling around in the shadows of Michigan Avenue.

Roy Rowan was also a fellow announcer of Paul's at WKZO. Rowan would soon head for Hollywood where he would make his mark as the voice for Lucille Ball productions, the Jack Benny Show, and later the popular game-show, the Joker's Wild.[14]

In the midst of the rising stars, Paul was continuing to develop, shape, and mold the signature techniques that would help make him and his delivery famous.

"In those days," Carl remembers, "an announcer controlled his own microphone and when he was finished, he would just hit a button and take himself off the air. One day I noticed that Paul seemed to be ending his newscast too abruptly. He'd finish with his last bit of news and then quickly say, "Good day!" and bang, off the air he went. I said, 'Paul, you shouldn't do that so quickly.' He replied, 'No, no, I'm working on something. It's O.K.'"[15]

Aurandt was simultaneously working on his use of the deliberate "pause" that punctuated and set aside his broadcasts from all the others. Ironically, the very mark that made him famous almost got him fired.

Station owner John Fetzer grew annoyed at Aurandt's use of the unorthodox technique. He hated the idea of dead air and considered

it a waste of valuable time. He called Paul into his office and told him
to cut it out or to find himself another job. Some diplomatic negotiations commenced. Paul pleaded his case and agreed to shorten but not
entirely eliminate the tactic. Fetzer grudgingly went along with the
brashness of his young announcer.[16]

★   ★   ★

On Saturday, June 13, 1942, the establishment of the Office of War
Information (OWI) was announced from the White House.[17] For the
first time, the government would be disseminating the news of the
two-front war under the auspice and authority of a single media
organization. Appointed to lead the new department was a Rhodes
Scholar named Elmer Davis, the distant and detached mentor of Paul
Aurandt. The WKZO announcer had listened and studied Davis
through the years, emulating elements of his style and admiring the
substance and scholarship of his newscasts. Originally from Indiana,
Davis was a highly respected newspaperman who was known for his
tightly written five-minute radio commentaries heard all across the
CBS Radio Network. His voice was laced with an air of sophistication
that he paired with an authoritarian yet statesman-like tone. Nevertheless, the humble Hoosier never let go of the common sense perspective of the quintessential Midwestern personality. This was the
secret to his success. When people heard Elmer Davis, they immediately thought of home and hearth, mom and apple pie.[18] Paul worked
towards becoming more like Elmer Davis.

History suggests that the whole idea for a concentrated and coor-
dinated management of war news came from one particularly opinionated Elmer Davis broadcast. Concerned that the public might be
hearing mixed messaging about the reasons America was at war—and
even worse, that her enemies might capitalize on information from a

rogue, carelessly filed report, Davis urged the formation of a unified news monitoring entity. Roosevelt agreed.[19]

Elmer Davis'd listeners expected such frank and sharp political assessments. During one such broadcast, Davis noted the reported sighting of an unidentified submarine inside neutral waters. He was incredulous but expressed it with a tinge of obvious sarcasm. "Of course the safety zone declaration doesn't say that belligerent war ships must keep out; only that they mustn't do any fighting," he said. "But what are they there for? American neutrality is a serious matter. It seems a pity that it threatens to provide the war with comic relief."[20]

Elmer Davis had great influence on the developing broadcast style of Paul Aurandt. Both men appreciated the power and punch of brevity and the stubborn, unrelenting nature of facts. "Every man has a right to his opinion," Bernard Baruch once said, "but no man has a right to be wrong in his facts."[21] By assuming command of the Office of War Information, Elmer Davis would be faced with the challenge of maintaining the balance of an unwieldy and still emerging new medium. At once he was to ensure that broadcasters were true to the facts—but not at the expense of American lives.

Upon hearing the news of Mr. Davis's departure for Washington, D.C. in the summer of 1942, a confident and cocky Aurandt made a deliberate and bold play for his broadcast spot. Sitting down before the WKZO's microphones, Paul began recording an audition tape for Mr. William Paley, the president of the Columbia Broadcasting System (CBS). It began, "Mr. Paley, sir, you are listening to the radio voice of tomorrow."[22] Unbeknownst to the 24-year-old, his Kalamazoo colleagues were determined to teach him a lesson and temper his insolence. In the midst of preparing the tape, he was set up for failure by several station smart-alecks. "[I was told that] the network preferred cosmopolitan pronunciations of such words as 'eye-ther' and 'neye-ther'." He then went on to remember they urged him, "... when you mention the concert at Carnegie Hall, it is 'car-nay-gee' and the violinist's name is 'yee-hoo-dee-main-wine.'" But wait, he countered, "I've heard it 'Yehudi Menuin.'" With straight faces they replied, "A frequent mistake." Ignorant of the set-up, he took their bad advice and the tape was mailed. He waited anxiously for a reply.[23]

Soon enough, a response was received. "A kind letter to Kalamazoo" was how Aurandt remembered it, but its content and evaluation was strikingly and decisively clear. "Not ready for New York," was the way Mr. Paley phrased the diplomatic letdown.[24] Disappointed but undeterred, Paul didn't miss a step and kept right on climbing.

★ ★ ★

Elmer Davis's story was a familiar one, filled with pitfalls and lucky breaks on an upward trajectory of hard work. Davis's big break came when he filled in for another radio hero of Paul Aurandt's, H. V. Kaltenborn, in August of 1939.[25] World War II was on the verge of breaking out in Europe and the network had sent Kaltenborn across the Atlantic to cover rising tensions. Faced with the prospect of substituting for the radio legend, Davis was excited but also somewhat overwhelmed. "I had done some broadcasting at odd times over the past dozen years," he later wrote, "had sometimes even pinch-hit for Kaltenborn during his absences; but to fill in for him in such a crisis as this was a little like trying to play center field in place of Joe DiMaggio."[26]

As the OWI's new chief, it was Davis's responsibility to hire a few dozen deputies to oversee domestic commercial radio facilities. When it came to filling the director role for the states of Michigan and Indiana, Elmer chose Paul Aurandt. In addition to his news broadcasting position, Aurandt became the Program Director and News Commentator at WKZO and the News Chairman in Michigan and Indiana for the Office of War Information by the second half of 1942.[27] In only a few short months, the Tulsa native had gone from being unemployed to juggling three jobs simultaneously.

Meanwhile, John Fetzer had emerged as an elder statesman for the radio industry and was appointed by President Roosevelt as the National Radio Censor within the U.S. Office of Censorship, a high-level position.[28] Apparently, all of Fetzer's trips to Washington, D.C. during the legal wrangling over his directional antenna made an indelible impression on the Roosevelt administration. WKZO emerged as one of the most important and highly respected radio stations in the country and was responsible for significant domestic wartime work.

Behind the scenes, John Fetzer was entirely uncomfortable with the concept of government censorship. It pained him to accept the assignment, but the peril of the times demanded it. But as soon as the war began drawing down, the principled radioman who believed strongly in the power of self-government and self-discipline began quietly laying off his deputies and deliberately reducing the organization's budget. He packed up all the files related to wartime censoring and shipped them off to the National Archives in Washington, D.C. "I'm convinced if we hadn't," he would later say, "the Office of Censorship would still be with us today, and I shudder to think how powerful it might be."[29]

Like all of the radio facilities around the country, the staff at WKZO jumped feet first into creating and producing patriotic radio programming that would encourage and complement the American war effort. Paul's wife, Lynne, hosted a weekly interview show on location at Fort Custer, an Army post halfway between Kalamazoo and Battle Creek, Michigan.[30] Paul hosted another program at Fort Custer, entitled

Hi Mom! that aired several days a week. The thirty-minute production was interwoven with Paul's upbeat and colorful commentary. Live music was interspersed with GIs who were given the microphone and afforded the opportunity to say hello to their moms back home. The ratings were terrific. Paul was always quick with a pep-talk and optimistic perspective on the capabilities of America's able-bodied sons and daughters.

The program was broadcast from inside the chapel on base, a place considered ideal for the necessary acoustics. On one memorable but sad day, Paul arrived for the show but was barred from setting up with his engineer inside. A brawl over racial tensions had broken out earlier in the day inside the chapel and military personnel were trying desperately to restore order. The bloodstained wooden floors were a disappointing spectacle and a reminder that, despite America's internationally driven focus, tending to the country's domestic social struggles was still a necessary and sometimes overlooked priority.[31]

Paul began to gather professional accolades and had the continued approval of John Fetzer, so the station began to send him on more remote broadcast assignments around the country. One such trip sent Evelyn and him, along with his chief engineer, Carl Lee, and his wife, Winifred, down to the Women's Third Army Corps Training Center at Fort Oglethorpe in Georgia. Arriving on site, the dapper and always pressed Aurandt was welcomed by a chorus of whistling, beautiful women. Paul didn't seem to mind, waving like a movie star on Hollywood Boulevard. He figured if the male soldiers could acknowledge pin-ups in such a manner, it was only fair to allow the women a similar expression of emotion. According to Lee, Evelyn took the GIs flirtatious overtures toward her husband in stride and even laughed the incident off. She likely thought it was just funny and, given the stature of her handsome spouse, could she blame them? Though still relative newlyweds, Paul's devotion to her had never been—nor ever would be—in question.

As an announcer, Paul was considered to be the consummate professional in and around the station. He was a good-natured soul, and his colleagues repeatedly would try to test his power of concentration. Once in the middle of an evening broadcast, a staff member came into the studio and shined Paul's shoes. He smiled and nodded, but never broke or lost his place. On another occasion, a shorter employee by the name of Hooper Waite put a pair of shoes on his hands and crouched down outside the window of Paul's studio. To the roaring approval of the watching staff, Hooper carried out a marvelous performance that would have convinced Aurandt that a man was walking on his hands outside the studio for over fifteen minutes. The gag was to no avail. Aurandt was a rock.[32] Broadcasting was serious business.

In the 1940s, radio stations were careful not to "commercialize" their news announcers, lest they lose their reputation of unbiased objectivity. As a staff newsman in Kalamazoo, Paul could not personally endorse products, as he would in later years, but all his broadcasts and announcements were made with such zeal and sincerity that listeners almost immediately trusted and respected him. The sales team at WKZO knew they had a winning commentator in Paul Aurandt, one who wasn't afraid of talking enthusiastically about his sponsors' products. Advertisers benefited greatly from placement in and around his newscasts. Paul brought such a big and important sound to every on-air opportunity, everything seemed more exciting when the Tulsan covered it. Fetzer once suggested that Aurandt could go to a parade of two people and cover it with such color and embellishment as to leave the listener with the impression he was really watching a forty-member, highly decorated military band walking down the middle of Main Street.[33]

As World War II dragged on, Paul Aurandt grew increasingly rest-
less with the level of his contribution to the cause. The GIs loved him
and he loved them, but he knew he could do more. His responsibilities within the Office of War Information were becoming fairly routine.
The meetings and reports were, while necessary, boorish and, in Paul's
opinion, unnecessarily layered and more difficult than they deserved
to be. This brief brush with bureaucracy further emboldened the radio
newsman to join the fighting and enlist in the Army Air Corps. By his
own admission, Harvey had to fight to have his previous medical defer-
ment overturned. Over the years, the broadcaster never elaborated on
the circumstances surrounding the change of status other than to say,
"I had left a comfortable deferment to enlist. . . . "[34]

An amateur pilot since the age of fourteen, he had never relin-
quished his dream of flying. He began to think about becoming a
bombardier. The Air Corps seemed like a perfect fit. He was following in the footsteps of his friend, fellow Tulsan and KVOO alum Gene
Autry, who joined the Corps in the middle of his *Gene Autry's Melody
Ranch* program on July 26, 1942.[35]

No man willingly and voluntarily leaves the comforts and securi-
ties of his home for war unless he holds in his heart a passion for his
country and an appreciation for her ideals. He needs to love them
more than he loves himself. When Paul Aurandt informed John Fetzer of his decision to leave the station and don the uniform, his boss
at WKZO didn't blink an eye. And so, Paul and Evelyn once again
were on the move. They packed up their apartment on Gull Road and
headed for Tulsa, Oklahoma.

Through tear-filled eyes, Paul left Evelyn with his mother over on
East Fifth Place. She then landed a job at the CBS affiliate downtown.
A pioneer in her own right, Paul's Angel literally ran the station,
including hosting an eight-hour on-air shift between 11:30 a.m. and

midnight, six days a week. "I was all alone," she remembered, "but it was a great way to learn the business."[36] The proud husband's only regret was that his deployment to boot camp prevented him from listening to her show.

He was officially inducted into the Army Air Corps on December 2, 1943.[37] He reported for basic training at Sheppard Field in Wichita Falls, Texas, eager to begin flight training. Having covered the military build-up in Hawaii and reported from dozens of bases around the country, the sights and sounds were familiar. But here he was on the inside and would soon be embroiled in a controversy whose details remain intriguing and unclear even to this day.

To be completely fair and honest, the facts of the story have never been fully known, or at the least, they haven't been fully reported without some ulterior motive assigned to their telling. Throughout his life, when asked about his brief tenure in the Army, Paul Aurandt was always fairly vague. "My time in uniform was abbreviated because I had volunteered for the Air Corps," he later wrote, "but before I could start training I was advised that the Air Cadet program had been abolished and I was 'in the infantry.' I resisted the arbitrary switch vigorously until I was mustered out of uniform with an entirely honorable discharge . . . and before I could be drafted back in we ran out of war."[38]

It's not clear why he would suggest that the Air Cadet program was abolished in the midst of his tenure. According to official records, the United States Congress didn't disband the Army Air Corps until July 26, 1947.[39] Having enlisted in the Army Air Corps and passed all of the required tests, Aurandt would have been assigned to one of four divisions: the Air Cadets, the Signal Corps, Artillery, or Infantry.

But regardless of Paul Aurandt's apparent confusion of circumstance, an accident on an obstacle course would only add to the murkiness surrounding his eventual discharge. Years later, in 1978, a left-wing "investigative reporter" from *Esquire* magazine penned a hatchet piece on Paul suggesting, among other things, that his father had been killed in a hunting accident—and that the radio broadcaster had received a 4-F discharge for mental instability manifested by deliberately cutting his foot.[40]

Angered by the accusations, yet prohibited by ABC from responding, Paul met with a Chicago-based Associated Press writer by the name of Marc Wilson and gave him a sheet of paper with a point-by-point refutation of Brashler's hit piece. He told Wilson bluntly, "You can't tell anyone where you got this."[41] Wilson's reflections on the meeting, some thirty years later, appear to put the issue to rest, once and for all:

> The allegation that most angered Harvey was that his father hadn't died in the line of duty as a policeman. The magazine article's author said he had checked through the records of the Oklahoma Police Hall of Fame, which didn't list [Paul's] father as killed in action. [Paul's] article said that his father was killed while on duty as a Tulsa police officer. (I double-checked, and Tulsa police records confirmed his story.)
>
> [Paul] was almost equally angry at the magazine's allegation that he had been given a 4-F discharge, which is given to men or women who have been found not qualified for service in the military because of physical, mental or moral standards. Harvey's article—and documents he showed me—showed that he had enlisted in the Army Air force in 1943, but was discharged within a year because of

an injury suffered during training. The U.S. Army con-
firmed to me that [Paul's] account was accurate.[42]

According to official records, Paul Aurandt received an honorable
medical discharge from the U.S. Army on March 15, 1944.[43]

Arriving back in Tulsa by train, a civilian once more, a beaming
Paul Aurandt would be met at the station by his blond-haired beauty
and bride, Evelyn. Their ivory Nash automobile was parked alongside
the tracks, its fresh coat of paint glistening in the sunshine. She had
brought with her a surprise—a gift for her returning man. In her arms
she held a tiny black cocker spaniel. He would name her Reveille.[44]

"One man's handful of love wrapped in black fur," he would later
write. "Just love. Reveille was almost worthless for anything else. If
there is anything else. Reveille has never been told she was a dog and
probably wouldn't have believed it, anyway. . . . Her bed was the foot
of my own . . . . My feeling for Reveille is just a mite absurd by the standards of sensible folks; I would not pretend otherwise."[45]

CHAPTER TWELVE

Hello, Chicago!

"A person's name," wrote Dale Carnegie, "is the sweetest and most important sound in any language."[1] But what does a person do if people are continually misspelling or mispronouncing his name? Or what if he was looking for a more lyrical or melodious-sounding appellation? If he was in television or radio in the early days, he simply changed his name.

The name Archibald Alexander Leach seems less dashing than the moniker of a debonair beau known as Cary Grant. Nathan Birnbaum might have been equally hilarious but not nearly as memorable as a man named George Burns. Benjamin Kubelsky is a mouthful; a cheapskate called Jack Benny rolls right off the tongue. Before we laughed at him as Bob, he was known to everyone else as Leslie Hope. The name Frederick Austerlitz seems somewhat clunky for a dancer, but Fred Astaire evokes a gentle and graceful ballroom scene. Lawrence Zeiger would have been regularly misspelled, but the name Larry King is pretty difficult to get wrong and now impossible to forget.[2]

The name "Paul Harvey" is so natural now that it is almost hard to believe that sixty-five years ago, his name was Paul Harvey Aurandt.

He didn't do it at first—his loyalties ran deep. After all, "Aurandt" was the name of his father and his father's father; an only son doesn't set it aside without great consideration. But with competition steep and network positions limited, Paul was going to have to give himself every available industry advantage. He couldn't control much, but he could make his name easier to remember and repeat. Paul was committed to working harder than anyone else in the business, and he certainly wasn't going to allow his name to set him back, so in 1944 he dropped "Aurandt" and started going by "Paul Harvey."

The couple was resolved to work like it was all up to them, but pray knowing that it was really all up to God. They held their blessings and dreams lightly. "God answers prayers 'yes' and some 'no' because if a father, however loving, did all his son's homework . . . he would ruin the son," Paul once wrote. "The ancient Greeks had a saying that, 'If you want to destroy a man give him everything he wants.'"[3]

When Paul and Evelyn Harvey were reunited in Tulsa, Oklahoma in April of 1944, the young couple was faced with the daunting prospect of making decisions that would carve out the course of the rest of their lives.

Cruising around the familiar streets of downtown Tulsa in Evelyn's shiny beige 1938 Nash, the couple exhibited an unusual openness to break from the cultural and social mold of modern twentieth century America.

"He told me, 'You do the on-air work, and I'll back you,'" Angel remembered, "but I thought he should do the commentary. With that beautiful voice, he was a natural."[4]

As the Harveys began to look for work, they were encouraged by the industry's receptivity to them as a broadcast team. It was tempting to head for the broadcast mecca of New York or even fall back on the familiarity of the past friendships forged at former radio affiliates. "Paul had offers for radio all over the country and also for theater," Mrs. Harvey recalled. "It was I who focused him and decided that news would be his best venue."[5]

In April of 1944, Evelyn Harvey, in a stroke of pure genius, suggested that they to move to Chicago to launch *Paul Harvey News*, but at first Paul resisted. "He didn't care to go 'big time,'" Angel said. "Paul was content with the small city broadcasts. But I told him he'd be sorry if we didn't at least try. I was always confident he would become a network news commentator."[6]

At the time of their move in June of 1944, the windy city was a hotbed of radio talent. Popular serial shows like *Fibber McGee and Molly*, *The Breakfast Club*, *Little Orphan Annie*, and *The National Barn Dance* all emanated from studios alongside the shores of Lake Michigan. Powerhouse stations like WGN (owned by the *Chicago Tribune*— the "World's Greatest Newspaper") and WLS (operating under the corporate umbrella of the retail giant, Sears and Roebuck—the "World's Largest Store") dominated the radio dial.[7]

"When we decided to sink our roots in Chicago, we drove to the North Side," Paul remembered. "We were looking for a room to rent. This sounds like we had elegant ideas, but it was actually a very modest room with a shared bathroom in a building that was across the street from the Ambassador East Hotel."[8]

He continued,

> We pulled up in front of the building, and I was taking our luggage from the trunk. I was starting toward the door when suddenly two police cars pull up, and I'm surrounded. They were saying: "Turn around. Put your hands on the car. Who are you?" and so forth. I finally showed

them a driver's license or whatever credentials I carried in
those days. The officers then backed off and showed me an
all-points bulletin they had that described a young blond
man in his 20s and a blond woman in a white car. Who-
ever this couple was, they were really wanted, from the
looks of the rather elaborate wanted poster. Anyway, that
was my introduction to Chicago. Kind of a shaky one. I ate
dinner that night trembling.[9]

Still without a permanent position, Paul continued to lift up his wife's
career potential and appeared willing to take the back seat profes-
sionally. "When we first came to Chicago, he said, 'Which way should
we go? Do you want your own programs? Should I back you?' I said,
'With all your air experience, let me back you.'" Evelyn continued, "I
stayed behind him, keeping focus and editing. Listening."[10]

As the American troops were storming and securing the beaches of
Normandy along the bullet ridden shores of France, Paul and Lynne
Harvey began to set up their shop in Chicago. It was a bittersweet start
to their soon-to-be historic adventure. Anxious to dig in and begin
bringing the good news of the United States' forthcoming victory over
the Axis powers, Paul could only wonder what might have been had
he been given the opportunity to fly his coveted bombardier over the
waters of the warm Pacific. But it wasn't meant to be. Instead, the couple was familiarizing themselves with the city that would be their
home for the next sixty-four years.

He had reservations. "I was scared about coming," he would say,
"but Angel had all the foresight and the daring to make the move."[11]

At first, they struggled to find a position. Paul was able to land substitute work and filled in at various stations around the city. Finally, a
break materialized. "I broke into the radio business . . . through the help
of a friend, a well-known name in broadcasting and advertising who told

me Longines (a Swiss watchmaker) was dropping its evening program and that they had decided they wanted to try a 10 p.m. newscast," Paul reminisced. "So I initiated the tradition of the 10 p.m. news in Chicago, and that was the beginning of a program that went on the network."[12]

Selling themselves to station management as a broadcast pair, two for the price of one, the Harveys landed at WENR, an affiliate of NBC's Blue Network. By their own account, they were broke, eager for the work, and down to "one meatball sandwich" between them.[13] It would be just enough, a recurring theme for the Harveys, in a narrative that evoked the biblical account of the multiplying loaves and fishes—everything in its proper time and proportion. Answers never came late, but neither were they ever too early. And in those first few years, they had nothing too much, but neither was there not enough.

"I remember sitting on a bench overlooking Belmont Harbor near to where we first moved and looking out on the city's skyline, wondering whether we could make it," Harvey recounted. "Angel simply told me we could and that if I believed in myself, I could accomplish anything."[14]

The Harveys' new broadcast home of WENR in 1944 was in the midst of transition. After the FCC ordered NBC to sell one of its networks upon complaints of a broadcast monopoly, WENR was acquired, along with fifty-nine other stations, by Edward Noble, famous owner of the Rexall Drugstore Company and Life Savers candy, for approximately $8,000,000.[15]

Originally named "the Blue Network" for the color of the pushpins NBC used to keep track of the stations, Noble renamed his new acquisition "the American Broadcasting Company," or ABC, in 1945, just after Paul and Lynne arrived at WENR. (Noble's name choice, to which he bought rights from broadcast mogul George Storer, caused CBS to then change its New York flagship station from WABC to WCBS.)[16]

Paul Harvey News was officially launched as a fifteen-minute, six days a week news program over the WENR ("The Voice of Service in

Chicago") airwaves in the middle of June 1944.[17] (It would become *Paul Harvey News and Comment* in April 1951.) At the urging of Paul's sidekick, wife, and producer Lynne Harvey, the couple convinced station management to allow them to broadcast at 10:00 p.m., Monday through Friday. The Sunday night newscast was aired at 9:15 p.m. During the week, Paul's closest competition was the popular conservative newscaster Fulton Lewis Jr., whose fifteen-minute program aired across the Mutual Broadcasting Network. Harvey's reporting had hints of Lewis's, who always ended with the familiar sign-off, "That's the top of the news as it looks from here!"[18] In the Chicago market, Lewis's network program occasionally ran opposite Harvey's on WGN, but its normal time slot was two hours earlier at 8:00 p.m. Central. But though the Tulsan's newscast may have inherited elements from the legendary broadcasters in his orb, *Paul Harvey News* was immediately unique. The decision to end the show with a humorous or poignant kicker at the end ("For what it's worth . . . ") resonated with an audience eager to close out their day with a laugh and a slice of perspective. "For though languages differ all over the earth," Paul observed, "all laughter and all pain sound the same."[19]

For many at WENR, the late nighttime slot seemed like a gamble. But Lynne believed the placement allowed Paul to reach a larger and more varied audience. She had convinced the executives that at 10:00 p.m., listeners were home and winding down from their day, ready to get caught up on the news. They would train them to change their listening habits. As it turned out, it was another brilliant move. Their local competition was pretty thin. Across the dial, *The Music Shop* ran on WMAQ and *I Love a Mystery* aired on WBBM. Paul's timing was perfect.[20] With the war reaching its final climax, more Americans than ever were eager for news. Paul's upbeat style coupled with the generally good news from across the Atlantic and Pacific Oceans was a natural and timely fit.

The pioneering Harvey duo had very deliberately and successfully introduced the concept of the late evening newscast to America. A precursor to the now familiar 10:00 television newscast, Lynne Harvey is now widely credited for hatching the idea. Thirty years after their arrival in Chicago, Angel Harvey said, "I remember those days like they were yesterday... I would ring the gong at the opening of the broadcast. I was always ready to substitute for him if it was necessary, but it never was. He never missed a broadcast. Even when he had the mumps once—he broadcasted from home."[21]

Almost immediately, the ratings for *Paul Harvey News* went through the roof, and it quickly became the most popular and listened to program on Chicago radio. According to the "Hooper" rating—a dependable media measure in the 1940s, an astonishing 26 percent of all Chicago radios in use each night were tuned in to Paul Harvey's program. He began to receive and accept extracurricular speaking assignments all over the Midwest as part of the "Redpath Lecture Bureau" circuit. "One of the most dynamic personalities in radio," read the brochure promoting his availability, "An exceptional speaker with a fine sense of humor."[22]

Anxious to further capitalize on his popularity, the WENR management began using Paul on other programming within the station. One such example was a broadcast entitled the *Bureau of Missing Persons*. Promoted as a "new series with Paul Harvey as MC of the program bringing to air persons seeking missing heirs and relatives," it pulled on the newscaster to conduct "interviews with Chicago civic leaders identified with Missing Persons Bureaus."[23] He was a natural, adding a dramatic flair to the interviews and an air of mystery to the investigative reporting.

World War II had rattled the usually unflappable and upbeat Paul Harvey. In addition to his own ordeals regarding his enlistment in 1943 and discharge in 1944, the radio commentator had lost his boyhood friend Harold Collis to a mine explosion overseas. Another close Tulsa classmate, Fred Markgraff, was also killed in action. Paul wasn't necessarily bitter, but he said for some inexplicable reason, he would long blame Tulsa for taking his two good friends.[24] The trauma of the years had taken its toll. Not one to dwell on discomfort, a sad-dened Harvey plowed on—determined to keep ahead of further sorrow.

Clear and definitive confirmation of Mr. Harvey's meteoric rise came the day following the death of president Franklin Roosevelt on April 13, 1945. When Harvey eulogized the late president with an essay from the perspective of FDR's dog that began, "A great tree has fallen and left an open place against the sky..." the switchboard of the station lit up. Over 25,000 responses and requests for copies rolled in.[25] Management was incredulous. "It was unprecedented for any one station to get that much mail on one broadcast," Paul remembered. "Most of it was people wanting copies; a lot of it was just people shar-ing our tears."[26] Ironically, Paul Harvey's politics and ideological per-spectives ran generally counter to the government-friendly FDR. "If your government is big enough to give you everything you want, it is big enough to take away everything you have," he would say.[27] But the young newsman knew how to capture the drama and the emotion of the historic moment. He had that magical broadcast quality, an abil-ity to connect with a stranger over the airwaves and leave the broad-cast having made them a friend.

At the time, Paul Harvey was a fresh and exciting talent. He was truly, as he promised Mr. Paley of CBS in the brash 1942 audition tape, "the voice of tomorrow."[28] And as the tide was turning in World War II with an imminent victory in the offing, Chicago listeners saw in Paul Harvey the emergence of a new Uncle Sam. He was honest, forthright, optimistic, and a patriot who appealed to their better natures. As John Gambling, a popular third-generation New York radio host said,

"Paul Harvey is John Wayne and Jimmy Stewart—the quintessential patriot all wrapped up in one. He is the American personality we wish and hope to be."[29]

When the peace was finally declared, Paul celebrated with the rest of the country and settled in to enjoy postwar life, relieved that American boys were finally out of danger. He created and hosted a popular program called *Jobs for G.I. Joe*. It was a patriotic but practical show designed to help returning unemployed soldiers find work upon their return home. Harvey's interview skills and uncanny ability to relate to anyone, anywhere were on full display. During one memorable program, Paul learned that his guest had once been injured and spent a miserable week aboard a converted cruise ship. Ironically, it was the very same ship that Paul and Angel had sailed back on from Hawaii in December of 1941. Following America's entry into the war, almost all of the available cruise ships had been converted to hospital or military transports. As the G.I. regaled Harvey's listeners with his sad tale, Paul alluded to his intimate familiarity with the ship but purposely left out the context, lest he ruin a good story. Responding in a dramatically low and sympathetic tone, Harvey said, "Oh, how I knowww that ship. How I knoooow that ship!"[30]

★   ★   ★

On Sunday evening, February 15, 1948, the skies were overcast and the temperatures were falling to the predicted low of five degrees when the Harveys arrived at WENR's studios inside Chicago's Merchandise Mart. Snow was likely. Perusing the wires in preparation for the Sunday evening program at 9:15 p.m., there was no shortage of bad news. Out in Aspen, Colorado, the body of 34-year-old Memphis resident Alexander McFarland had just been recovered from an avalanche a day earlier.[31] The tragedy had a local edge to it. At the time, Vail was a new ski resort, the brainchild of prominent Chicago businessman Walter Paepcke.[32] That would definitely make Harvey's cut. Further out west, two boys from Everett, Washington had gone missing in a twelve-foot skiff. Pounding rains and wind gusts of 50 mph slowed any hope of imminent rescue.[33] And in New York, there was a dramatic tale of a $39,000 jewelry heist from a private home, the maid gagged and tied up.[34] The evening's script quickly came together.

But amid all the bad news there was something very good, too. Evelyn Harvey was expecting their first child, due any day now, and the couple was ecstatic. It was their first. The proud parents couldn't wait. Their prayers and petitions had been answered. On this Sunday night, the Harveys completed their radio program but then rushed off to Chicago's Lying-in Hospital.[35] The moment had arrived. At the corner of East 59th Street and South Maryland Avenue, the medical facility was considered among the finest maternity hospitals in the entire world with a reputation for "safe deliverance." Its chief surgeon was Dr. William Dieckmann, a top shelf professional and a personal family friend.[36] Evelyn was in good hands. She would need to be.

It was a difficult and dangerous birth. Writing about the ordeal several years later, Paul would say that his Angel was "snatched back from the door step of death."[37] The hopes and dreams of all their years were fulfilled when a bouncing boy named Paul Junior made his grand entrance into the world shortly before midnight.

"And then one day a dream," Paul would later reflect. "The valley of the shadow. A miracle. A son. Soft, strong chains."[38] "Little Paul" would bring light and laughter—and perspective and purpose—to the man who was about to become a star on the national stage.

"Oh, God of little boys, be near bedside," he wrote regarding his newly born son, "unveil tomorrow with the gentlest touch for those two bright eyes. . . ."[39]

CHAPTER THIRTEEN

From Sea to Shining Sea

*P*aul and Evelyn's offices were owned by Joseph P. Kennedy, former Ambassador to Great Britain and the father of a future president. When he bought Chicago's Merchandise Mart in 1945, it was the largest business complex in the world. A shrewd businessman, Kennedy purchased it for $12.5 million—half of what its original owner, Marshall Field, paid to even build it.[1]

The art deco masterpiece, marked by its marble piers and terrazzo floors, was immense and far beyond any other comparable property. It contained 4,000,000 square feet of commercial space. A customer would have to walk approximately six and a half miles to see all its display windows in a single trip.[2]

As the Chicago headquarters for NBC, the network took up over 76,500 square feet on the eighteenth, nineteenth, and twentieth floors.[3] It was a virtual "radio city," with several stations emanating from the massive but elegant studios. Several of the facilities were full-scale theaters that could seat hundreds of people. There was always something going on. According to radio logs, over 1,700 different programs, or a total of 500 hours per month, were broadcast from its studios.[4]

In a short while, Paul and Evelyn Harvey grew familiar with the building's navigational complexities. Arriving together each day, they would head for the studios of WENR via the dedicated elevator labeled "NBC—EXPRESS TO 19." There they would often share the ride with developing legends Mike Wallace (he was known as Myron at the time and was a spokesman for Peter Pan Peanut Butter), Hugh Downs, Danny Thomas, Studs Terkel, or Dave Garroway. Occasionally, the Harveys met or mingled with colleagues over a meal or coffee in a drug store along the Wells Street side entrance of the building.[5]

Since his arrival in 1944, Paul Harvey had been cultivating a bit of a local following which included the owner of his building. Joe Kennedy, a political ally of President Roosevelt and a strong supporter of the "New Deal," saw the world much differently than the young broadcaster, yet they struck up a great friendship. It was a surprising relationship to some, but Harvey had a knack for getting along with everybody. Few people of such prominence had so few enemies.

One day, over a cup of coffee, Joe told Paul that he thought he should expand his reach beyond Chicago's airwaves and join ABC's national network. The next thing he knew, Kennedy had called the president of the network, and told him to put Paul on.[6]

To hear Harvey tell the story, the casual observer might get the idea the network brass were doing him a favor when they began putting him on the national network. The reality is quite the opposite. Clearly, the seasoning of the last seventeen years was evident. The 32-year-old broadcaster had become a favorite of the network executives in both New York and California. ABC's Network News Director, Cornelius O'Dea, had an especially strong affinity for Harvey. To the staff inside the Merchandise Mart and the thousands of WENR listeners, it seemed like only a matter of time before Harvey's

mellifluous voice would move beyond only the reach of Chicago's airwaves. Kennedy's call likely served only to confirm his talent. But following the conversation, Paul was asked to substitute on the network
more frequently.

Harvey caught a big break in February of 1950 when the ABC
Radio network sent him across the Atlantic on special assignment.
The hotly contested British elections, the first general vote in that
country since 1945, were slated for February 23.[7] Sailing from New
York several weeks earlier, Harvey was excited. With significant
worldwide interest in the election mounting, it was a prime opportunity for the Oklahoma orator to further display his talent and unique
reporting abilities. He couldn't help but think of the Arthur Mosby's
admonition eight years earlier that he give up newscasting. How
quickly had his fortunes changed—but not without dedicated toil and
the wise counsel of his Angel.

Much to Harvey's delight, he arrived to discover that the British
campaign was raging red-hot not only in the Parliament, but also in
the press and in pubs on nearly every corner. It was a reporter's
dream—a timely topic of great interest accompanied by people eager
and willing to talk. Harvey would traipse all over the countryside in
search of insight and perspective. He darted and dashed with his
microphone from the busy streets of London to the rolling countryside of Cambridge, to Birmingham, Liverpool, and Manchester, "like
a prospector panning for gold" as he often liked to say.[8]

Ever since former Prime Minister Winston Churchill had been given
the "order of the boot" in 1945, the people of England had been debat-
ing the merits of socialism versus capitalism. At the time, the country's
government was ruled by the Labor party and its socialist-inspired programs were promoted by Prime Minister Clement Attlee. Among
Attlee's serious challengers in 1950 was Winston Churchill of the

Conservative Party. Turnout was strong, Harvey reported, 26 million or nearly 80 percent of the electorate. Reports from the night of the 23rd suggested a party-like atmosphere with thousands of citizens streaming through city streets holding balloons and signs and chanting slogans. In the end, Attlee would hold on—but only barely. Harvey noted that a change was afoot, though it was imperceptible at a quick glance. Prime Minister Attlee won reelection by a narrow margin, and the Conservative Party would ultimately call an election again in 1951—and reelect Sir Winston Churchill in a move of great emotion and political significance.

At the time of the 1950 elections, Paul Harvey's assessment of a struggling Great Britain was starkly and strikingly clear. Upon arriving back in Chicago, he sized up the situation across the Atlantic. "[This] is a bowed, bombed out, compromised, austerity starved ghost of the England that once was," he reported. "A ghost without pride, dignity, or even much honor any more. England that is old and mixed up and tired and scared and seeks feebly to reflect on its former place in the sun. A place remembered by Englishmen quite vividly... as it never was."[9]

It was this frankness, delivered with a poignant and dramatic flair, that continued to set Paul apart from his otherwise talented colleagues. His analysis and commentary was also beginning to run counter to the wisdom of intellectual elites, those in Washington such as Adlai Stevenson. Stevenson, a one-term governor of Illinois and two-time Democratic nominee for president in 1952 and 1956, was widely considered an eloquent orator with a high IQ. But Harvey would often bristle over Adlai Stevenson's speeches and calls for "moderation" in pursuit of Cold War victory. In acknowledging Stevenson's well-spoken views, Harvey would reference his "painfully mature philosophy" that was nevertheless naïve and ineffective.[10]

When Stevenson would later advocate for big labor and greater utilization of the United Nations, Harvey would dismiss him as being nothing more than a "fundamental Fabian Socialist."[11]

His voice was resonating strongly with Mr. and Mrs. Middle America. A man of strong opinion, Harvey was certain of America's superiority but irritated by its willingness to embrace or accept socialist principles. It frustrated the young reporter that the United States, led by President Truman, suggested that they had no preference in the outcome of the British elections, beyond that the margin of victory be decisive.

And so Paul Harvey began to say what most people back home were thinking, which was that capitalism had always been a good master—why should any nation on earth make it a bad one?[12] "No government in history," he would say, "ever gave its citizens what hard-working Americans with their sleeves rolled up, have earned for themselves."[13] He had given credence to those without a voice and spoke with an authoritarian vigor rarely seen in a man so young yet so well traveled. Some of the network executives grew nervous, but the calls from listeners and affiliate managers continued to pour in, almost all favorable to Harvey. It appeared that a grassroots type movement was afoot—but Harvey still didn't have his own show.

It has become common or even fashionable to mock those in post-World War II America who expressed concern about the rising menace of communism. Reduced to nothing more than a "Red Scare" in the late 1940s and 1950s, an entire generation of citizens has grown up without an understanding of the magnitude of the threat of communism when it was on the rise after World War II. Between 1945 and 1950, Poland, East Germany, Rumania, Bulgaria, Estonia, Latvia, Albania, Yugoslavia, Czechoslovakia, North Korea, and China were all taken over by Communist regimes.[14] Over 400,000 American lives had been sacrificed during the four-year world war with the expressed purpose of defeating the very socialist and totalitarian ideals these newly installed Communist countries governed by and celebrated.

Out in Hollywood, the motion picture industry was rumored to be a hotbed for Communist spies and sympathizers. When a group of congressmen in the House established the Un-American Activities Committee [HUAC] in 1947 to investigate Communist influence on the motion picture industry, it was only a matter of time before actors and actresses who refused to testify were placed on a so-called "black-list."[15] Of the forty-seven invited to Washington, nineteen refused. The remaining twenty-four "friendly witnesses" included future President Ronald Reagan and a future ABC colleague of Harvey's, actor Robert Montgomery.[16]

It would be Montgomery whose decision to take a ten-week summer vacation would help propel Harvey into the national spotlight.[17]

Robert Montgomery cut a dashing figure on the silver screen. Tall and handsome, he had grown up dreaming of becoming a writer, but soon found himself acting on the stage. Before long, the Fishkill, New York native had signed a contract with MGM. Montgomery served in the Navy as a lieutenant during World War II and, upon returning to Hollywood, interspersed his acting with some writing. In the early days of radio, it was common to try to lure big name actors into on-air network positions. When the ABC Radio Network came calling, Montgomery signed on as a news commentator in the fall of 1949.[18]

By the following June, Montgomery had either grown tired of the assignment or ABC had become disillusioned with their star. He requested a break, not quite sure if he'd return. ABC's O'Dea knew just who to call. On June 15, 1950, Paul Harvey assumed Montgomery's network time slot for a ten-week assignment.[19] His voice was now officially being heard coast-to-coast.

The affiliates loved him—and more importantly, so did their listeners. Calls flooded the network's switchboard. He was a hit. In time, Robert Montgomery gave up his slot as a news commentator, taking on a plum job with President Dwight D. Eisenhower when he was elected in 1952.[20] He was to help craft both Eisenhower and Vice President Nixon's television images. But there was still no permanent spot on the network for Paul Harvey. After the temporary stint was completed by summer's end, he went back to doing his regular Chicago show on WENR—but it wouldn't be long before he returned to the national airwaves.

Momentum was now on his side.

As the Harveys' profile began to rise within Chicago and beyond, Evelyn and Paul began to talk about the possibility of purchasing a retreat away from the hustle and bustle of the city. "Like most city boys, I had always figured a farm meant 'security' somehow," he would write.[21] The young couple would settle on a 300-acre farm just south of St. Louis, north of a small town called Kimmswick, purchasing it in the late 1940s. Though always struggling to pull back from the grind of responsibilities and enjoy the solitude of the Ozarks, the Harveys quickly fell in love with their slice of heaven. Named for their dear dog, "Reveille Ranch was intended to be a 'retirement' place," as Paul wrote.[22] It was a place to dream about growing old together in, with a house overlooking the Mississippi and a barn for cattle. Family had their doubts. As his brother-in-law predicted, "Paul will retire the day they bring his body down here in a box; not one day before."[23]

From their first day at the ranch, the Harveys battled the predictable success paradox that follows any accomplished family. They could enjoy the luxury of such trappings because they worked so hard; but because they worked so hard, they rarely had time to enjoy the spoils of their efforts. Still, the family would be deliberate when making plans to break away from their apartment on Lake Shore Drive in Chicago, and later, the family house in River Forest. To help bridge the gap between the professional demands and family priority, a small radio studio was installed inside the house. Paul would make good use of it.

Over the years, Reveille Ranch would be home to many fond family memories, times now faded in the pages of albums and lost but for the memories of those few still left. It was common for the Harveys to host Thanksgiving and Christmas holidays in their cozy farmhouse. "Traditional Christmas dinner at Reveille Ranch is like something out of Dickens," Paul would write. "Relatives, all sizes, all shapes and all hungry, will be stamping the snow from their overshoes by the back door and filling the house—kitchen first—with a torrent of talk and laughter."[24]

Of greatest poignancy and purpose were Paul and Evelyn's memories of those early days at the farm with their son, Paul Jr. Only a toddler when they purchased it, the ranch was the site of priceless moments that all the money from radio could never buy. It was a magical sight to see the boy roaming around the barn at his father's side. Of Paul Jr.'s interest in it all, Paul would write, "There is something very basically American about being a cowboy and this, his energetic young spirit prefers."[25]

And so for the Harvey trio plus beloved dog, Reveille Ranch quickly became a treasured destination. In time, when the lights grew even brighter and the demands more intense, it would be their lifeline to normalcy and perspective.

A favorite spot for Harvey's writing was inside the farmhouse, beside the stone fireplace. Many a column and commentary was penned in that cozy spot. An oil painting of Reveille hung over the mantle. Outside the window, a marble headstone on the south lawn marked the final resting place of the cocker spaniel. Beside her lies another—the remains of a little white poodle named Mr. Tip Toes who came to the family in the late 1950s. Though he died in 1965, the canine captured some headlines, reportedly living for three and a half years with diabetes.[26]

"I was very glad for the patch of green and the bit of blue that is mine on the hilltop in the Ozarks," Paul reflected shortly after the purchase. "For here in this good earthly place my family will always 'belong'.... This is my land. I have watered it with my sweat and fertilized it with my footsteps."[27]

Whether by good fortune, providence, or more likely than not, a combination of both, opportunities for extended substitute positions continued to open up for Paul Harvey. As 1950 drew to a close, famed ABC commentator Hilmar Baukhage requested an early Christmas break. A no-nonsense broadcaster of German lineage who originated his newscast from Berlin before World War II, the 61-year-old was beginning to lose favor with the network. Starting each program by simply saying "Baukhage talking," he was known to sometimes talk about the same topic for his entire fifteen-minute broadcast. Younger listeners were tuning out, frustrating both network executives and advertisers.

As he was for Montgomery, Paul Harvey was called on to temporarily take the commentator's shift. His eclectic and electric style contrasted so devastatingly from Baukhage's long and often boorish yarns that it was clear something had to give. This time, the six-year Chicago native would stay for good.

"That's how I started out, substituting for regulars. After I went on the air, the managers of the little affiliate stations insisted that the network keep me on," Harvey said. "If it were up to Madison Avenue, I still don't think I'd be on the networks. It was grassroots support that brought me where I am."[28]

He didn't know it at the time, but when Paul signed on to do Baukhage's broadcast on December 3, 1950, it would be the last time he filled in for anyone. The boy from Tulsa who had leaned on his elbows listening to the faint sounds of radio newsmen and been mesmerized by the medium had officially made it. He was finally home, a permanent and steady voice across the network.

By 1951, Hilmar Baukhage left ABC for the Mutual Network. He retired from radio two years later.

Although it wouldn't be formally designated as such until April 1, 1951, *Paul Harvey News and Comment* was now airing from sea to shining sea.

CHAPTER FOURTEEN

Britches on
Barbed Wire

A reporter on the run is a normal yet amusing sight to see. In an industry controlled and constrained by the unrelenting nature of the clock, many people tend to be in constant motion, eager to meet their deadline or beat another reporter to the punch of an exclusive story. Movement can be a predictor of passion and an indication of hunger. Journalists, print or broadcast, are always going or returning from somewhere; rarely are the good ones satisfied to stay in one place.

But it's a little odd to see a newsman, his tie flipped back over the shoulder, shirt sleeves rolled up, running up and down the hallway of his radio station—several times in a row—with no place to go.

Paul Harvey, a tall, robust, and handsome network news anchor, sprinted back and forth along the corridor outside his ABC studio, huffing and puffing, with a cast iron weight belt around his waist. He spoke as he ran, exercising the vocal chords with a sing-song series of chants and chatter. He didn't appear self-conscious. He could not care less that some staffers smiled and chuckled or that visitors considered it strange. It was a pretty good workout in its own right, but it was his chosen method of warming up in the moments before he took to the national airwaves.[1]

Still a relative newcomer to the network, Harvey would regularly exercise for a broadcast much like an athlete prior to competition. Harvey told people he did it because he wanted to get his blood flowing, and wanted to enter the studio with an edge of excitement in his voice, and a breathless tone in his delivery. The world's events were fantastic and fascinating in their own right, but a newscaster, Harvey would say, needed to ensure that his voice matched the emotion of the moment.

The network edition of *Paul Harvey News* began with a bang. Settling down behind his RCA microphone on the cold Chicago night of Sunday, December 3, 1950, Harvey suffered from no shortage of news. As usual, he struggled to pare things down and condense the spirited and informative offering to a mere fifteen-minute program. If he had been preparing for his usual local show, he might have spent some time crafting a commentary on the Chicago Cardinals 20–10 upset victory over the Bears at nearby Comisky Park.[2] But tonight, his report was going out across the network. There would be no time for native favoritism.

Over in Korea, the Chinese Communists were moving on Pyongyang. American forces were in retreat, desperate to avoid being trapped or cornered. By December, the Korean War was now nearly six months old and growing from bad to worse. The new ABC star would grow increasingly frustrated with the Truman administration's handling of the conflict. Over the next few weeks and months, his opinions about the raging conflict were lost on no one.

"We are told that what is happening in Korea is not really a war," he declared shortly after going national, "but a lot of American boys are just as dead as if it were. I am going to call it what it is: a bloody, rotten, thankless war...at home the headlines are all about truce talks, because a truce that is a dream is easier for the home folks to sleep on than a war that is a nightmare."[3]

A quick take of Harvey's perspective might suggest the newsman was a pacifist, a dove in search of peace. However, Paul Harvey's opposition to the war at the time of his broadcast wasn't based upon a belief that America was doing too much or acting too aggressively. In fact, it was just the opposite. The ABC commentator's objections were based upon a concern that the United States government was doing too little.

"Past a point, patience is no longer a virtue," Harvey offered in exasperation. "Impatience with the old war led us to the new one. It was our impatience that stopped Hitler at the Channel instead of the Hudson. There is a time to lose your patience and use your temper."[4]

A student of MacArthur and Eisenhower, his commentaries were resonating with an audience now weary of war and anxious for normalcy. Phone calls and letters poured in, most positive and supportive of his strong pro-militant positions.

Finishing his thought, he opined: "I vote that we make this phony war a real one and I recommend, on the basis of General MacArthur's proposal, that our first battle maneuver be to silence our little guns and stop killing Chinese and stop killing Americans and get out our big guns and get this over with...I vote we call a war a war and aim for a knockout before we get whipped on points."[5]

On the very same night of Harvey's first official broadcast, President Harry Truman was preparing for a visit with British Prime Minister Attlee. At the time, there was a growing sense that both Attlee and Truman didn't fully appreciate the magnitude and worldwide threat of Communist expansion. In the middle of it all was Joseph Stalin, the longtime general secretary of the Communist Party of the Soviet Union.

A murderous tyrant on all accounts, Stalin's grand vision of Soviet domination was chilling. Of particular concern was intelligence showing that he was providing weapons to North Korea's Kim II Sung's army.

Emboldened by the power of his new network perch, the brash Harvey was blunt about the day's events and opened his program with a stinging commentary:

> "Britain's Prime Minister Attlee is aloft at this moment . . . . And in Moscow, the sun is rising over Red Square. And the Politburo is brushing its collective teeth and shaving its collective cheek and tying its collective tie. And right after breakfast I'd like very much to have a second cup of coffee with Joe Stalin."

He then went on to mock Russian claims that they had invented the electric light bulb, submarine, telephone, and radio. His sarcasm reached a climax: "The Russians first learned the secret of the atom bomb and [the] Russians discovered the North Pole!"[6]

The personal message aimed at Stalin continued:

> You've heard from Washington, Uncle Joe. And what you heard was weak. But wait till you hear from Kokomo. That's where our secret strength is that nobody has yet discovered. In Kalamazoo and Oshkosh and Corpus Christi and Kokomo. Remember this, Uncle Joe, you've never heard from the United States until you've heard from Kokomo.[7]

The message grew more pointed:

> If you could get this through your head it might save you a lot of trouble: We do things backward from you. In this

> country the people . . . tell the government . . . what to do.
> Washington is up to its knees in little men. It's in the fields
> and the factories of this country where you find the giants
> of our time . . . . Here are America's real bosses. They're the
> men who grow the food and buy the bonds and run the
> machines and carry the guns that win our wars . . . . And there
> is not one of them who wouldn't deliver a loaded, triggered
> atom bomb to the Kremlin and drop it on you personally![8]

The switchboards began to light up with callers responding to Harvey's populist and patriotic message, echoing his sentiments with both incredulity and appreciation: "Who is this man?" "Send him to Washington!" "He gets it!"[9]

"It is understandable that you should underrate us," he continued.

> We underrate ourselves. Free competitive American capitalism, in less than 200 years has surpassed all the combined progress of the world for four thousand years before.
> Now we, in these 48 states, seven percent of the world's
> people, enjoy more than half of the world's good things . . . .
> Now, Uncle Joe, you've heard from Kokomo and you can
> see why I thought you ought to know. . . . An American has
> a warm heart . . . because there's hair on his chest.[10]

Thus began Paul Harvey's network career. His themes never changed over the years. For the next six decades on his network show, he consistently advanced the same steady, predictable perspective of the "quiet American" from which America gleans its true strength. The first show was a stirring success. Newspapers reprinted his commentary in the days leading up to Christmas. Speaking requests poured into his Chicago offices.

The Harvey wisdom was rooted in logic and practicality. "I'm going to shuck the corn right down to the cob" he would say, "and speak to you in shirt-sleeve English." His wife's sister, Aunt Betty, was his mental audience of one. Each morning, he would sit down and try to reconcile "what I think our countrymen need to know and what I think they want to know. I could be a profound authority on the machinations of the Middle East, on the potential for another oil embargo. But if I can't explain it in dime-store words so that Aunt Betty cares, then I just don't bother to try. I leave those expositions to the intellectuals."[11]

One of his favorite philosophers was a man named Joseph Wood Krutch. Both Paul and Lynne read his textbooks in school and enjoyed his essays in the *American Scholar*. A prolific writer who also taught at Columbia University, Krutch would eventually move to the Arizona desert. The two men became fast friends over the course of several winters. He left Harvey with three distinctive thoughts that further shaped his perspective and regularly found their way into the writing of his commentaries. "He taught me that living is more important than making a living; that what makes news is rarely what makes history and that invention is the mother of necessity."[12]

Harvey knew how make important things sound interesting—and acknowledged the importance of stories of everyday interest.

The new network star, with his Midwestern charm and gentlemanly manner, was liked by nearly everyone. He also instinctively understood that kindness and professional courtesy paid dividends. Robert Mulholland, a Chicago journalism professor and former colleague of Harvey's in the 1950s, remembers how staff members would jockey for position around the Teletype machines, hoping to find a story Harvey might use on the air. The staffer who handed Harvey the story was rewarded with an on-air mention, such as, "A late breaking story has just been handed to me by Robert." The aspiring news hounds loved it. "It was the cheapest form of insurance ever invented to make sure that nothing ever broke while he was on the air that he missed," reflected Mulholland.[13]

Another former colleague of Paul Harvey's in the early 1950s was a rising star in his own right, Chicago radio host Art Hellyer. A beloved and colorful character, he was a clean precursor to the shock jocks of the 1980s and 1990s. Hellyer became known for his unorthodox style. He would deliberately mock advertisers' products. Pepto-Bismol became "'that yucky pink stuff' called Pepto-Dismal."[14] He'd purposely announce the wrong time during the morning commute, and during brutal Chicago heat waves, Hellyer would play hours of Christmas music.

But Hellyer, along with famous Chicago radio personalities Fred Kasper (*The Breakfast Club*), Charles Homer Bill (*Is Anybody Home?*), and Wayne Atkinson (*ABC Network Announcer*) all shared announcer duties on the *Paul Harvey News* program. As Hellyer remembered, "The thing I most liked about Paul Harvey was his complete devotion to his lovely wife, Angel. On one occasion she was in the studio with him as I walked in at 10:58 a.m. for the daily 11:00 a.m. broadcast. Paul had to leave for the airport immediately after the program, so he turned to Angel and asked, 'Would you rather have a two-minute kiss now, or a ten second one after the show?' She, obviously just as devoted to him, chose the former."[15]

A father of a toddler and the sole breadwinner for the family, Paul Harvey began searching for other means of income. In addition to his growing popularity on the radio, he quickly became a favorite on the lecture circuit. When Evelyn secured representation with talent agency The Redpath Bureau, they began promoting six popular speeches he had written, each with their own clever twist and all tinged with humor. The first was entitled, "Radio and Peace," followed by "Let's Talk Television," "Let's Keep Radio Clean," "Slips That Pass in the Mike," "Questions and Answers on Current Problems," and "An Adventurer Retires."[16] His speaking fees would grow with his popularity. Originally charging only a few hundred dollars plus expenses, the commentator would eventually command over $30,000 per appearance.[17]

Writing was also a natural fit, serving a dual purpose in those early days on the network. Not only could Harvey garner an extra paycheck for freelance contributions, but he always considered writing to be a bit like exercise—the more frequently he did it, the easier the words would come. Harvey had begun contributing to various "pulp" magazines, popular inexpensive fiction, in the 1940s. He also contributed a number of sports stories to various national publications including *Collier's Weekly* and the *Saturday Evening Post*. In the February 1951 edition of *Man's World*, Harvey penned a piece entitled, "Is Joe DiMaggio Finished?" In the classic Harvey prose he wrote, "Nobody wants to see the Clipper leave baseball. For one thing, he's the greatest 'inspirational' team player that ever lived. . . . [but] Joe is, today, a battered and frequently pain-wracked man . . . Joe DiMaggio may be able to earn big money in the entertainment field . . . if he retires from baseball before he slips too badly, he is likely to become a legend that will pay off handsomely."[18] Of course, "Joltin' Joe" retired from the game only months later and went on to become a beloved cultural figure.

By January 3, 1955, Paul Harvey had etched a deal to pen a nationally syndicated newspaper column, distributed through the General Features Corporation of New York. Three essays a week were distributed to several hundred medium-sized newspapers. "The column," it was promised, "ranges through all areas of human interest, including

economics, philosophy, art and literature." Billing Harvey as a "leading spokesmen for old-fashioned Americanism, as opposed to the
other 'isms' which threaten to engulf the world," the feature only
added to his explosive appeal.[19]

If President Eisenhower had stepped down in 1956, and Paul Harvey had run for the presidency, he very well may have won. In only a
few short years, the stentorian voice of Tulsa had quickly become one
of America's favorite sons.

"Controversy is only dreaded by the advocates of error," wrote Benjamin Rush, a leading member of America's Continental Congress.[20]
Indeed, Paul Harvey's meteoric rise had been attributable, at least to
some degree, to his willingness to tackle the tough topics with direct
and precise language. Listeners might have disagreed with his opinions, but they never could argue with his facts. Not one to try to curry
favor with politicians, Harvey's stinging rebukes and chastisement of
the United States' war handling, along with its pitiful record of waste-
ful public spending had helped the ABC newsman make both friends
and enemies in Washington.

Harvey leaned heavily on the dependability of hundreds of sources
from around the country for fresh news and first hand accounts of
developing and otherwise unreported stories. Most were reliable. A
few were not. He would soon learn a painful lesson about jumping too
eagerly on tips that seemed too good to be true.

In late December of 1950, only days after his show had gone
national, Paul Harvey received a news tip that security was lax, even
inadequate, out at the Argonne National Laboratory. He was told
unchecked cars were regularly driving in and out of the property.
Patrols appeared non-existent. A top-secret atomic energy facility
located twenty-five miles south of the Chicago loop, Argonne was a
key site for the development of American nuclear energy.[21] Dating

back to the early 1940s, the Atomic Energy Commission managed the highly sensitive compound. Harvey's sources were sound—two security guards and John Crowley, his friend, who was a Reserve Naval Lieutenant employed in Naval Intelligence inside the laboratory. Reinforcing the validity of the information was Harvey's own knowledge of the facility's checkered history. On February 8, 1948, a bottle of enriched uranium went missing from the Argonne storage vault. Most of it was later found, but a small amount was discovered in its landfill. Security appeared to be sloppy, if not downright dangerous.[22]

Confident of the opportunity for a high profile scoop, the buoyant Harvey set out from the city in his Cadillac around midnight, February 6, 1951. Crowley and an off-duty guard by the name of Charles Rogul accompanied him on the late-night caper. Stashing his car alongside some bushes, Harvey quietly but very deliberately began to scale the ten-foot security fence that ringed the perimeter of the property. It was just after one o'clock in the morning. All was quiet. His sources appeared to have provided an accurate description of the lax security detail.[23]

WHen Harvey was seconds away from slipping into the shadows, a guard by the name of Emmett Dalton spotted him starting to jump off the fence. Racing over in his Jeep, Dalton shouted for the intruder to halt in his tracks. Startled, the ABC newsman stumbled, but stopped upon command, his coat inadvertently caught and dangling from the top of the barbed wire fence. The two accomplices, Rogul and Crowley, still standing outside along the road, fled as soon as they saw the patrol vehicle. The Tulsan was immediately placed under arrest and brought back for questioning to the FBI headquarters in Chicago.[24]

Listeners couldn't believe it. "Radio Reporter Detained" headlined a two-paragraph blurb in the next day's *New York Times*.[25] Newspapers around the country ran the story on page one. An aura of mystery and intrigue surrounded the event. Because his driver's license identified him as "Paul Aurandt" and the country now knew him as "Paul Harvey," there was some initial speculation that he was a spy. The confusion was only amplified by Harvey's own statement, issued the next day. While not commenting directly on his arrest, the release suggested that he had "been working in cooperation and conjunction with the investigating divisions of several government departments for several months" and that he was "not at liberty, nor . . . authorized by the government investigating divisions to release any story or information concerning the matters upon which he [had] been working."[26]

Although the Federal Bureau of Investigation determined that Mr. Harvey had not broken any federal law, government officials announced their intent to seek an indictment on March 15.[27] The filing charged the popular commentator with "conspiracy to obtain information on national security and transmit it to the public." On March 20, the case was presented to a grand jury, and a two-week investigation ensued. More than a dozen witnesses testified. It turned out to be an exercise in futility as it quickly became clear the broadcaster had no malicious or treasonous intentions when he breached security at the Argonne Laboratory. The grand jury declined to indict him, and he was cleared of the charges on April 4.[28]

There was widespread agreement that Harvey was fortunate he hadn't been shot or killed. Given the circumstances and the cover of darkness, another guard might have opened fire on the intruder. The impetuous Harvey, realizing the folly of his actions, assured ABC executives that he would employ a greater degree of discretion on future assignments. A favorite among the network brass, he kept his job. In the end, how someone viewed the incident normally depended upon their politics. Conservatives appreciated his courage. Liberals resented it, considering the move arrogant and egotistically inspired. When President Truman was briefed of the incident, he reportedly scoffed and ordered law enforcement officials to "Roast that Republican good."[29]

Years later, Harvey would chuckle at the memory of the incident. "No indictment was filed," he would remember, "but Harry Truman had me picking barbed wire out of my britches for about a decade."[30]

CHAPTER FIFTEEN

Birth of a Salesman

When heaven came calling, Paul Harvey had a pretty good idea how he hoped the conversation would go.

> I'd like to have a couple of minutes with St. Peter, just long enough to say, "Sir. Do you see that little bitty bowl of mud out there in the middle of the Milky Way? That little fly-speck in space includes a nation which is only 6 percent of its land surface and less than 6 percent of its population. It's called the United States of America, and Sir, they have the first government ever created in your hand, under God."[1]

So far, so good.

When the discussion turns to eternity and his credentials for his place in the heavenly realm, the country's most-listened-to broadcaster planned to respond with a one-sentence synopsis of his own life. "St. Peter, Sir," he planned to say, "I did what I could while I could to keep that little United States of America sold on itself."[2]

A salesman, even to the end.

"We have been unselling ourselves and our offspring on a way of life which is, in fact, the envy of the rest of the world," Harvey added.

Fellow Oakie and friend of the newsman, the late Will Rogers once quipped, "Advertising is the art of convincing people to spend money they don't have for something they don't need."[3] Though the two men saw eye to eye on most other things, the Tulsan would most certainly and assuredly have objected to such cynicism. Paul Harvey could sell anything from cars (the Buick Road Master) to radios (the Bose Acoustic Wave) or vitamins (Citri-Cal: "C as in citrus, Cal as in Calcium ... Citri-Cal!"). In the course of his sixty-year relationship with the ABC Radio network, Harvey generated a little over $1 billion in revenue for the company.[4]

Fellow radio legend and storyteller Garrison Keillor once wrote about attending a memorable dinner with the commentator and finding him to be the affable and predictably gregarious man he imagined on the air. "When the salad plates were whisked away and the entree brought in, he leaned over toward me and said, 'Page ... 2,' just like he does on the radio," Keillor recalled. "In fact, Mr. Harvey was exactly as he is on the radio. He read me a number of stories from a script in his pocket, most of them about ordinary Americans and their struggle to deregulate industry and give large corporations the freedom to do good in the world, and during all of this, he sold me a tin of liver pills and a utensil that dices, slices, chops, minces and prunes."[5]

Since he was a boy, Paul Harvey had exhibited the principles Dale Carnegie espoused in his national bestseller, *How to Win Friends and Influence People,* which Harvey read when he was eighteen.[6] The essential life doctrines translated to sound sales strategies as well.

Become genuinely interested in other people. Smile. Remember that a man's name is to him the sweetest and most important sound in any language. Be a good listener. Encourage others to talk about themselves. Talk in the terms of the other man's interest. Make the other person feel important and do it sincerely. Avoid arguments. Show respect for the other person's opinions. Never tell someone they are wrong. If you're wrong, admit it quickly and emphatically. Begin in a friendly way. Start with questions the other person will answer yes to. Let the other person do the talking. Let the other person feel the idea is his or hers. Try honestly to see things from the other person's point of view. Sympathize with the other person. Appeal to noble motives. Dramatize your ideas. Throw down a challenge.[7]

Dale Carnegie's cousin, the famous steel magnate Andrew Carnegie, commissioned a man named Napoleon Hill to research principles of personal achievement in 1908.[8] Hill would go on to author a series of inspirational bestsellers. The first was entitled *Laws of Success* and later the blockbuster book, *Think and Grow Rich*.[9] A student of Hill's was the late W. Clement Stone, a wildly successful entrepreneur who formed the Combined Insurance Company of America, which was later merged and became the Aon Corporation.[10] Over the years, Stone and Harvey became fast, dear friends. They would often share the stage together out on the lecture circuit. Stone, a Chicago resident, loved to fly back home in Harvey's personally piloted plane. Conversation always flowed freely, one learning from the other, each assuming they were getting the better deal. From Stone, Harvey would glean perspective and an appreciation for the power of positive thinking. In time, it would be known as "PMA"—a positive mental attitude. Stone also helped to further instill in Harvey a love and appreciation for the hopes, beauty, and prospects of American business. Meeting personally with advertisers and writing the commercial scripts himself, Paul regularly, but subtly, injected the wisdom and attitude of Stone in every piece of copy.

"In a climate where bigness was suspect, [Stone] altered that climate with persistent integrity and decency," Harvey once wrote. "In an era when rich men begat mostly resentment, this one earned respect [and] inspired emulation."[11]

Harvey saw his role as a salesman as indistinguishable from his duty as a patriot and man of integrity. During an interview on CNN, fellow talker Larry King once said to Harvey, "Arthur Godfrey once told me that on his license plate his occupation should be 'salesman.' Do you think you're a salesman?"[12]

Leaning forward, hands clasped, a wide and thoughtful smile emerging, Harvey responded.

> Oh, I hope so. I sure hope so, Larry, because I'm trying with all my might to compensate the people who put their money where my mouth is, for one thing. And also, I want to try to keep our American people sold on their "ism," because we in the news business are so constantly preoccupied with nagging about what's wrong—page 1 is always malfeasance, misfeasance, mistakes—that our citizenry and, more significantly, our offspring, come to figure that this nation that's always apologizing for itself must not be worth very much. And, of course, it's still the one place in the world where people are standing in line and waiting to get in—instead of braving stormy seas in small boats, dying, trying to get out.[13]

King pressed a little further, addressing the criticism most often lobbed against the commentator. "You've never had a question in your own mind that in doing commercials, that would take away from what might be considered objective news reporting?" he asked.

Harvey appeared glad he asked.

"No," he said simply.

> This dates back, of course, to the years when almost every-
> body did his own commercials. I guess I'm the last of the
> newspeople allowed to do it. We walk kind of a tightrope
> to be sure that journalism doesn't get mixed up with the
> others, so I always say, "Page 1," "Page 2," "Page 3," and
> the listeners over the years learn where the news leaves off
> and the commercial begins, but sometimes the best part of
> a broadcast might be in the essence of a commercial. There
> really is a battery that'll last the life of your car and there
> really is a way you can keep your natural teeth from here
> to hereafter. I'm not sure that some of the commercials
> aren't more significant than most of the news.[14]

Harvey had relationships with his advertisers that were more significant than some friendships. One of *Paul Harvey News'* earliest and
longest-tenured advertisers was the Bankers Life and Casualty Company. First signing on in 1952, he would serve as their spokesman for
thirty-three years until the company was sold in 1985.[15] At the time,
the previous record for program-advertiser affiliation had been Jergens' sixteen-year sponsorship of Walter Winchell's program. (Unlike
Harvey's peaceful and pleasant sponsor relationships, Winchell's
tenure with Jergens ended badly when the newsman refused to read a
commercial for deodorant.) In 2004, Bankers returned to the lineup
with then-president and CEO Edward Berube stating simply, "Who
better to share [our] message than the voice of America himself. . . ."[16]

   As a rule, Paul Harvey had a longstanding policy that he would not
endorse any product he didn't personally use and enjoy with enthusiasm.

"I'm very selective," Harvey said of his evaluation process. "I guess my office turns down 12 to 20 sponsors for every one that I accept."[17] Still, his detractors accused him of incessant hawking, a curious charge given his unblemished record for only advertising reputable products and services. Once deemed "Salesman of the Year" by the National Association of Direct Selling Companies, Harvey was hardly ashamed of his record or willingness to partner with his sponsors. "I don't well my mouth for dollars, but I'm not above endorsing the guy who endorses me."[18] In a later interview about the same topic, he was even blunter: "I cannot look down my nose at people who pay the bills."[19]

But did he really use all the products? Phil Gulley, a popular author, pastor, and personal friend of the Harvey family, vividly remembered his first visit to their home in River Forest, Illinois for lunch. "We went to the living room to wait for Mr. Harvey," he wrote. "There was a Bose Wave radio on the table. Mr. Harvey's been telling us for years how wonderful they sound."[20] Harvey exemplified putting his money where his mouth was.

Over the years, Paul Harvey's on-air comments in the midst of a newscast about books, music, and even local restaurants would unexpectedly spike sales and increase foot traffic in stores all around the country. A mention on his program translated into major dollars for many people. During his time at WKZO in Kalamazoo, Harvey became acquainted with Win Schuler, a popular restaurant proprietor in nearby Marshall, MI. Though he was never an advertiser on his national program, the commentator would regularly tout Schuler's (now over 100 years in business) steaks and the down home atmosphere of its dining room. When Harvey listeners from other parts of the country came through Michigan, many made a point to come visit. When Mr. Schuler convinced United Airlines to replace their free peanuts with breadsticks and the restaurant's famous beer butter, a Schuler's staple, Harvey was happy to report the development. He found it particularly entertaining and satisfying that Chicago-based United Airlines had chosen a small business's product over that of a Chicago giant—Kraft's cheese. It was typical Harvey—always eager to celebrate the power of the little guy.[21]

There was no simple reason for his success as a salesman. Studies have found that salespeople with "variable intensities" in their voice tend to be more successful than those with a more even-keeled and predictable vocal tone.[22] Other findings suggest it pays for salespeople to speak at a pace quicker than that of a normal conversation.[23] All of this might be true, but throughout Harvey's career, those who knew him best typically boiled down his advertising dominance to modest and basic principle.

"He doesn't simply sell widgets, he tells stories," said John McConnell, the former ABC Radio vice president and longtime Harvey colleague and friend. "No one has spoken to more people. He has no equal. He's a master, writing his own copy, talking about his own personal use of the advertiser's product."[24]

Chicago's WGN vice president and general manager Tom Langmyer echoed McConnell's sentiment. "As a terrific salesman, Paul told a personal story about the product," he said. "It was not about reading a script or running a highly produced spot with music and cute effects. He stood out in a sea of noise. He did this by simply using the power of personal experience, storytelling and his unique voice to talk about the product with *one* listener, one-on-one. So many broadcasters think they are on stage, talking to thousands of people. Paul knew that broadcasting is a bit of a misnomer. It *really* is about talking to *one* person. That way, each listener feels more connected because it is a personal connection."[25]

Neill Walsdorf Jr. is president of Mission Pharmacal, another longtime sponsor of *Paul Harvey News*. It wasn't his highly paid marketing team that came up with the catchy slogan for the product—it was Paul Harvey. "'C' as in 'citrus.' 'Cal,' as in 'calcium.' *CIT-ra-cal*." According to Walsdorf, calls came in "like a tsunami" immediately after the campaign began. "I was actually [standing] at the buyer's desk at Walgreens when [the buyer] manually overrode the ordering computer to accommodate the high turns...we never looked back. He has a way of taking the essence of any product and putting it across in a conversational manner that rings true with consumers."[26]

Every advertiser has a story. Norm Miller, chairman of Interstate Battery System of America, said, "We're still known by many people as "Paul Harvey's batteries."[27] Ross Advertising CEO, Wayne Flittner, who introduced the Wahl Clipper Corporation to the commentator's program, once said, "Harvey's legendary ability to create mental images in the listener's mind really works."[28]

It wasn't always a smooth ride, though. Even the most successful spokesman will inevitably run into challenges with some of his sponsors over the course of sixty years. Towards the end of his life, clients grew weary of Mr. Harvey's reduced broadcasting schedule. The ABC network made billing adjustments in order to accommodate and retain them, but there was still a level of tension. Revenue was down from previous historic levels.[29] When Harvey made a comment about the violent nature of militant Islam in 2003, the Council on American-Islamic Relations urged listeners to boycott his program and its advertisers.[30] General Electric, a longtime client, responded to the initial pressure. "GE certainly doesn't endorse the comment and regrets any offense that it may have caused," they wrote. "While we look into the matter further, we have pulled GE's advertisements from Mr. Harvey's show."[31] An avalanche of pro-Harvey support followed, and GE quickly reversed itself. In 2005, another popular sponsor, Hi-Health, was forced to pay a fine of $450,000 to the Federal Trade Commission for allowing certain "unreliable" scientific evidence to be included in the Harvey spots.[32] In 2007, the United States Attorney General John W. Suthers announced a $4.5 million settlement against the General Steel Corporation. According to the file charges, General Steel erroneously advertised they were selling buildings at factory-direct or clearance prices.[33]

"Advertisers in the United States are going to spend $249.3 billion this year—and, by the way, that's 5 percent more than last year—telling us all of the good things, real and imagined, about their respective products," Harvey said in a speech shortly before he died.

> Isn't it a rotten shame that with noisy, distressing, depressing news hour after hour, day in and day out, by our own emphasis on all of the bad things, crime and inflation and pollution and floods and fires and discords and disaster and discontent, by our persistent preoccupation with negatives, we tend to unsell ourselves and our impressionable offspring on a way of life, which is the envy of the rest of the worlds? And repetition is effective. Repetition is effective. Repetition is effective.[34]

When Paul Harvey suggested that ads are often the best part of the news, he was just echoing the sentiments of America's third president. Thomas Jefferson once famously said that "advertisements are the most truthful part of a newspaper."[35] He might very well have been right. As the late Charles Revson, a pioneer in cosmetics whose courage, innovation, and persistence led to the creation of the Revlon Corporation, once said, "In our factory we make lipstick. In our advertising we sell hope."[36] Perhaps that's why Paul Harvey was such an effective salesman. Being unequivocably sold on the merits of America made it infinitely easier to embrace and promote its products. But the ABC commentator, always deferential towards his sponsors, had a simple explanation for why he was able to sell so effectively for so long. The most effective advertisement, he would say, is a great product. And Paul Harvey loved great products.

Radio executive, writer, and editor Al Peterson was once asked to address charges that Paul Harvey's shtick was just that—all foam and no beer. Was Paul Harvey really as passionate about his products as his advertising copy suggested? Peterson didn't hesitate. "Of course he believed it," he responded. "Even the world's greatest actor couldn't fake it that well—for that long. Even Paul Harvey wasn't that good."[37]

The turbulent decade of the 1960s was coming, and one of America's most effective salesmen was about to embark on one of his toughest assignments yet—selling the American people on his strategy for ultimate victory in the rice paddies of a jungle called Vietnam.

CHAPTER SIXTEEN

Drive It or Park It

The newspaper columns tell us the story. Like a time capsule emerging from the cornerstone of an old brick building, Paul Harvey's thrice weekly essays of the 1960s and 1970s captured in real time the mood and tenure of now faded and previously contentious cultural moments. At once pithy and poignant, the reflections reveal what he was thinking and how he was feeling about the waging of war and the prospect for peace.

The language is strikingly crisp, opinionated, and swiftly decisive. He was obviously comfortable in his own skin, never shying away from controversy or afraid to contradict the consensus if it contradicted his reading of the United States' Constitution. At the same time, in paper and after paper, he appeared to be wrestling with big thoughts and serious ideas.

It is possible he was struggling with the reality of mortality. His beloved mother died, aged seventy-seven, in 1960. Like other topics of deep personal grief, such as his life without a father, he didn't say much about his mother's passing. But it shadowed his perspective on the turbulent decade that began with America at war. Despite his sober frame of mind, his reputation was growing.

Numbers can often obfuscate reality, but in the case of quantifying Paul Harvey's popularity in the 1960s, they are, if anything, insufficient. At the beginning of the decade, the ABC newsman was heard each day by more than 14 million listeners on nearly 400 stations across the ABC network.[1] His office reported an average annual receipt of 31,000 letters, many demanding a reply or posing a question and making a request.[2] He was elected to the Oklahoma Hall of Fame in 1955.[3] New York's *Radio-Television Daily* bestowed upon him their "Commentator of the Year Award" in 1962 and "Man of the Year" in 1963.[4] His General Features syndicated column was being carried by over two hundred newspapers. His first two books, *Remember These Things* and *Autumn of Liberty* were bestsellers, selling briskly at retail outlets nationwide. Not surprisingly, the Harvey Empire extended into the recording industry as well through Word Records in Waco, Texas. His first album, entitled *The Testing Time*, was released in 1958.[5] By 1962, he had recorded another called *The Uncommon Man*.[6] Both sold extremely well. Supporting and complementing all of these entrepreneurial endeavors was Harvey's tireless speaking schedule. At its height, he was booked a minimum of four nights a week. A conservative estimate suggested that well over one million people per year were in attendance at his functions all across the country during the 1960s. In addition, *Paul Harvey Comments*, a daily three-minute television commentary feature, launched nationwide in 1968.[7] Ratings were strong right out of the gate.

From a marketing and business perspective, Harvey was a promoter's dream with no near equal in his field. Under the tutelage and direction of his wife Lynne, the Harveys established Paulynne Productions to manage and direct his extracurricular non-radio endeavors. But Lynne was more than a creator, producer, and shaper of content. As requests poured in, Mrs. Harvey helped her husband keep his focus, turning down hundreds of requests each year, even high profile ones such as an invitation to host the Miss America Pageant. The arrangement allowed them to engage in a "good cop/bad cop" routine with strangers. Publicly, Harvey always expressed a desire to accommodate every request. When Angel would turn someone down or cut an interview short, Paul was quick to jokingly refer to her as Simon Legree, the cruel slave dealer in Harriet Beecher Stowe's famous novel, *Uncle Tom's Cabin.* No tag team ever worked more efficiently or effectively.

"As you know," Harvey remarked, "anyone with talent gets lots of offers. Angel, my wife, goes over them all. She asks, 'Is this on course?' If it isn't, we turn it down."[8]

The disciplined strategy would help keep the commentator on message, especially regarding the decade's most controversial subject.

Between 1962 and 1974, Paul Harvey had quite a bit to say and write about the escalating war in Vietnam. But between then and now, an inaccurate narrative has evolved concerning the popular radio commentator's position on the bloody conflict in Southeast Asia.

That line, repeated on websites and in papers everywhere, goes something like this: the patriotic and militant Harvey was a resolute hawk who strongly supported the campaign at its outset. Even as casualties began to mount and victory became even more elusive, the belligerent newsman's backing for the long engagement held firm until around 1969 or 1970. But then, according to the much repeated story, two things happened to turn him from a hawk to a dove and a vocal, outspoken Vietnam War protestor. First, Angel finally convinced him of the war's folly, her reasoned pleas finally falling on receptive ears. And second, as the legend goes, Paul suddenly realized that his beloved son, Paul Jr., was of draft age—and he couldn't bear the thought of sending him off to a war with no end in sight. It was all of these factors, concludes the popular story, which led him to utter the now famous phrase on Friday, May 1, 1970, "Mr. President—I love you—but you are wrong!"[9]

It all makes for a neat and tidy tale. Too bad it's not entirely true. As contrived, the simplified narrative casts the war's opponents as the enlightened ones and, conversely, its supporters and defenders as brutish and simple. But facts are stubborn things. From Harvey's penned columns and hundreds of broadcasts and speeches through-out the 1960s, it's clear his own words tell a very different story about his wartime perspective.

As early as 1962, Harvey was asking his listeners, "If it were up to you to push the button, would you send American troops to rescue those lands of elephants and opium poppies....Would you send American sons into those steaming jungles...?"[10] In August of 1964, he accused President Johnson of creating a "crisis atmosphere" in Southeast Asia in order to justify an expansion of troops in the region. "A little exaggeration is an accepted part of politicking," he wrote. "Southeast Asia is infected with a festering, ugly, uncomfortable social sickness which is contagious if not quarantined, but there is no acute crisis threatening us."[11] As Labor Day of '64 approached, Harvey's col-umn bluntly asked the question, "Is Vietnam worth one American life?"[12] When he concluded by stating, "We fight for a harvest of opium poppies in Vietnam," his answer to his own question seemed brutally clear.[13]

After President Lyndon Johnson was elected in his own right on the night of November 3, 1964, Harvey's rhetoric rose by several deci-bels. Frustrated by the fact that the South Vietnamese government wouldn't draft their own sons to fight (at the same time Americans were being drafted), the 46-year-old commentator wrote, "It's time somebody called this war a war—and worse, a useless, pointless and apparently endless war....A military victory in Vietnam is not now foreseeable."[14]

Still, Harvey appeared willing to straddle the fence, even vacillating at times with his own opinions, hoping against hope logic would prevail and the tide would turn. "The embarrassing truth is that I don't know which course to urge," he wrote on February 23, 1965. "In decisions so critical, the blind must not presume to lead....An emotional harangue without a constructive conclusion seems somehow sadistic."[15]

American unease across the heartland was growing. Based upon the measure of his continuously high ratings and the steady stream of mail flowing across his desk, it was clear his audience saw things similarly. He found the conflict of emotion to be unsettling. "Man's extremity is God's opportunity," he would say, quoting Lord Belhaven's Scottish Parliament objection concerning the union of England and Scotland in 1706. "There is a remedy for most all that ails us which is as simple as 'love thy neighbor...' as uncomplicated as 'do unto others...' but a fellow has to be careful talking like that."[16]

The rationale for Paul Harvey's opposition to the Vietnam War mirrored the same objections he voiced so vociferously during America's stalemated foray in Korea. Frustrated by bumbling bureaucrats pulling the strings of messy and imperfect military campaigns, Harvey crisscrossed the country with the following message:

> [I]n world wars past, we who admittedly are not students
> of military weapons and tactics and strategy have gladly
> left these decisions where they belong—in military hands.
> Our civilian Commander-In-Chief historically has always

prescribed when and where we should go to war, but it's
been left up to military men to determine how. With that
formula we never lost a war. Since we switched we've
never won one![17]

Time marched on. With only two weeks off the air each year, Harvey
continued to sprinkle his newscasts each and every day with the eclectic color of popular culture his listeners had come to expect. It wasn't
all war, all the time. In the midst of offering serious reflections on
worldwide crises, he still found time to poke fun at developments
such as the Custom Tailors Guild of America's declaration of him as
one of the ten best-dressed men of 1964. Prior to the honor, in a self-
deprecating though not entirely honest comment given his reputation
as a jaunty dresser, he wrote, "Around the athletic club I, in a sweat-
shirt, am accustomed to looking like an unmade bed. Not any
more . . . [but] I'm trying to appear modest—like an undertaker tries
to appear sad at a seven thousand dollar funeral."[18]

    Few commentators could so deftly and subtly season their broad-
casts with such a mixture of bitterness and sweetness. "I've tried to
make the hard, cold sometimes acrid news palatable and interesting,"
he said. "If I did otherwise, we'd abandon that vast, decent, middle-
income, middle-IQ audience to the rabble rousers—to the professional anti-Communists, the white klan, and the Black Panthers!"[19]

    As the presidential election of 1968 approached, Harvey grew even
bolder with his politically pointed commentaries. Regularly lamenting
the United States' reluctance to use bigger weapons and even unorthodox methods of attack, he graphically wrote: "It is permissible for us
to burn the enemy to death with flaming jellied gasoline; that is a military decision. But gas? Horrors!"[20] He went on to point out that dis-
abling the enemy—but not killing or permanently maiming—with

liquid mustard gas was possible yet foolishly prohibited by Washington regulations. Harvey sided with the opinion of retired Brigadier General J. H. Rothschild, the chief chemical advisor for the UN Forces in Korea. General Rothschild had unsuccessfully argued for the use of mustard gas as far back as World War II when U.S. troops landed on Japanese islands throwing phosphorous grenades. "We could have dropped mustard-gas on those islands," Rothschild told Harvey, [and] "incapacitated the people and walked ashore with no resistance."[21]

"Mistakes are no disgrace if we profit from them," he wrote when the death toll reached an average of 1,200 troops per month in 1968. "A strategic retreat can defeat a Napoleon....Time and time again, our diplomats, seeking to cover up mistakes, have compounded them." With startling frankness, he concluded, "We goofed. We meddled where we should not have. Seeking to rescue an unworthy Saigon government, we alienated the Southeast Asians we had hoped to encourage."[22]

In coming to embrace a belief that America would be wise to steer clear of foreign entanglements, Paul Harvey was identifying with classic neo-isolationist ideology. But it's critical to note there is a significant distinction within "isolationism" itself. Whereas modern, liberal-minded isolationists believed America's influence would negatively affect the culture of a foreign country, Harvey, like other neo-isolationists, believed a foreign country's influence negatively affected America. Though the desired outcome is similar, there was a profound difference in motive. During the Vietnam years, Harvey lamented America's pulled-punches approach to fighting on many levels, but mostly because he feared it was damaging the morale back home in the United States of America. In contrast, anti-war activist Jane Fonda protested America's presence in Vietnam because she feared the United States was negatively impacting Vietnamese culture and its people.

Harvey, a devoted student of the founding fathers, regularly invoked their perspective in his books, speeches, and on his broadcasts. He would argue that patriots like Thomas Paine and George Washington had strongly advised against the formation of foreign alliances. In his famous farewell address, Washington stated, "The great rule of conduct for us, in regard to foreign nations, is in extending our commercial relations, to have with them as little political connection as possible."[23] The broadcaster was openly advocating for a return to such doctrine, though with an admittedly modern twist. Harvey was a realist who supported the alliances forged in World War II and those that evolved on economically philosophical terms. Simply put, he loved and embraced capitalism and despised anything remotely associated with socialistic policies. "We must seek after self-sufficiency," he said. "When that earl pioneer first turned his eyes toward the West he didn't demand that anyone else look after him . . . there was an old fashioned philosophy in those days that a man was supposed to provide for his own and for his own future."[24]

Throughout the early decades of his meteoric rise, Harvey regularly addressed the criticisms lobbed against him from conservatives who didn't appreciate the fundamental nuance of his position. Taking their comments to their logical extreme, he warned about the consequences of allowing American interests to be subjected to international rule. "Isolationism," he said, "you call it selfishness. Don't you see? It doesn't make any difference what names we call it because eventually we're not going to have any choice."[25] His nationalistic appeal strongly resonated with his expanding, enthusiastic audience. In fact, he had his finger on the sources of widespread American frustration in Vietnam. Alluding to the fact that President Johnson had decided not to run for reelection and that the new Nixon administration gave initial indications it planned to adjust Vietnam strategy, Harvey continued. "However tardily," he went on, "official Washington is beginning to reflect the ground swell at grass roots—enlightened selfishness. Now I'm not excusing the violent peaceniks and their vulgar degradation of our flag. I'm just trying to help us all understand some the frustrations and exasperations of this upcoming generation because I share it and because some of their grievances are valid."[26]

Paul Harvey was significantly though subtly influenced in his formative years by several key minds who advocated an isolationist approach. Governor Alfred Landon of Kansas, a candidate for the presidency in 1936, became good friends with the radio commentator over the years. Long talks on Landon's screened porch in Topeka most assuredly resonated with the maturing Harvey. These philosophical thoughts likely began with the growth of the *America First* movement that Harvey appreciated as he made his way up the professional ladder. With its leadership concentrated in Chicago in 1940, it claimed nearly 135,000 members, including such notables as famed aviator Charles Lindbergh, General Robert E. Wood, the CEO of Sears-Roebuck, Sterling Morton of the Morton Salt Company, H. Smith Richardson of the Vick Chemical Company, and publisher William H. Regnery.[27] The onset of World War II and America's forced alliances to defeat the Axis powers pushed the group into retirement. Though not an active member of the movement prior to the war, Harvey's elevated profile permitted him the pleasure of regularly crossing paths with the ideological giants of the group.

The tumult of the times was ripe for righteous indignation. As the decade unfolded, Harvey's stinging commentaries took few prisoners, and became a forum for him to challenge individuals on both sides of the aisle. He would reflect that over time, he began believing less and less in black and white political labels. "Basically," he said, "I believe

in Big People, as opposed to Big Government—to the extent that a
sardine society will allow."[28]

Admonishing his fellow members of the media for highlighting an
isolated city riot or any otherwise insignificant uprising: "Some argue
that it is the responsibility of the press to throw light on these situa-
tions rather than let them fester in the dark. But when it's flashbulb
light, it draws kooks like the porch light draws bugs."[29] Harvey had
observed that there was a near fatal attraction developing between
protestors of all sorts and the television camera. An otherwise peaceful demonstration would grow violent when a camera showed up. Yet,
careful not to trample on First Amendment rights, Harvey's chastisement of his fellow members of the press came with an acknowledge-
ment that he was more likely letting off steam than calling for a
journalistic revolution. "The free press has cost too many, too much
and historically it tends, eventually, to correct its own excesses."[30]

Addressing the rise of protest marches popping up and disturbing
business, especially during the Democratic National Convention in
Chicago in 1968, Harvey shared his perspective on the logical pro-
gression of lawlessness: "Demonstrators, allowed to parade without a
permit, soon will be smashing store windows. The next step is coor-
dinated smashing, burning, looting. If the looting eventually results
in bloodshed, somebody ends up dead because somebody else got
away with parading without a permit."[31]

The 1968 assassinations of the Reverend Martin Luther King in
April and Senator Robert Kennedy in June elicited a bold but still
stinging observation from the radio commentator. Bemoaning the
senseless violence and loss of life, Harvey again directed his fire to his
media cohorts. Both King's and Kennedy's funerals were covered on
every channel and station for hours at a time. "Yet one remembers,"
Harvey wrote, "that Senator Joe McCarthy and General Douglas
MacArthur and President Herbert Hoover and Helen Keller got no

such astronomically expensive, elaborate send-off. So it must be deduced after two-all assassination extravaganzas that it is at least possible that Martin Luther King and Robert Kennedy were in death the beneficiaries of a 'prejudice' which they in life renounced."[32]

Continuing to crisscross the country giving speeches for nearly $10,000 per engagement, Harvey was a master at serving up a dosage of outrage coupled with a measure of hope. In a single address he might lament "professional baby makers"[33] on welfare, or "goof off students defaulting on loans and using food stamps to pay for booze and drugs."[34] While acknowledging his continued concern about the Soviet Union and other socialist governments, Harvey would tell his audience, "I'm not nearly so anxious about the lousy Communists as I am about lazy Americans."[35] But then he would strike a note of hope: "How frequently a healthy outlook begets a healthy body. . . if you can keep a cheerful, optimistic outlook, your body is not likely to turn sour."[36]

On the evening of April 30, 1970, President Richard Nixon announced to the nation that he had ordered American troops into Cambodia, a small "neutral" country of seven million people that borders Vietnam.[37] He reasoned that the expansion was the most efficient means to quell North Vietnamese aggression that had been regularly spilling over into the tiny country and causing more American casualties in the region. "I realize that in this war there are honest and deep differences in this country about whether we should have become involved," Nixon said, "that there are differences as to how the war should have been conducted. But the decision I announce tonight transcends those differences."[38]

Meanwhile, back in Chicago, Paul Harvey was frustrated. Relieved when President Johnson decided not to run for reelection and encouraged when President Nixon announced plans for removing 150,000 troops earlier in the year, the commentator decided he would share his unfiltered perspective the next day on the air. While his regular listeners knew of his growing objections to military strategy, this would be the first time he addressed the president so directly.

Relaying the news of Mr. Nixon's announcement, Harvey was blunt. "Mr. President, I love you," he said on May 1, 1970, "but you are wrong! America's six percent section of this planet's mothers cannot bear enough boy babies to police Asia—and our nation can't bleed to death trying." He continued, "And quite frankly, Mr. President, out here in the unterrified nine-tenths of this country that's still country, we don't think there's anything in Indochina worth that."[39]

Even though his admonishment was not really new, over 25,000 letters arrived at the door of the Harveys' River Forest home office on Monday, May 4, 1970.[40] The vast majority of the mail was positive, thanking him for his statement and further enshrining him as the "voice of the silent majority"—a self-appointed title that resonated with his predominately mid-American audience.

He never had any regrets about his statement. "I had always been reared with the old MacArthur feeling that the only excuse for getting into a war is to win it," he reflected. "The only justification for war is to win it. And then, one day, I realized that in spite of the expenditure of all of our gold and all of that blood, in Vietnam and in Korea, the most we were able to deliver was a stalemate on the 50 yard line. We'd paid much too high a price for that. And it was then that I suggested that we drive it or park it."[41]

Paul Aurandt paid his dues at many stations across America. This photo was likely taken during his tenure at KFBI in Salina, Kansas in 1937. (*Public Domain Photo*)

Paul Harvey's childhood home on East Fifth Place still stands today. The extension to the right with the red door was one of the apartments Paul's mother built in 1922.

Paul Harvey Aurandt was a proud member of the Hi-Y Club at Tulsa's Central High School and is pictured here in 1935, top row, center.

PAUL AURANDT
OKLAHOMA
His pleasing voice is appreciated
over KVOO

MIRIAM BAILEY
WASHINGTON, D. C.
If you are lonesome,
seek out Miriam

JOY AYERS
OKLAHOMA
A demure little person; a
willing worker

WARREN G. BAILE
WASHINGTON, D. C.
A gay young Lothari
out for a lark

BEVERLY BADGER
NORTH DAKOTA
He possesses the ingredients
of a good mixer

DONALD BAIRD
OKLAHOMA
It is impossible to corr
a square man

JULIA MAE BAER
KANSAS
If silence is golden, she is
poverty str.cken

BETTY JANE BAKE
MISSOURI
Endowed with gifts
chic and charm

Paul Harvey Aurandt Central High School Tom Tom Yearbook photo, 1936.

Paul broadcasts from the floor of the Missouri State Senate as Director of Special Events at St. Louis station KXOK.

WKZO engineer Carl Lee, far right, broadcasts with Paul and Lynne at a Western Michigan University baseball game from Haymes Field in Kalamazoo, Michigan in 1942.

Kalamazoo's WKZO promoted newsman Paul Aurandt's popular radio program on this downtown bulletin board, circa 1942/1943.

A family of artists who painted pictures with words. The three Harveys hard at work inside the ABC offices of *Paul Harvey News*. Circa 1956. *(Photo courtesy of the ABC Radio Network)*

Paul Junior's childhood nickname was Hoppy. This family portrait was taken around 1955.

"Radio Daze," by Jim Daly, hung in Paul Harvey's office reception area for years. *(Courtesy of Jim Daly: JimDalyart.com)*

Paul Harvey was initially a fierce supporter and always a friend of FBI Chief J. Edgar Hoover. Here they are pictured at FBI headquarters in Washington in the mid-1950s.

Harvey, who almost always wore a coat and tie during broadcasts, also always kept a pencil with him for last minute changes he would make during the program.

Paul's interest in aviation extended to piloting a floatplane.

Paul would visit his mother, Anna Dagmar, at the family home on 1014 East Fifth Place as often as possible. Here they are pictured on their porch swing, circa 1959.

Broadcasting from his Chicago Studios, early 1990s. (*Photo courtesy of the ABC Radio Network*)

Paul and Lynne Harvey, along with their son, Paul Aurandt, inside their River Forest home. *(Photo courtesy of the ABC Radio Network)*

Nov. 16, 1988: Paul and Lynne Harvey hold the street sign bearing his name in Chicago. A one-block stretch of East Wacker Drive became Paul Harvey Drive in honor of the well-known broadcaster.

With fellow honoree Andy Griffith looking on, Paul Harvey receives the Medal of Freedom from President George W. Bush on November 9, 2005. "This is the highest honor I have received since some 60-years ago when Angel said, 'I do,'" the commentator told his listeners. *(Photo by Carrie Devorah / WENN)*

Chicago Mayor Richard Daley proclaimed Friday October 4, 2002 "Paul Harvey Day" in the Windy City. Pictured here on the morning of the day. (*Photo courtesy of the ABC Radio Network*)

Paul Harvey striking a pose inside his Chicago-based ABC office in 2006.

CHAPTER SEVENTEEN

The Rest of the Story

Depending upon the person, there can be either an incalculable measure of comfort or a maddening degree of boredom emanating from the rhythm and pace of a daily routine. But personal attitudes notwithstanding, psychologists will agree that monotony can often provide critical career momentum—especially for a creative and easily distracted mind. Simply put, routine serves to keep the train on the tracks. "Habit," wrote the English novelist George Eliot "is the beneficent harness of routine, which enables silly men to live respectfully and unhappy men to live calmly."[1]

Entering his fourth decade in Chicago, and his twenty-fifth year with the ABC Radio Network, Paul Harvey had assumed an unrivaled and rarely varied daily regimen.

Monday through Friday, the alarm clock issued the wake-up call at 3:30 a.m. His Angel slept on. She'd meet him at the downtown office later in the morning. Often she was up till midnight, editing or polishing a script from her third floor office, likely taking care of an array of other responsibilities that accumulate when someone is juggling many creative projects at the same time. Quietly but excitedly, the newsman would spring out of bed inside the pink-walled bedroom of the stately 22-room stone mansion on Park Avenue. He claimd he was eager, anxious for each new day to begin. Nobody doubted it was true.

"Let me say I can't wait to get up every morning and watch the passing parade and call out to anybody who might be interested in the things that interest me," the commentator insisted. "I don't have to work myself up. I can't wait to get down to the teletypes and find out what goofy, hilarious, heroic things people have been doing."[2]

Roused from his seven and a half or so hour sleep, Harvey didn't dawdle, didn't allow for any precious time to slip away. He showered, shaved, and was quickly dressed in a suit and tie. Even though it was radio, he insisted on maintaining formality. "It is all about discipline," Harvey once told Rick Kogan of the *Chicago Tribune*, "I could go to work in my pajamas, but long ago I got some advice from the man who was the engineer for my friend Billy Graham's radio show. He said that one has to prepare in all ways for the show. If you don't do that in every area, you'll lose your edge."[3] At one point during his career, he compromised and began to dress a bit more informally. "I had Bob Benninghoff, fifty years an engineer on *Paul Harvey News*. He took me aside on one day and said, 'You're beginning to sound as casual as you dress.'"[4] The coat and tie made a comeback.

Breakfast was a bowl of oatmeal, brewer's yeast, an alfalfa capsule, and sixteen vitamins. Always. He claimed to have eaten oatmeal every morning of his life. With an evangelistic fervor, Harvey would share with audiences a detailed but fairly simple prescription for a happy and successful life:

> When you get up in the morning, do at least 20 push-ups, even you ladies. Smile at yourself in the shaving mirror...
> wear a bright tie, or if you're a woman who has to wear a

navy or gray dress, wear a bright scarf. Have bran or oatmeal cereal for breakfast. Greet your co-workers nicely.
Schedule scripture reading and prayer, preferable with
your spouse. And don't leave all your pep at the office. Play
tennis, swim or jog. If you jog, jog not less than one mile
every other day. Avoid downers. Forget the 10 o'clock
news, forget the newspaper. Just listen to Paul Harvey.
Before you go to bed read some of Dr. [Norman] Peale's
great works or read some Erma Bombeck.[5]

By the 1960s, success extended him the privilege of a car and a driver.
Each morning, in the predawn dark, Harvey met the limousine at the
curb outside their River Forest home by 4:00 a.m. The fifteen-minute
drive to the office afforded him the rare opportunity to listen to radio
or read the news, which he did with great enjoyment.

   As the first person to arrive at the studio, he would walk in alone,
flip on the reception area lights, and travel past a large painting that
poignantly framed the essence of his career. The oil mural was a gift
of a fellow Oklahoman, a talented artist by the name of Jim Daly. Paul
shared with visitors that the boy pictured, a young lad leaning on his
elbow and listening to an old radio, reminded him of himself. Paul
also enjoyed sharing the note that Daly sent with the picture. It read:

   There is no way for me to express in words the pleasure I
   received from listening to old radio programs. Only in my
   paintings can I attempt to share these emotions. What a
   joy it was to let my imagination run free. In my mind I created what those wonderful heroes looked like. They were
   magnificent. No movie or television program, or even real
   life, could have equaled what my own imagination could

conjure up, and amazingly, in my mind, all those heroes looked a little bit like me.[6]

It was Paul who made the coffee (Kava) and collected the overnight stories from the wire service machines. Taking off his suit jacket, he donned a blue smock emblazoned with the ABC logo and quickly sat down behind his IBM Selectric typewriter.

Even to his last day, he would not use a computer, jokingly referring to the machines as "confusers" and saying that he was hoping they'd somehow fall out of favor.[7] His typewriter worked just fine, thank you. (He did keep a computer in his office, but he claimed he only used it to check stock quotes.)

The first script for the 6:30 a.m. broadcast would be finished by 6:20. Arising from behind the office desk, he would stack and clip the papers of his script and stroll into the austere studio. Each story was typed on a single sheet of white paper; small pencil marks were all along the margins, clarifying a pronunciation, indicating a last minute edit—or reminding him of the place to insert the famous pause. Paul Harvey could say more with fewer words than anyone in the business. He would regularly ad lib, purposely appearing like he was grasping for a word in a delicate balancing act. If it was too polished, it might seem phony; too off the cuff and he would appear unprepared. A quick final review followed and suddenly, he was live on the air. With the famous, enthusiastic opening line of "Good Morning, Americans!" the broadcast would be underway.[8]

He would then go back to the office until 10:20 a.m. and prepare the lengthier fifteen-minute version of his morning program. He would eat another small breakfast on the go. Depending upon the current lineup of sponsors, it might be a specially fortified piece of bread or an extra large glass of Welch's purple grape juice. In between typing and composing, he'd work the telephones and his contacts around the country. The fact-gathering went two ways. Many of his stringers would call him. He had "eyes and ears" all over, including the highest and most powerful offices in the land. Prior to 9:00 a.m., Harvey would answer the phone himself with an abrupt and pointed "Yes?" He'd talk to anybody, but he kept it brief and on point. An unrelenting deadline demanded it.

Once the 10:30 a.m. program was completed, there was at least another hour or so of varied assignments, from talking and meeting with sponsors to recording special features. By noon, it would be time for lunch. Having arrived separately, Paul and Lynne departed together and either headed for a favorite restaurant or more often than not, headed for home to eat with their son.

Like many creations of genius, the *Rest of the Story* feature came about somewhat by accident. At first it was an element of his early newscasts in the 1940s. Harvey explained,

> I have always thought that history cheats the history student by telling him the end of the story from the beginning. If you tell the same story in chronological sequence you have that history student moving out toward the edge of his seat until you get to the climax and he finds out this fellow you've been talking about—this poor little misfit boy who had to be taken out of school because he couldn't speak at the age of 7, who was what we would now call retarded, turns out to be the great Albert Einstein. I started writing in the news that way.[9]

Based upon a favorable response and interest in the fascinating stories, the Harveys published a small book of eighty-two short stories in 1977 entitled, not surprisingly, *The Rest of the Story*.[10]

Lynne thought the idea could stand on its own as a five-minute radio feature. ABC's interest was piqued, and a special nightly series with an American historical emphasis was created for the bicentennial celebration of 1976.[11] The response to it across the network was overwhelming.

"My mother had suggested that it be continued as a regular radio series," Paul Jr. said. "But my father said he didn't have the time to write another set of radio scripts each week."[12]

Paul Jr., then twenty-eight and a rising concert pianist, happened to be recovering from a serious car accident and was quite literally laid up with little to do. Although there is no detailed account of the incident, Paul Sr. had mentioned that they first feared their son wouldn't live and later wondered if he would ever walk again.[13] Fortunately, he did both and recovered without any lingering limitations. During his recuperation, he volunteered to give the writing a shot.

"I had a free week on my hands so I locked myself up [in the piano room] with my father's book, a yellow marking pencil and a stop watch, like a fool. I had never written anything before and I was worried. But I was able to pick up where my father's scripts left off and began writing in the same style so that it would blend unnoticed."[14]

But did writing come easily for the younger Harvey? "I was raised by a scholarly mother who in many ways laid the foundation for whatever literary skill I have, so that part came rather naturally," he says. "Anything I am able to write grows out of a temperament that is musical. It is the same mentality and the same substance. I believe the writer needs a lot of what the musician has and that the musician needs a lot of what the writer is capable of."[15]

Stepping into the family business was a big decision for Paul Harvey Aurandt Jr. Known as "Junior" to ABC executives, he decided as a young boy to go by the family's actual last name, hoping to carve out his own identity apart from the broad shadow of the Harvey mystique. He is a towering and lean man, 6'5", who exudes the gracious and hospitable spirit of his late parents. Though he rarely agrees to interviews, when he does, he is usually open, introspective and endearingly candid about the challenges associated with growing up in the shadow of two broadcasting giants. Where his father and mother were drawn to radio, he gravitated to music in his mid-teens. Remarkably, he was, at first, self-taught. His parents were astonished. He somehow managed to memorize the "Emperor" concerto of Beethoven over the course of the first few months of engaging in the hobby. Finally, Paul and Evelyn arranged for some formal instruction. His first teacher found him to be too much of a prodigy to handle and reportedly sent him to a more experienced teacher, who apparently also considered the young talent to be above her teaching level.[16]

Everything comes with a price. With his father jetting across the country for much of his life, Paul Jr. turned to his music as a refuge and outlet. "The piano has been my friend for a very long time," he said, "particularly during my youth when my father was away from home a lot. So, I relate to life as a musician, not a writer."[17]

"I might have gotten interested in music because of something inherent, because my parents are interested in music and because my father loves to sing," Paul said. "But the piano served more of a necessity in my life, growing up in a community where my father was well known. . . . In order to find and reinforce my own identity, I had to find something else, something separate from his writing. When you don't even have your own name and you're number two, you get a complex about who you are."[18]

Aurandt never let the desire to make it as his own man prevent him from cultivating and maintaining warm relations with his parents. In fact, Paul Jr. remained extremely close to his parents—both literally and figuratively, his entire life. When the 29-year-old musician and writer married in 1976, his parents purchased the house next door as a wedding gift for their son and new daughter-in-law, Tanya. The quaint English Tudor home at 1027 Park Avenue was built in 1933 and extensively renovated by the Harveys prior to the newlyweds assuming residence. Paul Jr.'s mother, for years extremely active in a host of charitable causes, saw a double benefit in the purchase. "I knew Infant Welfare [Society] was looking for a showcase house and Paul and Tanya were also searching for a home," Mrs. Harvey reflected. "So I bought the house and turned it over to Infant Welfare for use as their 1977 Showcase House and after the show, Paul and Tanya [lived there]."[19] Unfortunately, Tanya and Paul's fourteen-year marriage ended in a contentious divorce in 1990. Chicago's tabloids seized on the sad news. The gossip columnists eagerly followed the lengthy and bitter four-year-long court battle.[20] In the end, Paul Jr.'s ex-wife didn't receive what her lawyers had been pushing for. When it was pointed out that her legal fees had far surpassed the settlement, she showed a sense of humor. "How will [the attorneys] be paid?" she asked. "That is the rest of the story."[21]

Already very private and reluctant public personalities, the trauma of the incident, observers say, drew the Harvey family further inward. They would become less and less likely to accept interview requests and were certainly more cognizant of the potential for being taken advantage of by seemingly innocent personalities. Stricken by the pain of it all, Aurandt carried on and would indeed find love again in a lovely woman named Dina Kinnan. To this day they remain happily married.

Prior to assuming his role with *Paul Harvey News* in the mid 1970s, Junior received a bachelor's and master's degree in piano performance from Chicago's Musical College of Roosevelt University.[22] A twelve-year performance career included numerous appearances at concert halls throughout the world. Aurandt is also a playwright. His original one-man play, "Burton," dramatizing the life and times of actor Richard Burton, is still being performed. Eventually an employee of ABC, he created, produced, and starred in *Holiday in Orange and Black* in 1994 and *Incident at Lexington Green* in 1995 and wrote, produced, and hosted two year-end news specials entitled *American Family Album*, the first airing in 1993.[23]

But over time, Paul Jr. would begin to move further and further away from performance and the stage. Assuming a more prominent role as a writer inside the Harvey office, Aurandt seemed almost relieved at the change of pace. "There is an edge that one has to maintain to weather the verticality and horizontality of playing the piano at that level," he commented in 2006. "It gets pleasant after a while not having to get that edge rehoned."[24]

He eventually took over *The Rest of the Story* feature, much to his father's delight. At the time of Paul Harvey's death in February of 2009, the *Rest of the Story* feature had been airing for 33 years on over 1,100 domestic stations and in 177 countries across the American Forces Radio Network. It has even been heard in outer space on the International Space Station.[25] Not bad for a feature that initially appeared likely to be cancelled.

Those who work closely with Paul Jr. admit that he's almost obsessive about the editing process. The musician in him demands precision, lyrical tone, and cadence to each script. But he's a stickler for accuracy and is patient when it comes to making sure the facts are right. "Many stories come in a rush and come superbly corroborated," he would reflect, "there are no questions and are so powerfully suggested that out they come—but there are other stories that take a year, two, three, five, ten, waiting for something to develop [until they] are eventually written."[26] Paul Sr. was always proud of his son's fastidiousness and demand for journalistic accuracy. "He has to have two independent sources for anything that he uses, and in controversial subjects, at least three," he once bragged.[27]

Inducted into the Radio Hall of Fame in his own right in 2001, the highly decorated Harvey Junior was awarded the Edward R. Murrow Award in 2004 for a *Rest of the Story* feature, entitled "Bar Mitzvah in the Dark."[28] Ironically, there was "a rest of the story" addendum to the piece itself.

"I was doing a story of a boy in the Nazi concentration camp Bergen-Belsen whose name was Joachim," Paul remembered. "He was approaching 13, and he goes to a rabbi named Dasberg . . . and he said, 'I want to be bar mitzvahed.' So in the middle of one night, in secret, in the dark, they performed a bar mitzvah. After the ceremony, Rabbi Dasberg gave Joachim his Torah scroll and said, 'I'm not going to survive this, I'll die here, but you are going to go on. Take this Torah scroll, and I want you to remind people who see it of what happened here.'

"Joachim grows up to become a physicist and grows up to work on one of the space shuttle projects, and so to remind the world of what happened in the dark at Bergen-Belsen during the second World War, he gave [an astronaut] the Torah scroll. I thought it was a real 'feel good' conclusion to the whole thing."[29] The date was January 31, 2003.

Setting aside the commentary for the night, Aurandt would awake the next day to a great and sad shock. "That Saturday morning [February 1, 2003] I woke up, and Space Shuttle Columbia went down, and aboard the space shuttle Columbia was an Israeli Air Force colonel named Ilan Ramone," he said. "It was he who had Rabbi Dasberg's scroll with him.

"It became this incredibly poignant story, which I finished immediately afterwards, still not able to get the full emotional lead on it, and we broadcast it on Monday."[30]

With the news of the disaster still so fresh, Paul Sr. was awash in tears. "He couldn't get through it," Paul Jr. said. "I could guess he started it eight, nine times, maybe more, and could not get past the ending of it without breaking up. Finally we said, 'Let's try to do the end alone,' and he barely got through it."[31]

Paul Jr. is fiercely protective of the feature and has always resisted the idea of the ABC Radio Network streaming the content online. "My feeling is that the more special the encounter, the more it will be prized by the person who encounters it."[32]

Prior to his father's passing, there was always a natural assumption that the son was eventually going to take over and carry on with news reporting responsibilities. On the record he says, "I'm suspicious enough to be a good reporter, to be a good newsperson, but I'm just too iconclastic to be so-called 'fair and balanced.' Only a contrarian could write 'The Rest of the Story.' I think I'm doing the right thing and in the right field."[33]

Off the record, network executives would say that ABC would have warmly welcomed seeing the franchise transfer from father to son— but it won't happen for the simple reason that Paul Jr. doesn't like to get up early or live under the pressures that a hard news program demands. What will become of the famed *Rest of the Story* feature now that its legendary voice is gone still remains to be seen. In the later years, with the health challenges of his parents mounting, Aurandt began voicing more and more of the features himself. Affiliate response was positive. But only time will tell if—or where—the popular program will air in the days to come.

CHAPTER EIGHTEEN

Give Me Some of That Old Time Religion

*P*aul Harvey Aurandt was likely the most overlooked and under-studied Christian evangelist on earth. His sermons, offered in the form of entertaining vignettes, poignant commentaries, and a million subtle asides, were often as powerful, insightful, and effective as the words spoken from the pulpits of America's most acclaimed preachers. His faith was the foundation of his life.

Anyone who brought it up to him received the same response, typical of a man of his generation. Scoffing at the suggestion that he had pastoral aspirations, he would say in a dismissive tone, the pulpit "is a responsibility infinitely higher than any to which I would aspire!"[1] Yet, formal distinctions notwithstanding, Harvey's on-air evangelistic fervor was unmistakable and undeniable.

During his last appearance on CNN's *Larry King Live* in 2003, a caller asked Harvey about a "religious" television program he supposedly hosted in the 1960s. They actually were misremembering his daily three-minute television commentary. "Oh, bless your heart," Harvey responded in his typical folksy manner. "You're the first person who ever considered it a *religious* program."[2] Turning to King,

Harvey noted that in those newscasts, he was only attempting "to separate rightness and wrongness"—not to proselytize and convert. Many in Harvey's audience heard Judeo-Christian themes in his broadcasts. At times the themes were subtle, like when he would refer to the "basic ten" rules of life, rather than quoting chapter and verse from Exodus of the Old Testament.[3] There were other times when he was more explicit. Each year right before Easter, Harvey would offer the "shortest sermon you'll hear all year": "Jesus lived a good life in a wicked world to show us it could be done. And he died. And he rose again. To show us . . . we could do that too."[4]

To be sure, Paul Harvey liked to talk and write about God. His faith not only shaped and framed his thoughts, but it also defined his view of the world and everything in it, both past, present, and future. "I am no preacher," he said, "but I am a student of history and therein our professions overlap. This is history. Jesus was born in Bethlehem less than two thousand years ago. Anybody could have known he would be . . . through the prophets of Israel, God spelled it out. Where He'd be born, how He would live, and when He would die—on a cross against a Galilean sky."[5]

He believed in the authority and authenticity of the scriptures. "There is but one lamp by which my feet are guided and that is the map of experience," he said. "This history book is the experience of the world. This is the Master Plan."[6]

"Men may ignore this history book or reject it," he reflected thoughtfully. "Scorn it, burn it, crown it with thorns, nail it to a stick. But when they have done their worst it will still be there. Judging them, shaming them, haunting them, calling out to them—Believe."[7]

Paul Harvey's demanding broadcast and speaking schedule always kept his circle of good friends small, but during the 1960s and 1970s, the Harveys enjoyed some delightful vacations with Dr. Billy Graham and his wife, Ruth. In his 1997 autobiography, *Just as I Am*, Graham referred to Harvey as his "best friend in the American media."[8] And he had many. "He has always been very supportive of us and often keeps his many listeners informed about our work," Dr. Graham continued. "We have been guests in his home many times, with his delightful wife, Angel."[9]

Celebrities are always in danger of losing perspective when they reach a certain level in their career—it's the point that they begin to believe the hype from their own press clippings. For the Harveys, the Grahams were a source of accountability and reason during their meteoric ascent in those early days of national radio. Both Billy and Ruth helped keep the rising stars grounded in reality. But the relationship went both ways. "I used to worry about Billy," Paul reflected. "When he started out, there was all that adulation. I was worried he might be tilted off balance by it. But then I met Ruth. Then I relaxed, knowing he had that strength on which to lean."[10]

Most of the time, they were just a fun-loving, down-to-earth pair of couples who enjoyed traveling, visiting, playing, and eating together. When Lynne and Ruth would shop, Paul and Billy would golf—and regale friends with stories of their exploits on the links. They made quite the pair, these two tall and dashing high profile men. Though they loved to play the game, both often joked about how bad they were at it. Paul used to quip that "golf [was] a game in which you yell 'fore,' shoot six and write down five."[11] Graham used to explain away his poor play by saying, "I never pray on a golf course. Actually, the Lord answers my prayers everywhere except on the course."[12]

During one particular vacation to the historic Greenbrier Resort in White Sulphur Springs, West Virginia, the two men encountered a swarm of bugs while out on the course. "They were everywhere," Paul said, "and no matter how you batted at them with your hand, they'd still be there when you started to putt."[13] Undeterred, the men played on. Paul described the scene. "The only thing that worked was to take the steel shaft of the club and arc it backward and forward at chest level. I don't know whether the reflected sunlight caused the insects some concern and made them disappear or not, but it sure worked the trick."[14]

Concerned about the appearance of such an alarming spectacle at the swanky resort, Harvey remembered confiding his embarrassment. "I remarked to Billy that the other folks on the course must have us classed as some sort of nuts, standing there flashing the golf clubs back and forth across our chests."[15] In his classic dry drawl, Graham responded. "Oh no, they won't think that at all. They'll just say that those folks are down there with Billy Graham and he's already got them doing some sort of fanatical religious exercise."[16]

The Tulsan once remarked that the benefit of a clean vocabulary was that its owner would never have to worry about cursing in front of an open microphone. During a golf outing with Graham, Harvey remembered watching the great evangelist tee off, but only hit a dribbler fifty feet. "All the caddies waited to hear what kind of expletive he was going to utter," Paul said. "He turned and faced them and quoted the bible: 'That which the Lord hath decreed hath come to pass.'"[17]

In his religious observances, Harvey was not overly concerned about the doctrinal differences within particular Christian denominations. Though a descendent of five generations of Baptist ministers, his earliest years were spent in First Presbyterian in Tulsa prior to his father's death. He later worshipped right near his house at the Church of God on Fifth and Madison in downtown Tulsa. For the rest of his life, he and Lynne would swing back and forth between varying congregations, depending upon where he was living on any particular Sunday. According to a 1979 Associated Press article, the popular commentator was named the 20,001st member of First Baptist Dallas during Dr. W. A. Criswell's tenure as pastor, though such a designation appeared to be mostly ceremonial.[18] While in Chicago, the Harveys attended the majestic Fourth Presbyterian Church on Michigan Avenue, even renewing their vows there on the occasion of their fiftieth wedding anniversary in 1990.[19] For a time, Paul even taught Sunday school. During the winter months, they worshipped at the Camelback Seventh-Day Adventist church in Phoenix. His pastor in Arizona, the Reverend Charles White, remembers how Paul, wearing a cowboy hat and boots, and Evelyn would quietly slip into the service at the last moment in an effort to not disrupt the service with their high-profile presence. Reverend White was also impressed that Paul took several of his sermons to heart. "I remember a sermon illustration I gave in 2004," White said. "I heard him use it on his show the next Monday."[20] Though not a baptized member of the Adventist Church, Harvey enjoyed a warm friendship with famed church author George Vandeman, author of the book, *Planet in Rebellion*.[21] The two men met in 1961 at the Campion Adventist Academy in Loveland, Colorado during a speaking engagement. Vandeman's book, Harvey said, "impacted my life so constructively."[22] Mr. Vandeman's daughter, Connie Vandeman Jeffery, recently reviewed her late father's file of correspondence between the two men and found it eclectic and colorful. In one exchange alluding to the Seventh Day Adventist focus on diet and health, Harvey encouraged Vandeman to cut out citrus and replace it with alfalfa—a remedy, Harvey noted, known to help cut down on joint pain. As was the case with much of Harvey's written correspondence through the years, most of letters to Vandeman were upbeat, brief, and to the point. Upon hearing the news of his dear friend's passing in 2000, Paul Harvey made the following comment: "George Vandeman has completed his earthly ministry in his 84th year. When the roll is called up yonder, and you and I hear that gently persuasive voice again . . . we'll know we made it to the right place."[23]

His theology was conservative, but for Harvey, the fellowship of the congregation and the quality of preaching were paramount. His popularity caused many denominations to claim his affiliation, but ultimately, Harvey was a man who felt at home in most any Christian church.

He was never quiet about his moral compass. As he traveled the country for his various speaking engagements, the ABC commentator would often frame America's ills as a mostly spiritual problem. "Not everybody wants to call sin 'sin'! Some call it mischief. Some call it rebellion. And hardly anybody can agree where we should draw the line . . . .Our courts are right now trying in vain to define pornography, yet moral law is very specific to any reader of God's Word."[24]

It was strikingly and vividly clear from Harvey's broadcasts and speeches that he believed America's survival was dependent upon its dependence upon God: "[W]hen they were obedient to the laws of God, Americans led this world . . . .Fear God again! I don't believe Almighty God is going to preserve this 'promised land' anymore than he preserved the previous ones, if its people are determined to destroy it. Nations are used of God as long as they serve his purpose."[25]

Through the years, the appeal of Christ to Harvey never abated. In 1960, he penned a commentary entitled "If I Were the Devil," that continues to be widely circulated. The piece was likely inspired by C. S. Lewis's famous work, *The Screwtape Letters*.[26] In the fictional classic, a senior demon by the name of Screwtape writes a series of letter to his nephew, Wormwood, advising him on how to help "the patient" (mankind) secure eternal damnation. "Do you know what I would do if I were the Devil?" Harvey asks rhetorically in his early recordings and speeches.

I would begin with a campaign of whispers... to the young I would whisper, "The Bible is a myth." I would convince them that man created God instead of it being the other way around. I'd whisper that what is bad is good and that what is good is kinda square. In the ears of the young married I would whisper that work is debasive. I'd caution them never to be extreme. Oh my goodness, don't be extreme in religion, patriotism or moral conduct. And the old, I would teach to pray. I would teach them to say after me, "Our father which art in Washington."[27]

And unlike many works erroneously attributed to the commentator, the passionate and poignant essay is legitimate.[28]

By the beginning of 1971, Paul Harvey held the world in the palm of his hand. His radio programs were continuing to add affiliates, ratings were edging further upward, television outlets numbered 126, the syndicated column was in over 250 newspapers, and he was being compensated for his three to four speeches a week at a rate of $5,000 per event.[29]

"Seemingly, I had achieved everything for which a man could ask," Paul reflected. "Everything, that is, except for a quiet heart. Something was missing. There was a vague emptiness in my life."[30]

In March of that same year, the Harveys were vacationing near Cave Creek, Arizona. It was Sunday morning. As the sun burned through the haze, they headed up a quiet mountain road to attend church services on an isolated hilltop. The building was old and primitive. Wooden folding chairs filled the sanctuary. It was a small congregation of approximately twelve people. It was hard not to stick out, but the couple slipped into their seats in the tenth row and the service commenced without any fanfare.

"I don't often talk about baptism," the minister said from the pulpit, "but today I'm going to talk about baptism."[31] According to Paul's
recollection, the preacher then explained how utterly alone man is
without a savior and how the only way to have any real purpose in
life is to surrender life to Him. "This baptism," the pastor suggested,
"through the symbolic burial of your old self and the resurrection of
a new one, is your public testimony to your commitment." The minister stressed there was no magic in the water. "One's immersion is
simply an act of obedience," he said, "a sign of total submission to
God."[32]

"But," Paul thought, "hadn't I done this?"[33] As it was, Paul had
remembered being moved by a preacher back in Tulsa who taught him
the words of the gospel writer, John. "For God so loved the world that
He gave His only begotten Son, that whosoever believeth in Him
should not perish, but have everlasting life."[34]

"I never made it to the altar in my church," he recalled, "but I liked
that promise of 'everlasting life.' So one night, alone in my room [back
in Tulsa], kneeling on my bed, I offered my life to Christ."[35] Reflecting on the experience years later, Harvey would say, "So I put that in
my pocket and went on about my own willful ways."[36] But something
was happening to him inside that little church on a Sunday morning
in March.

When the minister concluded and asked if anyone wanted to be
baptized, Paul immediately said yes. "I found myself on my feet, down
the aisle, by his side," he stated.[37] The little church didn't have a bap-
tismal font, so the pastor there helped Paul make arrangements for
the actual ceremony at another Arizona house of worship.

It was a transformational moment for the ABC broadcaster. At the
time of the experience he said, "I knew something life-changing had
happened. A cleansing inside out. No longer did there seem to be two

uncertain contradictory Paul Harveys—just one immensely happy one."[38] Reflecting on the difference, he said, "I've shaken off a lifelong habit of fretting over small things. A thousand little worries and apprehensions have simply evaporated."[39] When Harvey later reflected on his decision to recommit his life to Jesus Christ, he always spoke with warmth and relief, "Boy," he began, "that's where the fun begins, when you stop tearing yourself in half."[40] The Paul Harvey broadcasts continued to be peppered with spiritual themes and stories. In fact, two commentaries in particular were so popular that he continued to rebroadcast them on an annual basis. Each Easter, he would tell the story about a Boston preacher named Dr. S. D. Gordon, coming upon a bunch of boys in an alley playing cruelly with some tiny birds. As the story goes, the lads had trapped and shoved the creatures into a rusted beat-up old cage and were eventually planning to feed them to their cats. "How much do you want for them?" the preacher asked. The boys resisted, suggesting they had no value. At Gordon's urging they finally relented and sold them for two dollars. "In a sheltered crevice between buildings," Harvey recounted, "Dr. Gordon opened the door of the cage and tapping on the rusty exterior, he encouraged the little birds, one at a time, to find their way out through the narrow door and fly away."[41]

Harvey would deliver the kicker by suggesting there had been a similar negotiation between Jesus and the devil. "Satan had boasted how he'd baited a trap in Eden's garden and caught himself a world full of people," Harvey iterated. "The devil said, 'I'm going to play with 'em, tease 'em. Make them marry and divorce and fight and kill . . .'" With dramatic effect, Harvey would pause and then conclude, "Jesus said, 'How much do you want for them?'" To which Satan responded, "'All of your tears and all of your blood. That's the price.'" Another long on-air pause would follow. Finally, Harvey would sigh and say, "So, Jesus took the cage and paid the price—and opened the door."[42]

"The Man and the Birds" was another popular story, told each Christmas, about an agnostic man who tried to cajole some of his birds out of a snow storm on Christmas Eve and into the warmth of his barn. Try as he might, the man, standing in the swirling precipitation, just couldn't convince the birds to follow him into the warm shelter. He thought to himself, "If only I could be a bird and mingle with them and speak their language. Then I could tell them not to be afraid. Then I could show them the way to the safe warm barn. But I would have to be one of them so they could see, and hear and understand." Suddenly, the man heard the bells of a distant church ringing and he realized that his frustration was exactly why God sent His son to earth.[43]

Most of Harvey's commentaries were original compositions. A few, like "The Man and the Birds," were not. "I can't claim credit for it," he said. "The religion editor of the United Press and I tried for many years, while he lived, to search out and find the author of those words. But I think, maybe some things are written without attribution purposefully. Maybe we're not supposed to attribute those words to anybody in particular. But isn't it a very, very moving story? It moves me even yet."[44]

It would be inevitable that controversy wouldn't entirely elude such a regularly high profile professor of faith. Shortly after his recommitment in Cave Creek, Harvey remarked that he had "discovered a new unselfconsciousness in talking about my beliefs."[45] As the times changed and the religious plurality of America broadened, he would need just such a sense of conviction.

On December 4, 2003, at a time when violence in Iraq was escalating, Harvey took to the airwaves and reported with disgust the prevalence of cock-fighting in the Middle East region. "Add to the thirst for blood a religion which encourages killing, and it is entirely understandable if Americans came to this bloody party unprepared."[46]

Within hours, the Council on American-Islamic Relations accused Harvey of defaming Islam and demanded an apology.[47] A boycott of the network's advertisers commenced. A few days later, the Harvey team decided it wasn't worth the fight. Though they were careful not to explicitly apologize, they simply quoted the objection. Substitute host Doug Limerick put the issue to rest when he said: "Last week [Harvey] told you about bloody cockfights in Iraq and mentioned the relationship between Islam and violence. He says he received several letters from dear friends in the American Muslim community who expressed their disgust with those who have hijacked their religion to achieve their goal through violence. They reminded all of us that Islam is a religion of peace, that terrorists do not represent Islam."[48]

CHAPTER NINETEEN

Speechless

$\mathcal{I}$n November of 2000, on the verge of celebrating their fiftieth year with the network, the Harveys signed an unprecedented, ten-year, $100 million contract.[1] Offers from three other networks were tempting, but the couple decided to stay with ABC out of both loyalty and stubbornness. "It was not dollars" that kept them, Paul reflected. "It was the fact that I'm a reactionary and resist change. ABC has made me so comfortable in my little digs here on Michigan Avenue. Some of the other offers sought to move us elsewhere."[2]

Sources suggest that one suitor, the Premiere Radio Network, had offered the Harveys a deal amounting to 100 percent of all advertising revenue. In other words, for the mere privilege of having the Paul Harvey franchise headline their syndication offerings, Premiere was prepared to make no profit from the show itself. The ABC deal amounted to approximately a 70/30 split of revenue—with the Harveys claiming the lion's share of the income.

Asked about the prospect of changing homes after so many years, Angel Harvey, Paul's producer and manager of all his affairs, responded in breezy fashion. "It was fun," she said. "These other radio companies were coming to us and offering us so much. One man asked what kind of jet plane Paul liked, and said, 'How would he like a Gulfstream?'"[3]

Mrs. Harvey was clearly flattered by the attention and was especially taken aback when a competitor, upon rejection, wrote to say, "We'll reopen talks in 10 years. I'll get you yet."[4] Speaking with Rick Kogan of the *Chicago Tribune* she said, "That shows a wonderful faith in our constitution."[5]

Even industry executives were stunned by both the financial scope of the package and the overall duration of the deal. When asked why a company would agree to sign an 82-year-old to a ten-year contract, Harvey quipped, "I told them I was 55."[6] But the precise and detail-oriented radio man didn't leave anything to chance. "I wanted to be very fair with both my family and ABC," he said. "I went to Mayo [Clinic], and boy oh boy, did they put me through the mill—from the hair on the head to the balls of my feet. Then I asked my physician if I can sign for 10 more years. He told me: 'I'll qualify you for astronaut training if you want.' I'm just so grateful that the Lord's seen fit to keep me fit."[7]

But just over six months later, Harvey, though otherwise feeling fine and energetic, had literally no voice.

What was it like for the Radio Hall of Fame legend to be without the golden pipes? "How can I find the words to answer that question?" he told his friend Larry King. "Since I was 14, that voice has been my vocation, my avocation. It's been my life."[8] At first, the raspy voice was just an annoyance. It was late April of 2001 and Harvey hadn't given the prospect of the strained vocal chords much thought. "When the car's running, you don't look inside the carburetor," he would often say. "Just keep rolling."[9] Besides, after so many years of talking on the air, he had grown accustomed to the ebbs and flows of illness. Fastidious with his diet and exercise, and generally considered to be a "health nut," Harvey took great precaution to avoid illness. Though not a "germaphobe" on the caliber of the late Howard Hughes, Harvey would often discourage the practice of handshaking during his radio reports. Revealing his eccentric side, during the winter months he urged Americans to dispense with the hand-to-hand greeting tradition and suggested they "salute" one another instead. He even came up with a name for it for one Christmas: "The Harvey Holiday Salute."[10]

But by the end of his noontime broadcast on Tuesday, May 8, 2001, it was clear he would need to take some time off to heal.[11] The tea and the hot towels and vitamins just weren't working. The voice was nearly gone, cracking and fading to the very end of his newscast. Listeners half expected Harvey to turn over duties midway through, but he plowed on and somehow managed to finish the program. Assuring his staff that he'd only need a few days to whip the bug, he departed his Chicago office for home in River Forest. Little did he know at the time that he'd be off the air for the next three plus months.

With May turning into June, the voice only marginally improved, and Harvey still off the air, affiliates began to grow anxious, peppering the ABC Network with questions.[12] High profile substitutes like Sam Donaldson and David Hartman helped soften the blow, but they weren't the great Harvey. Was the network hiding something? Would Paul Harvey ever return? In an attempt to dispel the rumors and quell anxiety, Harvey released a printed statement. "I know it must seem that I have neglected my 'professional family' in recent weeks," he wrote.

The fact is that I've imagined that every "next week" I
would be back on your frequency broadcasting as usual,
but this bug is tenacious! The bad news is that it is not yet
the broadcast quality which ABC affiliates deserve. Also,
I'm told that to stress the voice prematurely could prolong
the hoarseness. I am indeed sorry this uncertainty has
dragged on so long, but the worst is past. The healing has
begun. God willing, it won't be long now.[13]

Splitting his time between Chicago and Phoenix, he continued to por-
tray an optimistic spirit, but inside, he was struggling emotionally. He
later confided in his friend, columnist Bob Greene, that he had felt
fear and profound despondency during his time on the disabled list.[14]
Beginning to face the prospect of his career being over, Harvey was
lost in a reserved state of grief.

"I spent a great deal of time feeling sorry for myself," he would
remember, "and then I settled down at the insistence of my wife and
son to start making some notes for a book that I had postponed writing. First, I read 25 and a half books—25 and a third books. That
third book, by the way, was on broadcasting. I couldn't finish that
book because it was so full of all those words that I consider inappropriate and offensive. So I spent my time as fruitfully as I possibly could."[15]

Finally, by the middle of July, there was a breakthrough. Harvey
was introduced to Dr. Robert W. Bastian, an internationally recognized
Otolaryngologist (ear, nose, and throat physician) popular with per-
formers at Chicago's Civic Opera House. After an examination, Bastian realized that a virus had settled in a muscle adjacent to Harvey's
vocal chord, severely weakening and rendering it useless. A procedure
was scheduled for the middle of July. Operating out of his Chicago

facility, the physician performed what's known as a "Medialization larngoplasty"—a surgical procedure that pushes a paralyzed, atrophied, or scarred vocal fold toward the other vocal fold to reduce flaccidity.[16] A tiny shim was inserted to support the weak vocal chord until it would be strong enough on its own.

The surgery was a 45-minute out patient procedure. Instantly, the voice returned, though still scratchy and hoarse. "I spent a lot of time on my knees that night," he recalled.[17] To the delight of everyone, Harvey returned to the airwaves on Monday morning, August 20, 2001.[18] As he neared the end of the program, the commentator became almost giddy and began to sing. "It's been a long winter without you," the serenade began. "It's been a long, long winter without you!"[19] He reported that he was so excited to be back behind the microphone that he was considering the possibility of singing the news from then on. "And you wouldn't want that," he said with a hearty laugh.[20] For several weeks, he limited his broadcasts to mornings before assuming full responsibilities in early September.

Dr. Bastian, officially designated one of America's top doctors, and known for his compassionate and dignified professionalism, took an instant liking to his celebrity patient. Agreeing to comment only because Mr. Harvey himself had revealed on-air their doctor-patient affiliation, Bastian said the broadcaster was "fabulous" to work with and a "true gentleman" throughout all the visits.[21] Shortly after the procedure, Harvey invited Bastian to his studio to watch the program and then have lunch. His voice seemed miraculously restored, but for Robert Bastian, it was just another day at the office.

Americans would be grateful to have Harvey's reassuring voice and perspective in the days following the terrorist attacks of September 11, 2001. "Bin Laden's press agents had told him that he had two billion loyal disciples all over the world. They had him convinced that if he could just knock the top off New York City, two billion people would rise up all over the world and on 40 different fronts overthrow us overnight. Not one did."[22]

With the voice restored and America at war, Harvey was energized. Chicago's mayor Richard Daley declared Friday, October 4, 2002, "Paul Harvey Day" throughout the windy city.[23] It was his second great honor by the city; they named a street after him in 1988.[24] Paul Harvey Drive was a one-block stretch of road located between Michigan and Wabash Avenues. Upon being handed the sign, Harvey said, "It is quite an honor for a country boy who started out in the business at the age of 14. It is the ultimate honor. I don't know what I could do for an encore." He would find a way.[25] Accepting the 2002 honor at the Union League Club during a special luncheon, the commentator spoke on a familiar topic. His speech was entitled "The Testing Time"—the title of his best-selling 1960 album that detailed the perilous state of a nation that refuses to embrace the principles of its founding fathers.[26] He was acknowledged with a standing ovation.

It was a glorious late fall day and the towering elm, maple, and oak trees ringing the perimeter of the Executive Mansion were in full splendor. Landscapers in brown uniforms scurried about, blowing and raking leaves and cultivating the color-filled gardens. Winter was approaching, but the golden hues of autumn gave only a hint of the coming change.

Paul Harvey was beaming. He was seated just inside and to the left of the double doors off the front driveway, up on a podium under the hot klieg lights inside the East Room of the White House. Dressed in a dark navy blue suit and a patterned silver tie with a white handkerchief tucked in the front coat pocket, the 87-year-old commentator was edging forward on his seat. To his immediate right was an old friend from afar, television legend Andy Griffith. To his left was the aging Mississippi congressman and famed veteran rights advocate, the Democrat Sonny Montgomery. The three men, along with another eleven of their fellow citizens, were about to be awarded the Presidential Medal of Freedom.[27] Considered to be America's highest civil award, the medals are presented for meritorious achievement in public service, in science, the arts, education, business, athletics, and other fields of endeavor.

Speaking to his radio audience just a few days earlier, Harvey reflected on the momentous nature of the award. Audibly moved and humbled by the coming event, he remarked, "This is the highest honor I have received since 60-some years ago, when Angel said 'I do.'"[28] His voice nearly broke with emotion.

Surrounded by his fellow inductees, each and every one now qualified as the top in their line of work, Harvey again leaned forward and looked up and down the single row of chairs. Among those waiting for the presentation of their medals and the reading of their respective proclamations was Federal Reserve Chairman Alan Greenspan. There was a great deal of warmth and respect between the two men. When asked his opinion of the famed economist, Harvey would say, "I would anoint him a saint if I could."[29]

Joining him on the dais was comedienne Carol Burnett, singer Aretha Franklin, golfer Jack Nicklaus, and the legendary boxer Muhammad Ali. *"How far a man of America can travel, if he keeps the faith and works hard to the end,"* he must have thought. Soon, it would be his turn in the spotlight and the unlikeliest of stories would now be nearly complete. From almost nothing to really something; that was the story of Paul Harvey's life. And it could only have happened in America.

Only in America could a fatherless son of a widowed mother, a boy with little means, zero influence, and only a high school diploma, grow up to stand beside the president of the United States and be declared the epitome of excellence in his field of professional endeavor. Where else but in America could an over-confident and arguably arrogant newsman get arrested for breaking and entry, and raise the ire of one president but then hug the same office's occupant fifty years later? Only in America could a Medal of Freedom recipient tell one president, in front of millions of listeners, that he was flat out wrong—and yet still be welcomed back to the Oval Office years later with all the fanfare assigned a hero.

In the business of radio, Paul Harvey started at the bottom. He was set up for failure, fired, ridiculed, lampooned, and written off too many times to count. His detractors deemed him a crank, a gadfly, a ruse, a mirage—even an eccentric entertainer. Parading around his studios in the ABC smock, some thought he looked more like Marcus Welby, MD, than he did a serious newsman. And yet here he stood with the titans and leaders of his nation receiving a star-studded salute, and by his own admission, the highest professional honor of his entire life. Only in America.

Paul Harvey had defied the conventional wisdom that pinned him as nothing more than a decent but folksy commentator, and a nice man with an odd voice who was funny at times but certainly not sophisticated or educated in the nuances of world affairs. To those of this opinion, he only appealed to country bumpkins and the corn-fed flyover states. In fact, when Ed McLaughlin, then the general manager for San Francisco's KGO in the late '60s and early '70s (later president of the ABC Network) proposed that ABC expand Harvey's show from its Midwest base to the big markets along the coasts, he was strongly rebuffed by the network bosses in New York. McLaughlin argued that Paul's appeal, assuming he was sufficiently and adequately marketed, would be as strong in America's large cities as it would be in rural

America. Still skeptical, the brass reluctantly agreed. Of course, Ed
was right and the rest was history.[30]

Whenever the Harveys were encouraged to move their broadcasts
out of Chicago and instead base them at ABC headquarters in New
York, they strongly and passionately resisted. The commentator would
often say that he was "too impressionable" and could be too easily
influenced by the media intelligentsia.[31] "New York's influence nationwide is disproportionate," Harvey would argue. "When the hub of the
wheel is that far off center, it's a distortion."[32] The *New York Times*
once charged the commentator with "reverse elite snobbism"—an
accusation that Harvey chose to ignore.[33]

At the White House on the afternoon of November 9, 2005, Harvey was thinking about how quickly the fortunes of a man can rise
or fall.

"Storms are a part of the normal year-in and year-out climate of
life," Harvey would say. "And if there were perpetual sunshine there
would be no victory."[34]

Paul Harvey's place on the stage in the East Room was even more
significant given his penchant for independent and sometimes politically rogue ideas, especially considering his genuinely conservative
bent. Over the years, the commentator had sparred with almost every
administration, including President George W. Bush's. A strong supporter of alternative energy, he had urged President George W. Bush
to vigorously pursue policies that would force the sheiks of the Middle East to practically drink their oil. "If by the dawn's early light
tomorrow the American flag were flying over every minaret in the
Middle East, if all of that were under our command," Harvey said, "oil
as fuel would still be doomed. The tomorrows are eight months preg-
nant. With wind power and assorted alternate energies, who else in

the world is growing enough fuel for most of us and growing enough bread for all of us."[35]

During the Reagan years, Harvey had been openly critical of the president's intervention in Central America, again preferring a hands-off, neo-isolationist approach.[36] When it came around to the subject of abortion, the commentator would frustrate some social conservatives by hinting at a personal objection to the act, but nonetheless assuming a libertarian stance by refusing to call for its abolition. "That is a subject that should be left to a woman, her God and her conscience. The government should stay altogether out of it," he would say repeatedly.[37] When the Equal Rights Amendment was being hotly debated in the 1970s and 1980s, Harvey broke with traditional Republican opposition and not only supported but also advocated for its passage. It was an act that would again raise the ire of many in his loyal base.

"There are places in the world where women are conspicuously and forever second class," Harvey intoned on his program in 1982. "But none of those places is any place you or I would want to live."[38] He went on to warn that "If nothing happens in the next eight weeks you will have voted women are not equal."[39] And then in classic Harvey style, the commentator further explained his rationale for switching sides on the issue: "We forgive criminals, embrace illegal immigrants, kowtow to the gimme-gimmes," he said. "Any hophead can get a free ride through three layers of jurisprudence demanding his 'rights' [but women] . . . don't rate as high as that sleazy night crawler."[40] He was hot and again the letters poured in. But he didn't mind—they were listening and they cared what he said.

Conservative opposition, led by the revered stalwart Phyllis Schlafly, was fierce. Ms. Schlafly and her colleagues argued that the amendment was actually worded in such a manner as to, ironically, *take away* women's rights and enshrine liberal policies in law. Barnstorming the country and testifying before forty-one state panels,

Schlafly's grassroots movement was wildly successful, and the window for state ratification of the amendment finally closed on June 30, 1982.[41] The ERA had failed.

There was a general consensus that Harvey had been heavily lobbied by his wife, Lynne, considered by most to be fiscally conservative but socially liberal. As soon as the matter was settled and it was obvious that Ms. Schafly was the victor, Harvey sent his worthy opponent a one word telegram that simply read: "Touche."[42]

And so one of the last stops on Harvey's improbable journey began as President George W. Bush opened: "This morning across the United States, millions of Americans started their day listening to Paul Harvey," said the president.

> People everywhere feel like they know the man and his wife, Angel, too. And for so many Americans, no morning, Monday through Saturday, is quite complete without "Paul Harvey News and Comment." This tireless broadcaster is up every day before the sun, writing his own scripts and ad copy for an audience tuning in to more than 1,200 radio stations and the American Forces Network. He first went on the air in 1933, and he's been heard nationwide for 54 years. Americans like the sound of his voice . . . over the decades we have come to recognize in that voice some of the finest qualities of our country, patriotism, the good humor, the kindness, and common sense of Americans. It's always a pleasure to listen to Paul Harvey, and it's a real joy this afternoon to honor him as well.[43]

Robust applause filled the room, echoing up and down the hallway of the White House. The smile on Harvey's face was wide and genuine. But for the Harvey family, life was beginning to get hard. "Crumbling

is not an instant's act,"[44] wrote Emily Dickenson, and signs were everywhere that life was about to change irreversibly for the seemingly
indefatigable first couple of radio. Though Paul Jr. was there, beaming with pride, keen observers noted that Paul's ever present companion, Angel, was missing from the White House that afternoon. For
her to miss a moment as significant as this one made it clear that the
92-year-old bride of Paul Harvey was slipping. At the time, the sad
secret was that she was sick—and that life around the Harvey house
would never again be the same.

CHAPTER TWENTY

An Angel Departs

The weather was unseasonably warm, a humid eighty-two degrees, and rays of cascading sunshine pierced the growing shadows in the streets below. A late spring storm was brewing. Rain was coming. The light breezes were beginning to gust as clouds gathered in the southeastern Chicago sky.

It was just past noon on Tuesday, May 6, 2008. Patrons of the renowned Tavern Club, a reserved enclave nestled on the 25th floor of 333 North Michigan Avenue, were taking in a quiet lunch and the magnificent vistas of the windy city's skyline. Many of the regulars were absent from their usual places. Of those who remained, the somber tone amid the tables and between the diners was palpable. They had seen it coming, even prepared for its inevitable arrival—but loss never comes easy and grief is always an unwelcome guest. Her regular chair had been empty for well over a year; hope had been hanging in the balance. But Lynne Harvey's death in the family home at 1035 Park Avenue in River Forest, Illinois in the early morning hours of Saturday, May 3, 2008 still came as a shock.[1] Her passing officially closed a charming chapter in the club's storied history. No longer would the regally attired couple step out of their offices down on the 16th floor, stride into the elevator, and ride together, hand-in-hand, up to lunch after a long morning of work. For once, there would be no happy ending to what had become the long and sad good-bye; no miracle to sing about or cure to tout. Heaven had claimed one of its saints. Paul Harvey had lost his "Angel," and Paul Jr. had lost his beloved mother.

At ninety-five years of age, she had succumbed to the ravages of leukemia, engaging in a year-long fight, always hoping, praying, and planning that she would beat it back enough to resume her regular routine.[2] The battle was valiant, but in the end, God had other plans. When she had exhausted all means of conventional treatment, her husband Paul went on the airwaves across the ABC Radio Network to announce her illness. His heart was heavy, his voice low, the pauses more pronounced. He was obviously burdened, the usual dose of daily optimism significantly diminished. "This is partly personal," he began, "but my Angel has a broken wing."[3] In a dramatic and poignant moment, Paul Harvey ended his newscast with an impassioned plea. He knew there was someone out there in his audience who had been working on an experimental treatment for cancer, leukemia in particular. It wasn't yet approved by the Federal Drug Administration, but it had shown some major promise. Please contact me, he asked, and sure enough they did. It led to a summer of promise with as many good days as bad, but her condition was mostly kept private. Conversations with people who possessed intimate knowledge of the struggle would go something like this: "She is hanging on, doing pretty well. But, well, you know... it's tough." They would change the subject, but the pause before the question was answered always communicated far more than the answer itself. Many now believe the treatment extended and improved Mrs. Harvey's quality of life. Nobody was about to complain. When the alternative is certain death, you're grateful for whatever additional time you can muster. But as good and temporarily effective as the new treatment was, it just wasn't good enough.

Barely three-quarters of a mile from the skyscraper headquarters of Paul Harvey News, mourners were beginning to assemble just north of the corner of Michigan Avenue and East Chestnut Street, home to the city's legendary grand gothic cathedral of Fourth Presbyterian Church. The hour long dreaded by the men of the Harvey home had come. It was time to officially bid farewell to the "First Lady of Radio." It was time to say good-bye to one of the first women to single-handedly run an American radio station—from manning the equipment, to making announcements, delivering the news, and even spinning records. And what a pioneer was this native of St. Louis, Missouri. As ABC Radio's official statement said:

> A director, writer, and editor, she was the creative and administrative heartbeat behind the number-one-rated Paul Harvey News and Comment, which reaches tens of millions of listeners. Her guidance and ingenuity helped shape many radio and television formats widely used today, such as the concept of news features within hard-news broadcasts and the humorous "kicker," which became a Paul Harvey trademark. In the late 1940s, Lynne suggested that her husband's news program be broadcast at 10 p.m. to take better advantage of adults' leisure time and thus gain a larger audience. That time slot soon became the national broadcasting standard for radio and television news programs.
>
> Lynne also developed and edited Harvey's best-known feature "The Rest of the Story."... Lynne created and produced

"Dilemma," a television program that became a prototype for today's talk-show genre, and also a groundbreaking syndicated television news feature that ran five days a week for 20 consecutive years.[4]

But all those days had come down to this sad and somber one. In a city full of sirens and noise, a morose hush descended over the arriving guests entering through the cathedral's narthex as they finally found their places in the dark wooden pews on either side of the family's Chicago church. As the hands struck one o'clock in the afternoon, the body of Evelyn Cooper Harvey was brought into the cavernous sanctuary of the 94-year-old building. Julliard-trained Dr. John W. W. Sherer softly played the prelude, the tune of "Brother James' Air," on the mighty 126-rank Aeolian-Skinner Organ.[5] The opening hymn, "All Creatures of Our God and King," a favorite classic selected long ago by Lynne herself, thundered outward, reverberating off the thick walls, capturing at once the sadness and hope of the moment. "Ye who long pain and sorrow bear," sang the gathered, and "praise God and on Him cast your care."[6] Dapperly dressed in a dark suit, the sadness of Lynne's husband Paul was obvious, his hands reverently clasped, a wistful gaze of loss and longing directed towards the closed casket. He stood and sang. There would be plenty of time—too much so—for tears in the days to come.

It was touchingly appropriate that the Christian funeral service for the woman nicknamed "Angel" unfolded under the witness of fourteen carved stone angels. Created by the famed Chicago muralist Frederick Clay Bartlett, the kneeling, seven-foot angels of Fourth Presbyterian Church ringed the perimeter of the sanctuary just below the rafters.[7]

The service of burial continued as Dr. John M. Buchanan, the senior pastor since 1985, first read the scriptures from the Old Testament.

"I lift up my eyes to the hills—where does my help come from? My help comes from the Lord, the Maker of heaven and earth . . . .The Lord watches over you—the Lord is your shade at your right hand [Psalm 121]." "God is our refuge and strength, an ever present help in trouble. There we will not fear, though the earth gives way and the mountains fall into the heart of the sea . . . [Psalm 46]." And finally, in unison, the assembled read aloud the ever familiar 23rd Psalm: "The Lord is my Shepherd, I shall not want . . . .Even though I walk through the valley of the shadow of death, I will fear no evil, for you are with me; your rod and your staff they comfort me."

Tenor Cole Seaton offered two solos, first the immortal and sweeping hymn "In the Sweet By and By,"[8] and then to close the service, "I'll See You Again."[9] Thomas O. Chisholm's famous composition, "Great is Thy Faithfulness," first penned in 1923 when Lynne was just seven years old, was also sung in soaring unison.[10] It was evident the pieces were painstakingly chosen and thoughtfully placed throughout the service.

If a memorial has its highpoint, Mrs. Harvey's would surely have come when her son, 60-year-old Paul, once nicknamed "Hoppy" (likely after his favorite character of the day, "Hopalong Cassidy"), would ascend the stairs of the sanctuary and offer his personal reflections on her life and legacy. "This is the story," he began in the distinctive and recognizable cadence and style of both father and son, "of a sandwich in a roll top desk."[11] Such an introduction would have been peculiar elsewhere and from others, but not Paul—the writer and creator of the popular award-winning, *The Rest of the Story* radio feature. Today he would go on to tell the tale of a woman—Lynne, of course; this young girl lost her own mother at a very young age, was raised by sisters and forever influenced by a beautiful cacophony of loving siblings. At first, though, she was afraid of being sent packing to a family of strangers; she was the youngest and her parents had been much older than most, so she made herself a sandwich and stashed it away in her desk to "fend off her ensuing privation."[12] Snuggled safely in her room, she knew that the desk, containing all the treasures of a young life, would follow her wherever she might wind up. Paul continued, "The family she made of all of us started with the family her sisters and her brother made for her...she'd want you to meet them."[13]

The list was long with an eloquent description of each sibling. Her older sister Helen was "the conscience of the sibling assembly." Bob was remembered as a man who taught a "precocious toddler the most raucous poetry of manly adventure" only to "hide and chuckle to hear the inevitable recitation for company." There was sister Virgie—an admired opera singer who would "submerge that golden voice in sing-alongs at hearth sides." Mabs "led them in laughter." June was noted as a woman of "dignity"—studious, conscientious, and an assistant to the St. Louis Superintendent of Public Schools. Finally, there was Betty. "Betty was my girl, my pal," he would say, "Auntie Mame, though even more ebullient." Musically inclined, she was known for playing the guitar and ragtime piano—along with reciting "silly, naughty poetry."[14]

The list of extended relatives continued, in a colorful cadre of characters. "A bouquet made of people," he concluded, "who for their good humor and their acceptance of everyone and their magnificent magnanimity comprised the greatest people I ever knew. They were the family who embraced my mother, who banished her childhood loneliness and encouraged her progress."[15]

Composed but visibly moved, Paul Sr. looked on, pensive; often appearing lost in thought. But the twinkle was obvious when Paul Jr. continued the memorable walk down through the years and across the corridor of time. "She grew up bright and positive and inspiring. Her young womanhood was high adventure, crossing the country by car with her handsome husband, settling here and then there and elsewhere, learning the craft of then fledging radio."[16] He would remark that his mother's legacy was that of "nurture"—and that she had "nurtured a talented young man into a legend." And indeed she had done so, and when the son was done and the end of the eulogy had come, the sound of the spellbound audience's silence was felt from the front to the back of Fourth Presbyterian Church.

He had spoken for only fourteen minutes. It had been a eulogy of layers; poignant, human, humorous, reflective—and it ended where it all began—back to that sandwich in the roll top desk in his young mother's room long, long ago. "She'd want you to hug your family a little tighter," he said softly, "as we sing this song at twilight. You have followed the bread crumb trail which leads from her presidency of the Infant Welfare Society and backward in time to a sandwich in a roll top desk . . . that house is full again, of laughter and light—because the baby has come home."[17]

The light was fading from the tall stained glass windows as the funeral service drew to a close. Pastor Charles White of the Harveys' winter church in Phoenix—Camelback Seventh-day Adventist—offered his words of comfort and consolation. "Often as Paul Sr. retired early to bed because of his early rising, he would bid Angel goodnight. He would say, 'Goodnight, Angel, sweet dreams.' We would join him in saying that today. Goodnight, Angel, sweet dreams. We will see you in the morning."[18]

Although her work was regularly recognized and publicly praised throughout her life, Evelyn "Angel" Harvey would likely have been humbled by the accolades privately shared among the gathered guests after the service, though she wouldn't have believed them.

Bruce DuMont, affable Chicago radio broadcaster and founder of the Museum of Broadcast Communications, was a longtime family friend who actually hatched the idea of the Radio Hall of Fame in the Harveys' home kitchen. Bruce said, "She was to Paul Harvey what Colonel Parker was to Elvis Presley."[19] Of Lynne's 68-year marriage to Paul, Bruce was equally reflective and sentimental, calling it "probably the greatest love story that I've ever experienced."[20]

Tom Tradup, Salem Radio Network vice president of News and Talk, said, "It will be hard to imagine her not at Paul's side, with his affectionate gaze fixed on her always."[21]

"I used to call her my girlfriend," John McConnell, former vice president of programming for ABC, mused. "She didn't mind. Lynne Harvey was the epitome of class and sophistication. She was just great. She was Paul's guiding light. Her passing has broken his heart—and mine, too."

Al Peterson, former editor of *Radio and Records* said, "Paul Harvey had the gift, but [Lynne] identified it, nurtured it, and helped bring it out of him. Though they did everything together, she was always content to live in his shadow."[22]

Those associated with the Harvey family, personal or professional, felt a sense of loss in the early days of May 2008, especially on this afternoon inside the oldest building along Chicago's Michigan Avenue. Unlike celebrity funerals known for their hyperbole, this service was marked by reserve and dignity. Little was said about how many people her death touched—and would continue to impact in the years yet to come. When a great and tall tree falls, it doesn't just leave an empty place in the sky. The ramifications are real. In this instance, the industry had lost one of its fiercest supporters—and dearest friends.

Tom Langmyer, the vice president and general manager of WGN in Chicago, was also misty-eyed that afternoon. Twenty-five years earlier, as a college student working at WGR in Buffalo, Langmyer visited backstage with Mr. Harvey. The veteran asked the rookie about his goals, and when they parted, put his hand on the young man's shoulder, winked, and said, "Work hard at it and live your dream, Tom."[23] Hurting for his dear friend, Tom reflected, "Angel's passing left an open place in the sky, but it also likely cleared the view to heaven and the connection between them. Her presence remains through her longtime influence on Paul. That part hasn't changed, but one can only imagine the effect of the loss of his life and work partner."[24]

At a small reception that followed the service, those gathered were given an opportunity to one last time confer their condolences on the bereaved. John McConnell approached Paul with a warm smile, and a hand outstretched on the tall, broad shoulder. John remembered a story and said, "I'll never forget San Francisco—and the skydiving adventure. Do you remember how that all came about?"[25]

"Oh my goodness," Paul responded, a broad grin creeping across his face and outshining the tears. And as John began to reminisce, Paul began to shake—with laughter.[26]

In November of 1990, Paul and Lynne Harvey were traveling in northern California and paid a visit to an ABC affiliate, the legendary KGO-AM in San Francisco. While at the station, Paul slipped into a sales meeting. "Did you know, Mr. Harvey," John McConnell told him, then News Director, "that we have a terrific advertiser on the station—a skydiving company—that suspends all their flights at 12 noon just so they can be on the ground to listen to Paul Harvey News?"

"Really? Oh my! That's loyalty! You know something . . . how I've always wanted to fly like a bird! We should do that sometime," he responded excitedly.

"Why don't we go do it right now?" John pressed.

"Now?" Paul said almost incredulously. "But what about Angel? She'd never approve."

A plan was quickly conceived and implemented. Several women at the station invited Angel into the city for a shopping trip to Sax Fifth Avenue and Nordstrom while Paul "tended to some business."

Unbeknownst to Mrs. Harvey, the group of conniving gentlemen slipped out the door and made their way to the KGO traffic helicopter. They were then shuttled over to the skydiving school at the airport near Lodi, California. A quick lesson ensued. It would be a tandem jump with the instructor; Paul wouldn't have to worry about pulling his own cord. He seemed a little disappointed, but accepted it.

As the team piled into the jump plane, McConnell called back to the station and proceeded to offer live, on-air reports of the historic jump. Word quickly spread. Network executives from New York caught wind of the fact that their franchise—their radio personality responsible for over 50 percent of the entire company's income—was about to voluntarily parachute out of an airplane.

"Don't let him do it! Stop him!" came the order from the East Coast. With engines roaring and the wind blowing, McConnell suggested he couldn't make out the message. But even if he could, it wouldn't have mattered. The 72-year-old Harvey had made up his mind.

There was no turning back.

The jump was flawless and the landing picture-perfect. McConnell's on-air reports tipped off the press, and there was an AP photographer waiting to snap pictures of the historic moment. The next day, a smiling Paul Harvey, strapped in his skydiving paraphernalia, would appear in newspapers all across the country. "It was so Paul Harvey," McConnell would say.

"I now know why birds sing," said Paul.

When Angel found out about it all, she leveraged it for a major shopping spree—and then some. "That stunt cost me more money," Harvey told McConnell. "She never let me forget it!"

The incident was classic Harvey. Always adventurous and curious, he once began to keep tabs on how many different hobbies he pursued in his free time—everything from golf and stamp collecting to flying and building model airplanes. He said he lost count at fifty.[27] One of his favorite pastimes centered around a love for automobiles. With a particular passion for fast cars, even into his seventies he attended racing legend Bob Bondurant's competition driving school.[28] In addition to the '38 Nash back in Missouri, residents of River Forest and Phoenix would see him driving a variety of cars through the years—everything from his coveted red Ferrari convertible to a 1908 antique Brush auto.[29]

For the historically resilient and healthy Paul Harvey, it had been a year of unprecedented struggle and strain. "Troubles," to paraphrase Shakespeare, "don't come as single spies, but in battalions!"[30] And indeed, such was the case for the now 90-year-old broadcaster. As he struggled to nurse his ailing Angel, and later mourned her passing, Paul was recovering from a series of personal health setbacks—pneumonia, bronchitis, and cataract surgery. The list of substitutes mounted, and a headline on Radio-Info.com, reprinted in the *Chicago Sun-Times*, raised the once unthinkable question: "Is Paul Harvey's Show Just Quietly Fading Away?"[31]

The pundits proved to be wrong. Though not on any consistent basis, in July of 2008, Paul Harvey returned to the airwaves—but with a chilling though not unexpected caveat. Still reeling from the passing of his beloved wife and recalibrating the production of his show without her steady hand of guidance, Harvey had this to say on his first day back on the air: "I will do my best with what remains, but it will be something less."[32]

CHAPTER TWENTY-ONE

American Original

"This is the story," began the voice of Paul Harvey Jr., "of a boy in a tree."[1] The 61-year-old only son of the legendary late broadcaster had ascended the chancel's steps and was standing quietly in the elevated wooden pulpit of Chicago's Fourth Presbyterian Church. His words came slowly but precisely, echoing off the walls of the cavernous downtown cathedral. The day of the sad and final farewell had come. On a rainy, dark, and cold Saturday afternoon, March 7, 2009, the world of radio and its listeners had gathered to pay their final respects to the American Broadcast Company giant, Paul Harvey Aurandt.

Loud claps and rumbles of thunder rolled up and down the wet and windswept Magnificent Mile of Michigan Avenue. But of the hundreds huddled inside the old stone church, there was an air of levity amid the sadness. Laughter arose from the crowd as the commentator's son recalled his father's attempt to fly a homemade airplane as a young boy back in Tulsa.

"He had his own inventiveness to blame," he recalled, explaining that as teenager, his dad had built the contraption "from spare parts, scrap wood, and bailing wire."[2] Having barely gotten it off the ground, a young Paul Aurandt was nearly above the treetops when he realized that a crash was imminent.

"Funny thing," the son said, "all the young boy could think was *even if I could jump out and save myself, I wouldn't, because life wouldn't be worth living without this airplane.*"[3] The young pilot slammed the plane into the upper limbs of a tree, but somehow managed to survive the accident and walk away. But, the son stressed, there was lasting significance in the event, far beyond the folly of youth. In fact, the long ago afternoon adventure foreshadowed great things to come.

"He was not nearly a boy in a tree," continued the grief-stricken Harvey, "he was a boy who could fly—through his own talent and inclination and inventiveness and determination—all by himself. He would grab hold of the sky and one day, that one voice grabbed hold of a nation—for a generation."[4]

In the years between now and then, the father remembered that infamous incident, but couched his comments in the form of a warning. "Isn't it strange how values change? At sixteen I wanted to go down with my plane—I figured if I couldn't salvage that beautiful bird, what's left? Isn't that terrible? I've tried to tell young Paul to be very careful that youth does not distort his perspectives."[5]

The mourners had initially gathered in a bright two-story room called Anderson Hall, directly off the main sanctuary of the cathedral. Outside, the rain, like tears from heaven, fell steadily against the wall of windows overlooking the church courtyard. In the final hour and a half prior to the 1:00 p.m. service, the body of Paul Harvey lay in an open black casket, heaped with a blanket of red roses and flanked by floral displays of bright and beautiful colors. "To my Dad" read the single ribbon draped across the rose bouquet. The Harvey family, now headed by the lone son, stood to the body's left, receiving the condolences and hugs of those in attendance. So close to the family was internationally renowned pianist Van Cliburn that the 75-year-old joined members of the immediate Harvey family to greet the mourners. Quiet and teary-eyed, Paul Jr. received every guest with a graceful and pleasant exchange, occasionally turning to look back at his father, pause, and slowly shake his head in a suspended state of disbelief.

In a span of just ten months, the announcer/writer had lost both of his parents. There may be little shock when a 61-year-old son is orphaned, but the loss is still devastating. The son mentioned to a visitor that when his mother, Lynne, had died, that was really it for his father, remarking the two were as close to being twins as any married couple could be. In fact, on the day when Paul Sr. first returned to his daily broadcast following Angel's death, the 90-year-old commentator said as much. "The loneliest days of my loneliest winter are still very much with me," he had reflected. "*Paul Harvey News* will never be the same as when we had Angel's 24-hour perspective."[6]

It was a room filled with strangers and old friends. Industry leaders like Farid Suleman, the chairman and chief executive of Citadel Broadcasting, Jim Robinson, president of the ABC Radio Network, Bruce DuMont, founder and president of the Museum of Broadcast Communications, were bunched together in groups of three or four, reminiscing and remembering. Longtime Harvey sidekicks, engineer Bill Karambelas and writer Ron Gorski, were also in attendance, each finding it hard to believe their dear friend of so many years was gone. Several of Harvey's unnamed and undisclosed sources—including an anonymous Vietnam veteran who would call the broadcaster during the war with inside perspectives and off-the-record intelligence—were there, too. Everyone in the room had a story.

Like the time an executive found the usually formal Harvey finishing up a broadcast in the studio inside his Phoenix home—decked out in a bright yellow sweat suit. That particular day they sat for hours and talked about everything from oil and energy to Harvey's long friendship with Billy Graham. There were a dozen stories of the commentator taking the time to attend a wedding of a staff member—or sending flowers to either congratulate or sympathize on various occasions. One mourner remembered Harvey telling him a tale from long ago. During his radio tenure in Honolulu, Harvey had encountered a professional wrestler on Waikiki Beach. "Show me your best move," the young radioman challenged. "You don't want me to do that," his new friend responded. "Oh, come on," Harvey insisted. "I'm a big guy, I'm in good shape. I can hold my own." The next thing Harvey knew, he was flat on his back in the warm sand looking skyward. "I never knew what hit me!" he had laughed.

June Westgaard, the venerable, trustworthy, and efficient assistant of Mr. Harvey, dressed in a black pant suit, greeted and welcomed old and new friends with smiles and a dozen embraces. Originally working for Mrs. Harvey out of the River Forest home office, she was transferred downtown and assumed managerial responsibilities in the 1960s. She was the gatekeeper, the protector, and the woman who kept Harvey's Chicago side of life in balance. "If you want a job done," Paul used to say, "ask a busy woman." Over the years, Paul would reflect she was "all the good things that a capable, conscientious secretary could be."[7] The two enjoyed playful banter. Harvey once joked that as good an assistant as she was, he was equally impressed with her ability to snap an unpeeled banana cleanly in two. In another moment of comedic candor, Harvey pondered the possibility of Westgaard penning a tell-all book of life inside the office. "I can imagine a chapter captioned: 'Harvey Flies Naked,' details of which would reveal only that he takes his jacket and trousers off before climbing into the cockpit so that his suit will appear freshly pressed when he arrives for whatever public appearance."[8] But there she was to the very end, standing steps from the body of her boss and friend, still scanning the crowd, still assisting, greeting, and serving—unto death.

If there was a common theme running through all of the tributes and conversations in the days and weeks following Paul Harvey's death, it might have been centered on just how much of an "original" the commentator had been. Born just four years before the first commercial radio station in Pittsburgh took to the airwaves, Harvey literally grew up with radio—or better yet, radio grew up with Harvey.

One of the best pieces of advice he ever received—and the one nugget that probably shaped his career more than any other—came from his boss at KVOO in Tulsa. Seeing that Harvey was trying to imitate national announcers, the manager told him, "Paul, if all you're going to do is imitate someone, the best you can ever hope to be is second best. Be yourself." It clicked. From that day forward, Harvey began to carve out his own identity and style. He decided in an instant to become an original—and his character grew and took shape.

At a time when most in the media focused their attention almost exclusively on the world's movers and shakers, Harvey remained true to the extraordinary exploits of ordinary people. Why? Because they were the interesting ones; most of the big stories were too predictable. He was always curious, always looking to learn a little more. Only months before he died, in the fall of 2008, he had called his good friend and fellow Hall of Fame broadcaster, Orion Samuelson, to inquire about a new form of sweet corn he had been hearing about on the radio. Orion suggested Paul speak with someone at Twin Garden Farms in Harvard, Illinois. Shortly thereafter, Harvey spent an entire day on the farm learning about the special seeds and just how they produced and manufactured them. He was fascinated by the experience.[9] He was always curious, even to the end.

In his sermon at the funeral, suggesting that the commentator considered all people "sacred," Dr. John Buchanan, the radio legend's Chicago pastor, summed up his appeal to the average American. "He saw the significance of everyday human life."[10] Indeed he did.

But a funny thing happened in this pursuit of carving out his unique role in radio. In time, personalities began to imitate him. Imitation has always been the sincerest form of flattery. But as the explosion of spirited and opinionated talk radio expanded and matured, so did the coarseness of some of its voices. As the Cultural Revolution raged, Harvey's appeal struck some as "square"—and maybe even irrelevant to a new and rising generation. Yet, Harvey kept on doing what he had always done and resisted any suggestions to adjust his style to accommodate detractors or industry malcontents. In fact, he really didn't care much what the critics thought of his style or his politics. He was confident because instinctively, he knew what he believed and knew how to appeal to the senses of the average American listener. He had a backbone. He took a long view of life and believed that everything old would someday be new again.

And just like that, he became an "original" once more.

The English novelist Evelyn Waugh once warned that "the only human relationships I abide are intimacy, formality and servility. What is horrible here and in America is familiarity."[11] To this argument, Harvey would have added his agreement. When Paul would greet his network colleagues, men and women maybe forty years his junior, he would say, "Hello, young American!" or "Greetings, good sir!" In front of guests at the office, he would refer to "Mrs." or "Mr." so and so. And of course, he always spoke of his wife in the most endearing of terms— she was his love, his dove, his beautiful one—would you expect anything less? Even when Angel could only get around with the use of a wheelchair, he would guide her from place to place by asking her,

"May I have this dance?" When others might question how a couple's togetherness could really be so idyllic, he would counter unapologetically, "I see our marriage through a soft pink light."[12]

The perspectives of the men and women of Harvey's generation were not colored or moved by the current swing of the stock market. They had been defined by seeing men die in the last big war. How grateful they have been in their conversations—there was an almost universal appreciation for God and His gifts in their talk and walk. Life's pettiness is reduced to irrelevance. They want to talk about who they love and who loves them. This is why any conversation with Paul Harvey always revolved around his devotion to his Angel and the beloved son by his side.

The music at the funeral mirrored the selections at Angel's. They truly were two peas in a pod. The same grand old hymns rang from the rafters—all six verses of "All Creatures of our God and King," along with a closing rendition of "Great Is Thy Faithfulness." Again, soloist Cole Seaton sang "I'll See You Again," as well as "In the Garden" and the moving and melodic "Beulah Land."[13] It was beautiful and poignant. Very majestic and very traditional; it was very Paul Harvey.

Legendary UCLA basketball coach John Wooden never met Paul Harvey—but Paul Harvey would often reference Wooden as one of the nice guys who finish first in life. Both men in their nineties, Wooden once penned a poem[14] capturing Harvey's perspective on the latter days of life:

On Growing Old
The years have left their imprint
On my hands and on my face,
Erect no longer is my walk
And slower is my pace.

But there is no fear within my heart
Because I'm growing old,
I only wish I had more time
To better serve my Lord.
When I have gone to Him in prayer
He has brought me inner peace,
And soon my cares and worries
And other problems cease.
He has helped me in so many ways
He has never let me down,
Why should I fear the future
When soon I could be near his crown?
Tho I know down here my time is short
There is endless time up There,
And He will forgive and keep me
Ever in His loving care.

"These were hard years, these last few, for my dad," Paul Jr. concluded during his father's funeral service. "Harder than even those who loved him knew."[15] He spoke of watching his dad standing by his mother's hospital bedside and saying, "I wish I were Peter Pan—I would come to your window and take you to Neverland."[16] The son paused and continued, "But you know, they're on their way—second star to the right...and he's a good pilot. He'll get them there."[17]

When Bob Collins, Chicago's popular morning man on WGN radio, died after colliding with a student pilot on a final approach to landing the plane he was piloting, friend Paul Harvey summed up his life in a sentence that inadvertently described his own legacy: "Somebody will take his job," Harvey said, "but nobody will take his place."[18]

Back at the church, Paul Jr. was concluding the eulogy for his father. "I can think of no other time in his career when my dad was needed more." But if Paul Harvey were still with us, said the son, he'd be telling us, "...don't you stop believing...don't you stop clapping for the extraordinary things we've done and do and will do...because all it takes is to believe...."[19]

"In flying they teach us when we can't see where we're going, go on instruments, and trust them," Harvey wrote once in an essay referencing the Bible. "Read your tested and proved charts and instruments. They will see you through."[20]

When George Washington died in 1799, he was eulogized by a former Virginia officer and member of the House of Representatives named Henry Lee, otherwise known as "Light Horse Harry"—father of Confederate military leader Robert E. Lee. Though the tribute is best remembered for its opening line, "First in war—first in peace—and first in the hearts of his countrymen...."[21] Lee's final words about the great Washington might also be said of Paul Harvey Aurandt:

> To his equals he was condescending, to his inferiors kind, and to the dear object of his affection exemplary tender; correct throughout; vice shuddered in his presence, and virtue always felt his fostering hand; the purity of his private character gave effulgence to his public virtues. His last scene comported with the whole tenor of his life—although in extreme pain, not a sigh, not a groan escaped him; and with undisturbed serenity he closed his well-spent life. Such was the man America has lost—such was the man for whom our nation mourns.[22]

The Gentleman

*L*ife is full of surprises. It was just past 2:00 on the afternoon of Tuesday, April 20, 1999, and New York City's Pennsylvania Station was its normal beehive of activity. As I made my way off the Amtrak train and upstairs to the corner of 34th Street and Seventh Avenue, Manhattan's streets were slick from a light spring drizzle. My destination was the headquarters of ABC Radio Today Entertainment on Madison Avenue and a routine meeting about Focus on the Family's syndication contract with the network.

I had just run the Boston Marathon a day earlier. The famous race is always held in conjunction with Patriot's Day in Massachusetts, a holiday commemorating the Battles of Lexington and Concord. It is a grand tradition marked by pomp and pageantry. To have qualified and finished was a sweet memory, and as I neared ABC, a conversation with a much older runner at the start of the race in the quaint town of Hopkinton came to mind.

"Are you ready, son?" the white-haired man asked me.

"I think so," I responded. "I didn't come all this way for nothing."

"Have you ever read Nikos Kazantzakis' book, *Report to Greco*?" he inquired.

I had not.

"There is a line to remember as you run," he said. "In that book, a character asks for instructions for life. First he is told 'to reach for what you can.' But he finds that too easy and boorish. He pushes back for something more difficult. 'Then reach for what you cannot,' he is told."

The older gentleman poked me in the chest and winked. "Go get 'em."

In the midst of my meeting with Geoff Rich, then executive vice-president for radio at ABC, the conversation somehow turned to Paul Harvey. I shared with him my fascination with the legendary broad-caster and a "wild" idea I had about writing a book about his faith. "But I would imagine a more seasoned journalist would be a more likely candidate," I offered.

"If you'd like to spend some time with him," Jeff replied, "I'll see what I can do."

I thought back to the exchange in Boston. The idea seemed clearly beyond my reach, but why not? "That would be wonderful," I responded. "Thank you."

It took a little over a year, but in June of 2000, I arrived in Chicago to meet Paul Harvey.

When you listen to someone your entire life and build up an image in your mind about who they are and what they're like, there is always a little apprehension and fear that you'll be disillusioned when you actually get to meet them. Not this time.

I actually heard Paul's typewriter first.

It was a bit jarring; I suppose my ears had become accustomed to the soft tap of a modern computer keyboard. Instead, the whirl of an electric typewriter filled the mid-morning air. There was a melodic tone to it all—the loud rap, clap, and whistle of metal keys hitting crisp paper.

Paul Harvey was busily preparing his noontime broadcast and I was his guest.

The reception area for *Paul Harvey News* was dignified but simple. The nostalgic painting by Oklahoma artist Jim Daly of a young boy in knickers earnestly listening to an old-fashioned radio hung prominently above the front desk. Proclamations and pictures with presidents lined the walls of the hallway.

June Westgaard, Harvey's assistant of nearly fifty years, escorted me to a conference room across from Mr. Harvey's office. It was a virtual museum. Mounds of memorabilia were on display. Over 500 keys to cities, more pictures, testimonials from longtime advertising sponsors, and an entire wall filled with framed, original sketches of Bill Keane's *Family Circus* cartoon, all with a Harvey theme.

Soon, the typing ceased and in an instant, the legendary broadcaster appeared in the doorway. He was dressed in a dapper brown suit, crisply starched shirt, and a solid silk tie. He carried a pair of eyeglasses and a stack of papers bound by a clip.

There was a bounce in his brisk step; his eyes were lively and anticipatory. His enthusiasm put me at immediate ease.

"Oh my goodness!" he offered warmly, "Paul Batura—my fellow American!"

His handshake was firm, his smile wide. He immediately began to ask *me* questions. Where was I from? Was I married? Did I have my eye on a special lady? What did I think of last night's Bulls game? Who looked strong from my perspective for this year's baseball season? Did I enjoy golfing in Colorado as much as he did?

Each time I attempted to swing the conversation back to him, he deftly returned it to me. This is the mark of a gentleman, I thought.

He knows what he thinks and what he believes, so he's more interested in finding out what he doesn't. Yet even when I did have an
opportunity to relay to him my appreciation for his broadcasting, the
response was fairly unique—especially for a man who has been on the
job since 1933.

"I've listened to you my entire life," I told him, "we even used to
turn your *Rest of the Story* broadcasts into a family game, competing
to see who might guess or identify the subject first."

He turned quickly on his heels as we made our way towards the
radio studio.

"Oh, my goodness," he responded, "thank you! Is that right? That
is wonderful, but do you know that my son, Paul, writes those pieces?
He is the one who deserves the lion's share of the credit."

The gentleman, I thought, accepts his due with gratitude, but he's
also always quick to properly assign commendation. To that end,
though, Paul Harvey had the habit of receiving a compliment with the
enthusiasm of a man who was hearing it for the very first time.

"You're the last of the lions," I told him.

"Thank you," he shot back. "The world needs people to report the
positive. I'm just one in a line that I hope will grow long."

We chatted both before and after his broadcast. When I broached
the subject of collaborating with him on a book about his faith, he
politely declined, citing his schedule and the very little time he had
for "extracurricular" writing. "But ask me again down the road," he
said with a smile.

I asked him again in 2003, and he again declined. Undeterred and
convinced of the value of the story, I pushed forward. It could be an
independent venture, I figured. But publishers weren't convinced and
considered the topic interesting but the focus too narrow.

By the summer of 2008, with Paul approaching his ninetieth birthday, it finally occurred to me that simply writing about the totality of Paul Harvey's life would be akin to writing about Paul Harvey's faith. But surely someone had already done this? There had been articles and essays, even documentaries, but to my shock, no biography. I was stunned. How did someone the caliber of Paul Harvey escape study these many years? I quickly sketched an outline. But could I really pull off this independent project?

"Reach for what you cannot," I thought.

And so began the adventure. The plan was to release the book on the occasion of his ninety-first birthday on September 4, 2009. But two weeks before the publisher's deadline for a first draft, the sad news of Paul's death turned the project on its head. Several chapters were added, others were rewritten, and all of them were adjusted to some degree.

Paul Harvey lived a little over ninety years—approximately 33,000 days. During that time, not a single writer or publisher ever devoted an entire book to a study of his life. Now somebody has. In memoriam.

P.J.B.

Remembering Paul Harvey

*N*ote from the Author: Rush Limbaugh once remarked that the only way to make millions is for half the nation to hate you. Paul Harvey would certainly have to be the exception to such a rule. When I began to reach out to colleagues and friends of the ABC Radio commentator, even months before his death, it quickly became apparent that he was a man of few, if any, enemies. Space does not allow for the inclusion of every response, but it's a pleasure to share several reflections.

★ ★ ★

Gil Gross is a nationally syndicated ABC Radio host
who currently broadcasts out of KGO-AM in San Francisco.
For several years he served as Paul Harvey's regular
replacement on Paul Harvey News and Comment.

I think Paul Harvey may have been the most gracious man I have ever met. I will take you back to 1971 when I was trying to disguise my youth behind a beard and showed up at the ABC News Chicago

Bureau at 4:00 a.m. in denim, boots, and the look of someone who had not only rolled out on the wrong side of the bed but somehow had gotten caught between the mattress and the wall. Paul arrived minutes later looking as if a team of Saville Row tailors had been working on him for days. The first time he saw me I would not have been surprised if he had called building security to find out how a Tribble had somehow been let loose in his office. Instead he nodded, said, "Good Morning" with a note of optimism that it would indeed be good, that by comparison made Norman Vincent Peale seem like a victim of depression considering his options on a ledge. There was no note of judgment on my looks.

Before the week was over I had simply taken a phone call for him when his staff was out and left him a note. That was hardly a task worthy of a mention, and yet the next day there was a handwritten note of thanks from him which I have to this day. He was courtly. I know that people may believe that was a mark of his generation, but Paul was of my parent's generation, and it was beyond anything I saw in all my relatives and their friends. He was probably old-fashioned in that regard even when being old-fashioned was in fashion, but it was one of his strengths. He brought people over to his point of view through humor and intellect. He drew them in through his personality and his stories. He accepted those who disagreed with him as long as he believed you were true of heart and your values were strong.

My final note from him came about a year before his death. Filling in for him, I had done a long piece about a dying aviator whose last wish was to be taken for a "final flight." I spent more time on it than I usually do because something in it struck a chord with me and I wanted to do the man the honor of getting the tone right. Paul sent me a note telling me, "I will never forget 'Final Flight.'" I think that was probably an overstatement, but when I got it I remember thinking

Paul, as he approached ninety, knew he was on his own final approach and was completely at peace with it, even though he had oh so many more stories to tell.

★ ★ ★

Philip Gulley has become the voice of small-town American life. A best-selling author, his newest book is entitled, I Love You, Miss Huddleston: And Other Inappropriate Longings of My Indiana Childhood.

When I was twelve years old, I got my first job delivering newspapers in our small town. My first paycheck was $7.50 and with it I bought a bottle of Coke and a paperback copy of *The Rest of the Story* at the Rexall Drugstore on the town square. So began my story with Paul Harvey.

Twenty-four years later, Mr. Harvey read an essay I'd written on his program, a book contract soon followed, and a friendship was begun. Thirteen years and fifteen books later, Mr. Harvey—one of the sweetest, kindest men you'll ever meet—still announces with every release, "Phil Gulley has a new book out. You'll want to read it." He never, not once, forgot.

If fame has been the ruination of some people, it has only magnified the many virtues of Paul Harvey. He was Mr. Approachable, Mr. Decent, Mr. Never Forgot His Roots, all rolled into one. He was what I hope someday to be—a friend to all.

★ ★ ★

Hugh Hewitt is an author, law professor and broadcast journalist. He is the host of the Hugh Hewitt Show, *broadcast live*

*from Southern California each afternoon. He conceived and
hosted the 1996 national PBS series* Searching for God in America.

From the time I began listening to the radio in the early '60s, Paul
Harvey was never not there. When I began my own career in 1990,
Paul Harvey was still a mainstay of AM radio, setting a standard for
excellence and, crucially, consistency. That's the secret to radio—
day-in and day-out delivery of the same high quality of broadcast.
Tens of millions of Americans got to "know" Paul Harvey though
they had never met or even corresponded, and the standard he
established for news with personality will endure as one serious
broadcast journalists will aspire to. Like Vin Scully, Paul Harvey
made it seem effortless, but of course he worked and worked and
worked at it. What a professional.

★ ★ ★

*Dr. Jerry B. Jenkins, a former vice president for publishing and now
chairman of the board of trustees for the Moody Bible Institute of
Chicago, is the author of more than 175 books, including the
70,000,000-selling* Left Behind *series.*

With the passing of the legendary broadcaster, I was reminded of
the privilege of my one personal meeting with him. I had been working with Billy Graham (Paul Harvey's same age, ninety, by the way) on
his memoir, and Mr. Graham was reminiscing about the 1957 Times
Square event. There at the conclusion of his several weeks of preaching at Madison Square Garden, hundreds of thousands jammed the
streets for a final meeting.

ABC television broadcast the event live, and Mr. Graham said, "Paul Harvey was their reporter." I said, "I would love to get his memories of that."

Well, I've worked with a lot of famous people, yet I remain amazed at their ability to get other famous people to take their calls. Mr. Graham asked his secretary if she could get Paul Harvey on the phone, and a few minutes later the two were talking.

The two giants were friends, and Paul Harvey was an outspoken believer in Christ. So we know where he is now.

★ ★ ★

Tom Langmyer is Vice President and
General Manager of WGN in Chicago.

My first time I met Paul Harvey was about twenty-five years ago when I was working at WGR Radio in Buffalo.

I was a kid still in college, and he certainly had been a longtime legend for a quite a while by then. Paul was in town speaking before a packed house at Kleinhans Music Hall. We met backstage and I still remember how I felt meeting him. Being a kid in awe of his talents and a bit nervous at the time, what would have been a brief encounter actually lasted for some time. He was very gracious and asked me questions. . . and that made it easy for me to then speak with confidence and ask him some questions. We talked about my school, Grove City College in Pennsylvania, the college radio station, and he encouraged me to live my life's dream. Before he went on stage, he winked at me, placed his hand on my shoulder and said, "Work hard at it and live your dream, Tom."

★ ★ ★

Roy H. Williams is New York Times bestselling
author of the Wizard of Ads trilogy.

Any success I've achieved as an author and public speaker is due to the fact that, in my mind, I'm doing what I think Paul Harvey would do. His distinctive structuring of stories with misdirection and surprise endings, his unusual phrasing and intonation when speaking, are imprinted on my mind. Strangely, not one person has ever realized that my style could easily be categorized as a very bad imitation of Paul Harvey. One of the highlights of my life was the day Paul talked about a column that I had written and mentioned me by name on the air. I play the audio file occasionally for students. I miss him deeply.

★ ★ ★

Ron Dentinger has worked the banquet circuit from coast to coast
for over 20 years. Unlike comedy club comedians, his humor
is clean and less aggressive, which is extremely important
to the associations and the corporations that book him.

Some years ago Paul Harvey was the keynote speaker in Las Vegas, for the National Realtors' Association. There were several thousand people in the audience, including a couple from my home in Dodgeville, Wisconsin. That night Paul Harvey quoted only one person, and the Dodgeville couple couldn't believe that, that one person was someone from their home town in little old Dodgeville. My point is that...Paul Harvey was not obligated to credit me for the quote, but he did. He cared enough to give that credit.

We lost an icon and it brought an end to an era. Rest in peace, Paul Harvey.

★ ★ ★

Argus Hamilton is the man Robin Williams once called "the Will Rogers of the Baby Boom." Argus Hamilton's daily column of jokes on the news, now carried in over 100 newspapers across the United States, is also read and heard by millions on the Internet and on radio stations across the country.

It was one of the greatest honors of my life when Paul Harvey began to quote my jokes on his daily broadcasts. As a comedian and columnist, I was accustomed to having people tell me they saw me on a television show or read my column, but the size of Paul Harvey's audience was unlike anything I'd ever seen. More people told me they heard me on Paul Harvey than saw me on the *Tonight Show*.

Paul Harvey never let his audience know how hard he worked preparing his sparkling commentaries, but he was up at three o'clock every morning going through all the news wire stories, every letter sent to him, and even the jokes I faxed late at night, trying to glean the most entertaining material for his listeners that day.

Acknowledgements

D r. Sol Tax is a former anthropology professor at the University of Chicago. He would often tell the story of carrying his granddaughter on his shoulders. Coming upon a friend who hadn't seen the girl in some time, the acquaintance looked up and said with astonishment, "My, oh my how you've grown!" To which the incredulous grandchild said in response, "Not really. Don't you see? Not all of this is me!"

Nearly every good thing in life is a collective effort, this book included. I am indebted to saints of many stripes; loved ones, old friends and new, close and distant colleagues, and even a few strangers whose kindness, interest, and general affability encouraged the adventure and effort.

The solitary and sometimes lonely task of writing can take a toll on a spouse. My wife and best friend in the entire world and the sweetest soul anyone could ever meet, Julie, deserves the heartiest thanks and the lion's share of all the credit for this work. Every idea and inspiration was first vetted through her—and she tolerated far more talk about my love of radio and a personal fascination with a commentator named

Paul Harvey than any human being should be asked or expected to endure. She believed in me long before I believed in myself. Our three-year-old son, Riley, is deserving of accolades, too. It saddens me that he'll be the first of a generation in more than sixty years to grow up without a daily dose of *Paul Harvey News and Comment* over breakfast and lunch. Nevertheless, he's a boy who has already enjoyed his fill of the broadcast legend. After months of overhearing conversations about the newsman and taking repeated trips to the mailbox to fetch archival clippings and tapes for research, he said with a sigh one late winter afternoon, "OK, Daddy. Enough with the Paul Harvey!" He'll learn. We all wish there was more Paul Harvey yet to come. I am blessed to share this world with Julie and Riley.

My parents, Jim and Joan Batura, were the first to instill in me an affinity and appreciation for radio. How wonderfully and beautifully that small kitchen radio on Central Avenue in Baldwin helped to order and make sense of our day and world. I first listened to Paul Harvey because they did. The conversations those broadcasts and commentaries launched and the pure enjoyment are the substance of priceless memories. The kindness and support of my siblings, Jim, Tommy, John, and Marie, also played a role in those early formative years. We all had a radio beside our bed. Today's culture would be better off if every kitchen in America was equipped with a radio and parents to help children process and appreciate the might, wonder, and majesty of the well-spoken word. My in-laws, the Reverend Jennings and Cindy Hamilton, are beloved and appreciated for their prayers, support, and feedback.

Every reader of *Good Day!*—but especially this writer—owes his esteemed editor at Regnery, Anneke Green, a robust round of applause. I am so grateful to her for guiding, shaping, molding, and sharpening this manuscript. She put in many long hours at great personal sacrifice. Anneke has a tremendous gift. My thanks also to her dear father, T. A. Green, a fellow Paul Harvey listener and unofficial manuscript advisor. Regnery's outstanding editorial and art team, led by Vice President Harry W. Crocker, are get-it-done people. Thank you to Christian Tappe, Mary Beth Baker, Amber Colleran, Kristina Phillips, Sally Brock, and Jeanne Crotty.

I'm thankful to enjoy the artful and dignified representation of my agent, Erik Wolgemuth of Wolgemuth and Associates, along with his colleagues within the firm, Robert and Andrew. They regularly extended me time they didn't have and generously shared their wisdom and perspective.

My colleagues at Focus on the Family offered guidance, feedback and friendship. I salute these treasured teammates: Ron Reno, Becky Lane, Sherry Hoover, Corinne Sayler, Vickie Koeppel, Gary Schneeberger, John Fuller, Brian Neils, Dr. H. B. London, Mark Frederiksen, Sherri Woods, Steve Reiter, Patty Watkins, Tim Goeglein, Olivia Yates, Joanna Brown, Sally Evans, Gail Hinson and Hortencia Perez. Having served under the leadership of Dr. James Dobson, I'm thankful for his support and encouragement—along with the privilege of finding my way as a writer by emulating several elements of his inspired style. My friend and colleague Bob West is founder of a fantastic organization called The Need Project which is devoted to helping families who have children with special needs. He generously donated precious free time editing and scanning many of the photographs within these pages. I also salute the memory of the late Bob Dobbs, a former boss at Focus on the Family and a tender man who helped further stoke a love of radio. I'd like to thank New Iron Media's Esther Fleece for helping connect me with several valuable contributors. My "running brothers" regularly offered insight and reaction to the developing story. I thank these good men with whom I've shared many miles and marathons: Fellow Harvey aficionado David Bervig, Dave Corsten, Al DeLaRoche, and Mark Hufford. Marlen Wells also belongs in this camp, but I'd like to reserve a special place of honor for him and his wife, Bobbi. Not only is Marlen a man with a gifted intellect and a regular contributor to my creative inspirations, but Julie and I will remain forever grateful to this Godly couple for facilitating the greatest "good day" of our lives. Retired Air Force Lt. Col. Dick Korthals, a decorated World War II pilot (and writer) who helped save these United States, is also a beloved hero of mine who encouraged, counseled, and offered insight on this work.

I'm deeply indebted to friends and current/former colleagues at the ABC Radio Network. President Jim Robinson, Vice President Carl Anderson, Louis Adams, John McConnell, Phil Boyce, Geoff Rich, and Ramona Rideout. John McConnell is deserving of special recognition for introducing me to so many friends and industry insiders. He is a prince and a gentleman. These are all tremendously talented men and women who shared my appreciation for Mr. Harvey and did everything they could to help me tell his story. I'm also appreciative of the courtesy of *Paul Harvey News and Comments*' June Westgaard and Rita Johnson.

Ironically though not likely coincidentally, our own beloved pastor, Dr. Jim Singleton of First Presbyterian Church in Colorado Springs, helped me initiate some key contacts in the researching of Paul Harvey's spiritual past. Jim's close friends, Dr. Jim Miller of First Presbyterian in Tulsa and Dr. John Buchanan of Fourth Presbyterian in Chicago, along with John's assistant, Barbara Cleveland, provided invaluable research and insight. I'm also grateful to First Presbyterian of Colorado Springs' dynamite music team of Jim DeJarnette and organist Don Dyck who helped me identify curious strains of music from recordings—which were a mystery to me but to them were no mystery at all. Thanks as well to retired Air Force General Jay Kelley for his insight and informal but keen counsel on various matters within the manuscript. I'm also indebted to Dr. John H. Stevens, pastor emeritus of First Presbyterian Church. How I love his teaching and preaching, whose art of sermonizing has helped me learn to tell a story.

So many people took the time to sit down with me and agreed to be interviewed for the research surrounding this book. Each conversation was critical. They include but were not limited to John Gambling, Al Peterson, John McConnell, Tom Langmyer, Dr. Ed Dumit, Calvin Swindell, Garvin Berry, David Crowell, Gene Allen, Dr. Ben Henneke, Bob Hille, Frank Absher, Stephen Trivers, Dr. Bill Knowles, David Hager, Dick Bott, Ken Jennison, Carl Lee, Peter Christian, Marc Wilson, Art Hellyer, Win Schuler, Connie Vandeman Jeffery, artist Jim Daly, Dan Vallie, Ron Dettinger, and Dr. Robert Bastian. Bruce DuMont and Gina Loizzo, at Chicago's Museum of Broadcast Communications, also offered critical insight and research for this endeavor. A special nod also to Art Vuolo Jr., "Radio's best friend."

What a phenomenal resource are the public libraries of America. I was the recipient of fantastic service and accommodation at research facilities in the city library of Tulsa, The University of Tulsa, Salina, Kansas, Oklahoma City, Oklahoma, St. Louis, Missouri, The University of Montana at Missoula, Kalamazoo, Michigan, Colorado Springs, Colorado, and Chicago, Illinois.

I owe ABC Radio host, former governor of Arkansas, and presidential candidate of the United States Mike Huckabee a sincere thanks for penning such a warm, affirming, and gracious word of introduction to the manuscript. Paul Harvey would be proud of *The Huckabee Report* and honored that Mike's program has already been cleared on many of his former and longtime affiliates.

Many busy people took the time to talk with me to offer reflections and delightful memories of Paul Harvey. Phil Gulley, House Majority Leader Steny Hoyer, President of the LDS Church Thomas Monson, author Marc Wilson, writers Doug Gamble, Harvey Mackay, President George W. Bush, ABC's Gil Gross, Salem's Hugh Hewitt, Radio Ink publisher and CEO B. Eric Rhoads, author Roy Williams, and comedians Ben Stein, Argus Hamilton, and Ron Dettinger.

The inclusion of the beautifully emotive and nostalgic painting Radio Daze by artist Jim Daly is most appreciated. Paul's office proudly displayed this portrait and it seems only fitting that *Good Day!* highlight it as well. Thank you, Mr. Daly.

Every human life is a gift from God worthy of respect and befitting the honor of honest evaluation. Paul Harvey's life was no more precious than any other, but I'm grateful that He allowed me the privilege of writing about one of His many faithful servants.

These (and many more) are the giants on whose shoulders I, and this book, rest. Paul Harvey used to say that he had over 200 million writers scattered about the American continent contributing to his daily broadcasts. So did I.

These are but a few of the noble citizens of the greatest country in the entire world. But again, insofar as my earthly encounters go, I return to my wife, Julie, to whom I am most thankful of all and always will be.

I salute each and every name on this roll. It's a privilege to be counted in their company.

Notes

PROLOGUE: TAPS AT REVEILLE

1. R&R Talk Radio Seminar Address, Marina Del Rey, CA, March 2003.
2. Paul Harvey, "A Message of Freedom with Responsibility," Landon Lecture, Kansas State University, September 19, 2003.
3. "Paul Harvey, Radio Broadcasting Pioneer, Dies at 90," *State News Service*, March 2, 2009.
4. Robert D. McFadden, "Paul Harvey, Homespun Radio Voice of Middle America, Is Dead at 90," *The New York Times*, March 2, 2009, p. A16.
5. Statement from Paul Harvey Jr., courtesy of the *ABC Radio Network*, February 28, 2009.
6. Stephen Vincent Benet, *The Saturday Review of Literature* 24 (December 6, 1941), 10.

CHAPTER 1: A BOY OF TULSA

1. The street name would change to East Fifth Place shortly after Paul's birth.
2. *Tulsa Daily World* edition of Wednesday, September 4, 1918. All pages of 9/4/18 edition accessed via microfilm, Tulsa City-County Library, Tulsa, OK.

3. Ibid.

4. Jeremiah 33:3 (King James Version).

5. *Tulsa Daily World*, September 4, 1918, p. 2.

6. Tulsa Area History, Tulsa County Library. See:
   http://www.tulsalibrary.org/tulsahistory/communities.htm#tul
   (Accessed March 13, 2009).

7. "A Bond is Denied By Judge Lawrence," *Tulsa Daily World*, September 22, 1907, p. 1.

8. K. D. Patterson and G. F. Pyle, "The geography and mortality of the
   1918 influenza pandemic," *Bull Hist Med* 65 (Spring 1991) (1):
   4–21.

9. Congressional Research Service, *American War and Military Operations Casualties: Lists and Statistics*. See:
   http://www.fas.org/sgp/crs/natsec/RL32492.pdf (March 13, 2009).

10. The Act of March 19, 1918, sometimes called the "Standard Time
    Act," established standard time in time zones in U.S. law. The Standard Time Act also established daylight saving time (DST), which
    was repealed in 1919 but was reestablished nationally during
    World War II.

11. Eleanor Flexner, *Century of Struggle: The Woman's Rights Movement
    in the United States* (Cambridge, MA: Belknap Press of Harvard
    University Press), 1996.

12. The Boston Red Sox defeated the Chicago Cubs four games to two
    to win a season shortened World Series on September 11, 1918.
    The Red Sox would not win another World Series until October 27,
    2004. See: http://www.baseball-almanac.com/ws/yr1918ws.shtml
    and http://www.baseball-almanac.com/ws/yr2004ws.shtml
    (Accessed March 13, 2009).

13. See: http://www.historyorb.com/today/birthdays.php (Accessed
    March 13, 2009).

14. Year: 1900; *Census Place: Harrisburg Ward 2*, Dauphin, Pennsylvania; Roll: T623_1402 Page: 10A; Enumeration District: 46; See:
    http://home.earthlink.net/~engtudor/paag11.htm#944C (Accessed
    March 13, 2009); and "Oklahoma to Honor Harvey," *Tulsa World*,
    October 22, 1955.

15. Ibid.

16. Year: 1900; *Census Place: Harrisburg Ward 2*, Dauphin, Pennsylvania; Roll: T623_1402 Page: 10A; Enumeration District: 46.

17. Ibid.

18. Year: 1910; *Census Place: Wichita Ward 3*, Sedgwick, Kansas; Roll: T624_456; Page: 5B; Enumeration District: 120; Image: 479.

19. Year: 1920; *Census Place: Tulsa*, Tulsa, Oklahoma; Roll: T625_1487; Page: 10B; Enumeration; and Paul Harvey Aurandt, "A Service of Witness to the Resurrection in the Celebration of the Life of Paul Harvey," The Fourth Presbyterian Church of Chicago, March 7, 2009.

20. Ibid.

21. Paul Harvey, "Friends with Ghosts," *The Gettysburg Times*, March 30, 1994, p. A4.

22. Nick Foltz, "Paul Harvey's Greatest Day Was Day Teacher Stepped In," *Tulsa World*, May 9, 1987, p. A1.

23. Paul Harvey, "Another Spring and Memories," *The News*, March 11, 1974, p. 4.

24. Ronald L. Trekell, *History of the Tulsa Police Department, 1882-1990* (Tulsa, OK, 1989).

CHAPTER 2: RIOT

1. INS Statistical Yearbook, 1993, p. 158; and K. Calavita, *Inside the State* (New York: Routledge, 1992), 217–18.

2. Michael LeMay and Elliott Robert Barkan, eds., *U.S. Immigration and Naturalization Laws and Issues: A Documentary History, 1999.* See: http://ocp.hul.harvard.edu/immigration/dates.html (Accessed March 13, 2009).

3. Grant, Madison, *The Passing of the Great Race*; or, *The Racial Basis of European History* (New York: C. Scribner, 1916).

4. Ibid., 228.

5. Kenneth T. Jackson, "Atlanta: The Imperial City," in *The Ku Klux Klan in the City, 1915-1930* (New York: Oxford University Press, 1967).

6. Richard Maxwell Brown, *Strain of Violence: Historical Studies of American Violence and Vigilantism* (New York: Oxford University Press, 1975); and George C. Rable, *But There Was no Peace: The Role of Violence in the Politics of Reconstruction* (Athens, Georgia: University of Georgia Press, 1984).

7. Final Report of the Oklahoma Commission to Study the Tulsa Race Riot of 1921, Oklahoma Historical Society. See: http://www.okhistory.org/trrc/freport.htm (Accessed March 13, 2009).

8. Larry O'Dell, "Ku Klux Klan," *Encyclopedia of Oklahoma History and Culture*, http://digital.library.okstate.edu/encyclopedia/entries/K/KU001.html (Accessed March 13, 2009).

9. Walter C. Rucker and James N. Upton, *Encyclopedia of American Race Riots* (Westport, CT: Greenwood Press, 2007), 260.

10. Brent Staples, "Unearthing a Riot," *The New York Times*, December 19, 1999, Section 6, p. 64.

11. "Tulsa, Oklahoma: Oil Capital of the World," http://www.legendsofamerica.com/OK-Tulsa2.html.

12. "House 176-55, Overrides Veto of Wartime Prohibition," *The New York Times*, October 28, 1919, p. 1; and "Senate Overrides Prohibition Veto by Vote of 65 to 20," October 29, 1919, p. 1.

13. *Tulsa Tribune*: May 27, 1921, p. 1; and *Tulsa World*, May 27, 1921, p. 8. (Accessed via microfilm.).

14. *Tulsa Tribune*, May 30, 1921, p. 1. (Accessed via microfilm.).

15. Tim Madigan, *The Burning: Massacre, Destruction, and the Tulsa Race Riot of 1921* (New York : Thomas Dunne Books/St. Martin's Press, 2001).

16. *Tulsa Tribune*, Series of articles: January 13, 1921, p. 12; February 12, 1921, p., 8; March 5, 1921, p. 10; April 5, 1921, p. 16; April 7, 1921, p. 16; May 1, 1921, p. B-14; May 3, 1921, p. 18; and May 13, 1921, p. 24.

17. *Tulsa Tribune*, May 14, 1921, p. 10.

18. *Tulsa Tribune*, May 25, 1921, p. 16.

19. Tim Madigan, *The Burning*.

20. Scott Ellsworth, *Death in a Promised Land* (Baton Rouge: Louisiana State University Press, 1982), 46.

21. Ibid.

22. Tim Madigan, *The Burning*.

23. *Tulsa Tribune*, May 31, 1921. Note: Though both the front and editorial page of this edition are missing from the official archive, the veracity and authenticity of the quote has been verified by numerous reputable sources throughout the years.

24. Ibid.

25. *Tulsa Tribune*: August 31, 1920, p. 12; and September 6, 1920, p. 1.

26. Ross. T. Warner, *Oklahoma Boy: An Autobiography* (privately published, 1968), 136; Petition No. 23325, B. A. Waynes and M. E.

Waynes vs. T. D. Evans et al., Tulsa County District Court. *New York Evening Post*, June 11, 1921. Testimony of John A. Gustafson, State of Oklahoma vs. John A. Gustafson, Attorney Generals Civil Case Files, Case 1062, State Archives Division, Oklahoma Department of Libraries.

27. *Tulsa World*, July 19, 1921, p. 1.

28. John A. Gustafson testimony; and handwritten notes to the testimony of W. M. Ellis; both in Attorney Generals Civil Case Files, Case 1062, State Archives Division, Oklahoma Department of Libraries. Stephen P. Kerr, "Tulsa Race War, 31, May 1921: An Oral History," unpublished manuscript, 1999. St. Louis Argus, June 101-1921.

29. James S. Hirsch, *Riot and Remembrance: The Tulsa Race War and Its Legacy* (Boston: Houghton Mifflin, 2002), 89.

30. Ibid.

31. Alfred L. Brophy, *Reconstructing the Dreamland: The Tulsa Race Riot of 1921: Race, Reparations, and Reconciliation*, (New York and Oxford: Oxford University Press, 2002), 53.

32. Ibid.

33. Final Report of the Oklahoma Commission to Study the Tulsa Race Riot of 1921, Oklahoma Historical Society. See: http://www.okhistory.org/trrc/freport.htm (Accessed March 13, 2009).

34. *Tulsa World*, June 1, 1921, "Third Extra," 1; and Charles F. Barrett, *Oklahoma After Fifty Years: A History of the Sooner State and Its People* (Hopkinsville, KY: Historical Record Association, 1941), 212–13.

35. Tulsa City Directory, 1921; Mary E. Parrish, *Events of the Tulsa Disaster* (1922), 41, 78–80; Eddie Faye Gates, *They Came Searching: How Blacks Sought the Promised Land in Tulsa* (Waco, TX: Eakin Press, 1997), 165–67; and *Tulsa Star*, March 6, 1915.

36. Maurice Willows, "Disaster Relief Report, Race Riot, June 1921," 6, reprinted in Robert N. Hower, *"Angels of Mercy": The American Red Cross and the 1921 Tulsa Race Riot* (Tulsa, OK: Homestead Press, 1993). Cited, Final Report of the Oklahoma Commission to Study the Tulsa Race Riot of 1921, Oklahoma Historical Society, online, 23.

37. Walter F. White, "The Nation," *Tulsa, The Nation* June 15, 1921. Available at http://www.thenation.com/doc/20010820/1921tulsa.

38. James S. Hirsch, *Riot and Remembrance*.
39. Ibid.
40. "States' Use of Police and Military Force to Arrest, Detain, and Confine American Citizens Because of Race," 27 *Oklahoma City University Law Review* 451–473, 451–455 (Spring 2002).
41. Ronald L. Trekell, *History of the Tulsa Police Department, 1882-1990*.
42. Paul Harvey, "Caught in Crossfire," *Oshkosh Daily Northwestern*, July 20, 1965, p. 31.

CHAPTER 3: AN INCALCULABLE LOSS

1. As quoted in official testimony in Cook v State, 1924 OK CR 155, 226 P. 595, 27 Okl.Cr. 215, Decided: June 7, 1924, Oklahoma Court of Criminal Appeals. Available at http://www.oscn.net/applications/oscn/DeliverDocument.asp?CiteID=32137.
2. Ibid.
3. Ibid.
4. Ibid.
5. Ibid.
6. Paul Harvey, "Life is Transient," *Oshkosh Daily Northwestern*, December 3, 1963, p. 4.
7. Cook v State; and *Tulsa Tribune*, December 19, 1921, p. 1.
8. *Tulsa Tribune*, December 19, 1921, p.1.
9. Ibid.
10. Now Admiral Place
11. Cook v State.
12. Ibid.
13. *Tulsa Tribune*, December 19, 1921, p.1.
14. Ibid.
15. Ibid.
16. Cook v State.
17. Ibid.
18. Ibid.
19. Ibid.
20. Ibid.
21. Ibid.
22. Ibid.

23. Ibid.
24. *Tulsa Tribune*, December 19, 1921, p. 1.
25. *Tulsa Tribune*, December 20, 1921, p. 1.
26. Ibid.
27. Ibid. See also: http://www.tulsaworld.com/webextra/
itemsofinterest/centennial/centennial_storypage.asp?ID=070925_1
_A4_spanc04513 (Accessed March 14, 2009).
28. *Tulsa Tribune*, December 20, 1921, p. 1.
29. *Tulsa Tribune*, December 22, 1921, p. 1.
30. Ibid.
31. Ibid.
32. Ibid.
33. "The Mystic Insignia of a Klansman," see:
http://www.kkklan.com/mioak.htm.
34. *Tulsa Tribune*, December 22, 1921, p. 1.
35. Ibid.
36. Ibid.
37. Craig W. Floyd, "Officers Who Became Off-Duty Victims of Violence," December 6, 2004. See: http://www.nleomf.com/
TheMemorial/tributes/offdutyvictims.htm.
38. Cook v State.
39. Gene Curtis, "Only in Oklahoma: Paul Harvey's Father Shot by Bandits," *Tulsa World*, September 25, 2007, p. A4.
40. Cook v State.
41. Riley Wilson, "Navy Dirigible Survives Storm," *Tulsa World*, January 17, 1924, p.1.
42. *Tulsa World*, November 20, 1923, p.1.
43. Riley Wilson, "Navy Dirigible Survives Storm."
44. Ronald L. Trekell, *History of the Tulsa Police Department, 1882-1990*.
45. Ibid.
46. Paul Harvey, "Life is Transient," *Oshkosh Daily Northwestern*, December 3, 1963, p. 4.
47. Ibid.
48. Paul Harvey, "Writer Confounded by Coincidence," *Lima News*, December 6, 1963, p. 19.

CHAPTER 4: STARS IN HIS EYES

1. Polk Directory of Tulsa, 1957.

2. Comments from S. Lee, *Tulsa 1957: A Porch Swing on East Fifth Place*. See: http://www.batesline.com/archives/2007/08/tulsa-1957-a-po.html.
3. Paul Harvey, "No Apologies," *Tulsa World*, September 8, 1961.
4. Paul Harvey Aurandt, "A Service of Witness to the Resurrection in the Celebration of the Life of Paul Harvey," The Fourth Presbyterian Church of Chicago, March 7, 2009.
5. Paul Harvey, "Friends with Ghosts," *Gettysburg Times*, March 30, 1994, p. 5.
6. Charles Francis Adams, *The Works of John Adams, Second President of the United States: with a Life of the Author, Notes and Illustrations* Vol. 10 (Boston: Little, Brown and Co., 1856).
7. Paul Harvey, "Friends with Ghosts."
8. Ibid.
9. Ibid.
10. Paul Harvey, "Another Spring and Host of Memories," *The Progress*, March 9, 1974, p. 16.
11. Ibid.
12. Paul Harvey, "Teacher's Pet," *Gettysburg Times*, June 30, 1994, p. 4A.
13. Ibid.
14. Ann Oldenburg, "This is Paul Harvey/Beliefs are as Rock Solid as His Voice," *USA Today*, May 16, 1994.
15. "Building Implosions," *Tulsa World*, January 26, 1997, p. A3.
16. Ben Henneke, Ph.D., "Fashion Street," *Quill of the Hill*, March 2007.
17. Gene Curts, "15 Killed in Edmond Post Office Massacre," *Tulsa World*, August 21, 2005, p. A3
18. Paul Harvey, "Hometown Has its Advantages," *The Brazosport Facts*, September 5, 1961, p. 2; Ben Henneke, *Type Script* (Tulsa, OK: Saint Simeon's Foundation), 72.
19. Charles A. Lindbergh, pilot, "The Log of the Spirit of St. Louis." See: http://www.charleslindbergh.com/history/log.asp (Accessed March 14, 2009).
20. Paul Harvey, "Friends with the Ghosts."
21. Ibid.
22. Paul Harvey, "Let Them Eat Bread," *San Mateo Times*, October 14, 1967, p. 16.
23. Paul Harvey, *Autumn of Liberty* (New York: Hanover House, 1954), 41–44.

24. Ibid.
25. "Lowell Thomas" Radio Hall of Fame Bio. See: http://www.radiohof.org/news/lowellthomas.html (Accessed March 14, 2009).
26. Liam Lacey, "Television Advertising Stoops to Conquer," *The Globe and Mail*, August 16, 1995.
27. "Recollections: Walter Winchell," see: http://www.shieldmedia.ca/print_this_story.asp?smenu=136&sdetail=5576 (Accessed March 14, 2009).
28. Edward Bliss Jr., *Now The News: The Story of Broadcast Journalism* (New York: Columbia University Press, 1991), 214.
29. Gerald Nachman, *Raised on Radio* (CA: University of California Press, 2000), 401.
30. Ibid., 402.
31. Gabriel Heatter biography, available at http://quotes-of-wisdom. eu/en/author/gabriel-heatter/biography (Accessed March 14, 2009).
32. "Up the Hill," *Time* Magazine, November 8, 1948.
33. Catherine Carter Fullerton, "The Youth's Companion Years: 1919-1925," in *Russell Gordon Carter, the Writer*, at http://www. geocities.com/~ccfullerton/rgc/ (Accessed March 14, 2009).
34. As quoted in Youth's Companion, 1923; and Ben Henneke, *Type Script*, 75.
35. Ibid.
36. Ibid., 42.
37. Ibid., 43.

CHAPTER 5: GOOD ADVICE!

1. Interview with Mr. George Winkert, Class of Central High School, 1936, conducted on January 27, 2009.
2. Joyce Saunders, "Central High School," Central High School Foundation, Inc. See: http://www.tulsacentralalumni.org/central.htm (Accessed March 14, 2009).
3. Ibid.
4. Ibid., "Oklahoma to Honor Harvey," *Tulsa World*, October 22, 1955.
5. "History of Central High School's Memorial Pipe Organ," Central High School Foundation, Inc. See: http://www. tulsacentralalumni.org/organ.htm (Accessed March 14, 2009).
6. Ibid.

7.   Ibid.

8.   Ibid.

9.   Central High School Yearbook, "The Tom Tom," 1935.

10. Ibid.

11. Interview with Mr. George Winkert, January 27, 2009.

12. James Hilton, "Good-Bye, Mr. Chips," *The Atlantic*, April 1934.

13. "Pretty Boy Floyd," lyrics see:
     http://www.woodyguthrie.org/Lyrics/Pretty_Boy_Floyd.htm
     (Accessed March 14, 2009).

14. Peter Pavia, "Marauders of the Midwest," *New York Sun*, July 14,
     2004, p. 17.

15. James Hilton, *Good-Bye, Mr. Chips* (Boston: Little Brown & Co.,
     1934).

16. Central High School Yearbook, "The Tom Tom," 1935, pp. 111, 118.

17. "Retired Teacher Isabelle Ronan Dies," *Tulsa World*, May 28, 1980,
     p. A9.

18. Ibid.

19. Ibid.

20. Ruth Sheldon Knowles, "Curtain Call," *Tulsa World Magazine*, April
     19, 1953, p 16.

21. Yvonne Litchfield, "Students Will Remember Miss Ronan," *Tulsa
     Daily World*, July 20, 1973, p. 18A.

22. Marc Fisher, "A Lifetime on the Radio," *American Journalism
     Review*, October 1998, p. 35.

23. Yvonne Litchfield, "Students Will Remember Miss Ronan."

24. "Retired Teacher Isabelle Ronan Dies," *Tulsa World*.

25. Ruth Sheldon Knowles, "Curtain Call."

26. Words of Alexander Woolcott, "Word and Music," *Tulsa World*,
     April 24, 2005, p. H1.

27. Phil Sweetland, "Danny Dark, 65, Whose Voice Spurned StarKist's
     Charlie Tuna," *The New York Times*, June 27, 2004, p. A32.

28. Ruth Sheldon Knowles, "Curtain Call."

29. Ibid.

30. Yvonne Litchfield, "Students Will Remember Miss Ronan."

31. Interview with Ed Dumit, Ph.D, conducted on January 6, 2009.

32. Yvonne Litchfield, "Students Will Remember Miss Ronan."

33. Jim Ruddle, "Tulsa Radio Memories," see: http://tulsatvmemories.
     com/tulradi4.html (Accessed March 14, 2009).

34. Rick Kogan, "Hello, America, This is Paul Harvey," *Saturday Evening Post*, September 1, 2003, p. 52.
35. Jim Ruddle, "Tulsa Radio Memories."
36. Ibid.
37. Tim Ashley, "For 62nd Consecutive Year, Pageant Tells Easter Story," *Tulsa World*, April 8, 1998.
38. Joanne Gordon, "Beloved City Drama Coach 'Stars' in Farewell Fete," *Tulsa Daily World*, April 24, 1953, p. 1.
39. "Retired Teacher Isabelle Ronan Dies," *Tulsa World*.
40. Yvonne Litchfield, "Students Will Remember Miss Ronan."
41. "Retired Teacher Isabelle Ronan Dies," *Tulsa World*.
42. Ibid.

CHAPTER 6: ON THE AIR

1. Larry King, "Interview with Paul Harvey," CNN *Larry King Live!* June 22, 2003.
2. Rick Kogan, "Good days for Paul Harvey," *Chicago Tribune*, August 4, 2002, p. C8; Interview with Ben Henneke, conducted on January 22, 2009.
3. Ibid.
4. Gene Allen, *Voices in the Wind: Early Radio in Oklahoma* (Loveland, CO: Western Heritage Books, 1993), 35.
5. "Mr. W. G. Skelly" history, available at http://www.skellylodge.com/w-g-skelly-hx.cfm (Accessed March 15, 2009).
6. Ibid.
7. Ben Henneke, *Type Script*, 56–57
8. Ibid.
9. Ibid.
10. Paul Harvey, "Ill Founded Sensationalism Finds Targets Among the Well-Known," *Fort-Worth Star Telegram*, June 12, 1996, p. 11.
11. Paul Harvey, "Four-Day Work Week," *The Ruston Daily Leader*, May 12, 1971.

CHAPTER 7: CLIMBING THE LADDER

1. Gene Allen, *Voices in the Wind: Early Radio in Oklahoma*.
2. Dana Simon, "New Owner of Historic, Tulsa, Okla., Wright Building Plans Renovation," *Tulsa World*, August 1, 1997.
3. Ibid.

4. Frank Morrow, "Tulsa Radio Memories," at
    http://tulsatvmemories.com/tulrkvoo.html (Accessed March 15,
    2009). Note: KVOO's frequency changed from 1140 to 1170 on
    March 24, 1941. Its signal strength increased from 10,000 to
    25,000 watts in 1931 and to 50,000 watts in 1943.
5. Tom Longden, "Oil-Rich Waite Phillips Shared Wealth with Boy
    Scouts," *Des Moines Register*, July 3, 2005, p. 2B.
6. Frank Morrow, "Tulsa Radio Memories," at http://tulsatvmemories.
    com/tulrkvoo.html (Accessed March 15, 2009).
7. Ibid.
8. Gene Allen, *Voices in the Wind: Early Radio in Oklahoma*.
9. Ibid.
10. John Wooley, "The King Of Swing; Bob Wills Crossed the Border
    and Put His Playboys On the Map," *Tulsa World*, August 24, 1997,
    p. H1; Gene Allen, *Voices in the Wind: Early Radio in Oklahoma*; and
    Gene Curtis, "Way Back When: Today in History," *Tulsa World*,
    February 9, 2008, p. A2.
11. John Wooley, "The King Of Swing; Bob Wills Crossed the Border
    and Put His Playboys On the Map."
12. Ibid.
13. Ibid.
14. John Wooley, "The King Of Swing; Bob Wills Crossed the Border
    and Put His Playboys On the Map."
15. Ibid.
16. Gene Allen, *Voices in the Wind: Early Radio in Oklahoma*.
17. Interview with Ben Henneke, conducted on January 22, 2009.
18. Julia Boorstin, "The Rest of the Story from Paul Harvey," *Fortune*,
    December 18, 2000.
19. John Wooley, "The King Of Swing; Bob Wills Crossed the Border
    and Put His Playboys On the Map."
20. Rick Kogan, "Good days for Paul Harvey," *Chicago Tribune*, August
    4, 2002, p. C8.
21. Lee, R. Alton, *The Bizarre Careers of John R. Brinkley* (Lexington,
    KY: University Press of Kentucky, 2002).
22. Erwin G. Krasnow, Jack N. Goodman, "The 'public interest' stan-
    dard: The search for the Holy Grail," *Federal Communications Law
    Journal*, May 1998.

23. "'Goat Gland Doctor' Memorialized," *The Topeka Capital-Journal*, September 16, 2002.

24. KFKB Brdcst. Ass'n v. FRC, 47 F.2d 670,672 (D.C. Cir. 1931).

25. Paul Harvey, "A Message of Freedom with Responsibility."

26. Dan D. Nimmo, Chevelle Newsome, *Political Commentators in the United States in the 20th Century* (Greenwood Publishing Group, 1997), 123.

27. Gary Demuth, "60 Years of Radio—From Live to Digital," *Salina Journal*, November 2008; "History of the Stiefel Theatre," http://www.stiefeltheatre.org/history.html (Accessed March 16, 2009).

28. Interview with Ken Jennison, Public Service Director, Salina Media Group, January 27, 2009.

29. David A. Haury, "Come Back to the Five and Dime," *Kansas Heritage*, Winter 2004. See: http://www.kshs.org/publicat/heritage/2004winter_haury.pdf (Accessed March 16, 2009); and Interview with Ken Jennsion, January 27, 2009.

30. Interview with Ken Jennsion, January 27, 2009.

31. Ibid.

32. Paul Harvey, "A Message of Freedom with Responsibility."

33. "Former Salinans Tell of Missions," *Salina Journal*, October 23, 1970, p. T-3.

34. Paul Harvey, "A Message of Freedom with Responsibility."

35. Ibid.

36. John Steinbeck, *The Grapes of Wrath* (New York: Viking Press, 1939).

37. "Brown Shares News from Decades Past," *Enid News and Eagle*, December 5, 2007.

38. Interview with Bob Hille, KXOK (retired), February 3, 2009.

CHAPTER 8: MEET ME IN ST. LOUIS

1. Frank Absher, "1938: KXOK Goes on the Air; Radio History," *St. Louis Journalism Review*, December 1, 2007, 22.

2. Ibid.

3. Interview with Bob Hille, February 3, 2009.

4. "KXOK," *St. Louis Star-Times*, September 9, 1938.

5. Bob Hille, "Original KXOKer," *St. Louis Journalism Review*, September 1, 2003.

6. Interview with Bob Hille, February 3, 2009.
7. Ibid.
8. Ibid; Paul Harvey, *Autumn of Liberty*, 179–80.
9. "On the Air," *Avalanche-Journal*, November 9, 1952, p. 53.
10. Ibid.
11. Walter Stevens, *St. Louis: The Fourth City, 1764-1911* (New York: The S. J. Clarke Publishing Co., 1911), 803.
12. Interview with Bob Hille, February 3, 2009.
13. Ibid.
14. "Exhibition Baseball," *The New York Times*, April 5, 1940, p. 33.
15. John M. McGuire, "The Rest of Their Story," *St. Louis-Post Dispatch*, May 10, 1998, p. C1.
16. Rick Kogan, "Good days for Paul Harvey."
17. Susan Wooleyhan Caine, "The First Lady of Radio," Washington University in *St. Louis Magazine*, Spring 2002.
18. "Who Bosses Paul Harvey? His Wife 'Angel,'" *The Gastonia Gazette*, September 3, 1967, p. D1.
19. John M. McGuire, "The Rest of Their Story."
20. Ibid.
21. Ibid.
22. Ibid.
23. "Nation says 'Good Day' to broadcasting pioneer Paul Harvey," *Anderson Independent-Mail*, March 2, 2009.
24. John M. McGuire, "The Rest of Their Story;" and "Paul Harvey's 'Angel' Dead at 92," *UPI*, May 4, 2008.
25. Year: 1920; Census Place: St Louis Ward 22, St Louis (Independent City), Missouri; Roll: T625_959; Page: 9B; Enumeration District: 422; Image: 21.
26. Year: 1910; Census Place: St Louis Ward 7, St Louis (Independent City), Missouri; Roll: T624_814; Page: 10B; Enumeration District: 119; Image: 359.
27. Mattie Jane Cooper, Missouri State Board of Health, Bureau of Vital Statistics, Certificate of Death, File No. 6065, 1924.
28. John M. McGuire, "The Rest of Their Story," *St. Louis Post-Dispatch*, 10 May 1998, p. C1. Special note: In the researching of this book, discrepancies continually came up regarding Mrs. Harvey's publicly acknowledged year of birth. The 1920 United States

Census data reports her birth year as 1913 and her closest sibling eleven years apart.

29. "Who Bosses Paul Harvey? His Wife 'Angel.'"
30. Susan Wooleyhan Caine, "The First Lady of Radio."
31. "Distinguished Alumni Award Winners, 1981—Present," Washington University Libraries, 1997. See: http://library.wustl.edu/units/spec/archives/facts/alumni-awards2.html (Accessed March 16, 2009).
32. Susan Wooleyhan Caine, "The First Lady of Radio."
33. "Who Bosses Paul Harvey? His Wife 'Angel.'"
34. Ibid.
35. Missouri Marriage Records, 1805–2002 (database online). Provo, UT, USA: The Generations Network, Inc., 2007. Original data: Missouri Marriage Records. Jefferson City, MO, USA: Missouri State Archives. Microfilm.
36. "Who Bosses Paul Harvey? His Wife 'Angel.'"
37. Paul Harvey, *Remember These Things* (Garden City Books, The Heritage Foundation, 1952), 164–67.

CHAPTER 9: ALOHA

1. Interview with Bob Hille, February 3, 2009; Interview with Ben Henneke, January 22, 2009.
2. "SOME BIG WARSHIPS TO STAY IN PACIFIC; Navy Splits Forces as Fleet Is Ordered East for Atlantic Manoeuvres 140 VESSELS ARE COMING Craft Destined for World's Fair Events Include Plane Carriers, Destroyers Submarines Stay at Hawaii," *The New York Times*, December 29, 1938, p. 7
3. Ibid.
4. Hanson W. Baldwin, "Our Gibraltar in the Pacific," *The New York Times*, February 16, 1941, p. SM4.
5. "Development of the Naval Establishment in Hawaii," The U.S. Navy in Hawaii, 1826–1945: An Administrative History, Department of the Navy. See: http://www.history.navy.mil/docs/wwii/pearl/hawaii-3.htm (Accessed March 17, 2009).
6. Hanson W. Baldwin, "BIG FLEET WILL SAIL TODAY IN WAR GAME; 134 Warships Will Move From San Pedro and San Diego in

Preliminary Phase of Plan. OTHER UNITS JOIN LATER 50,000
Men and 450 Planes Will Take Part in Far-Flung Pacific Manoeuvres," *The New York Times*, April 29, 2005, p. 5.

7. Hanson W. Baldwin, "ISLAND DEFENSE PLANS ALTER PACIFIC
    PICTURE; Change in Policy Toward the Orient Is Implied in Pro-
    posals for a Strong Advanced Fleet Base," *The New York Times*, Feb-
    ruary 12, 1939, p. 77.

8. Pear Harbor Revisited: United States Navy Communications Intelli-
    gence, 1924–1941, "Pacific Build-Up," Department of the Navy, 36.

9. Hawaii Journalism History. See:
    http://www2.hawaii.edu/~tbrislin/jourhist.html (Accessed March
    17, 2009).

10. "Paul Harvey" Promotional Speaker's Brochure. See:
    http://sdrc.lib.uiowa.edu/traveling-cul-
    ture/chau1/pdf/harvey/3/brochure.pdf (Accessed March 17, 2009).

11. Interview with Carl Lee, GM and President of Fetzer Broadcasting
    (retired), February 7, 2009.

12. Ibid.

13. Laura Bly, "Settle in for nostalgic ride through old Waikiki," *USA
    Today*, November 18, 1997, p. 10D.

14. Interview with Bob Hille, February 3, 2009.

15. Paul Harvey, "President Can't Forget Lesson of Pearl Harbor," *Jef-
    ferson City Post-Tribune*, April 17, 1969, p. 4.

16. "Paul Harvey" Promotional Speaker's Brochure.

17. Hanson W. Baldwin, "Our Gibraltar in the Pacific."

18. "Paul Harvey News" and Comment, The ABC Radio Network,
    Noon broadcast, January 25, 2002.

19. Paul Harvey, "Nothing Too Much; That Is the Law," *The Lima News*,
    September 16, 1963, p. 14.

20. "Dynamic Commentator From ABC Airs Views Daily at 12:15 PM,"
    San Antonio Light, July 2, 1951, p. 24.

21. Paul Harvey, "Surprise Attack," *The Rest of the Story* Broadcast,
    ABC Radio Network.

22. Hearings of Joint Congressional Committee on the Investigation of the
    Pearl Harbor Attack, U.S.Govt. Printing Office, 1945/46; Gordon W.
    Prange, *At Dawn We Slept: The Untold Story of Pearl Harbor*, (Colum-
    bus, OH: McGraw Hill, 1981); Ruth R. Harris, *The "Magic" Leak of
    1941 and Japanese-American Relations* (CA: University of California

Press, 1981); and Robert B. Stinnet, *Day of Deceit: The Truth About FDR and Pearl Harbor* (New York: Free Press, 2000).

CHAPTER 10: MOVING ON

1. Paul Harvey, "Mansions Inspired Ambitions," *The Daily Times*, September 29, 1968, p. 34
2. Aline Mosby, Oral History, Washington Press Club Foundation, May 8, 1991, pp. 1–34. See: http://wpcf.org/oralhistory/mosby1.html (Accessed March 17, 2009).
3. Missoula Historical Walking Tour, Missoula Downtown Association. See: http://www.missouladowntown.com/guide/historical.phtml (Accessed March 17, 2009).
4. Arthur James Mosby, Montana Broadcasters Association Hall of Fame. See: www.mtbroadcasters.org/hall_of_fame/arthur_mosby.html (Accessed March 17, 2009).
5. William Knowles, *Montana's Pioneer Broadcasters: Service, Adventure and Fun* (MT: University of Montana, 2009).
6. Interview with Peter Christian, KGVO Radio Missoula, February 11, 2009.
7. Paul Harvey, "North and North and North," *Flying*, February 1958, p. 22.
8. Paul Harvey, *Remember These Things*, 175.
9. William Knowles, *Montana's Pioneer Broadcasters: Service, Adventure and Fun*.
10. Thomas L.Greenough, 1851–1911, Thomas L. Greenough Ledgers, Maureen and Mike Mansfield Library, K. Ross Toole Archives, The University of Montana—Missoula.
11. Paul Harvey, ""Paul Harvey News," *The Anderson Herald*, October 1, 1968, p. 4.
12. The famous writer who wrote "rags to riches" type tales.
13. Ibid.
14. Ibid.
15. Milton Freewater, "American Style: Gas Pumping Poet," Associated Press, April 10, 1980.
16. Interview with Peter Christian, February 11, 2009.

17. Ibid.
18. Ibid.
19. Benjamin Franklin, Constitutional Convention Address on Prayer. See: http://www.americanrhetoric.com/speeches/ benfranklin.htm (Accessed March 17, 2009).
20. William Knowles, *Montana's Pioneer Broadcasters: Service, Adventure and Fun*.

CHAPTER 11: LEANING INTO THE WINDS OF WAR
1. "John Fetzer, 89, Dies, Baseball Team Owner," Associated Press, February 22, 1991; and Erik Barnouw, *A History of Broadcasting in the United States* (New York: Oxford University Press, 1966), 236; and Ewald, Dan, Kaline, Al, and John Fetzer: *On a Handshake* (Detroit, MI: Wayne State University Press, 2000), 32.
2. Ewald, Dan, Kaline, and Al, *On a Handshake*.
3. Ibid.
4. Ibid.
5. Ibid.
6. Interview with Stephen C. Trivers, Kalamazoo, MI, February 10, 2009.
7. Ibid.
8. Interview with Carl Lee, February 7, 2009.
9. Kalamazoo Phone Directory, 1943.
10. William Knowles, *Montana's Pioneer Broadcasters: Service, Adventure and Fun*.
11. "2007 Inductees for NBA Hall of Fame Announced," Nebraska Broadcasters Association, June 2007.
12. Interview with Carl Lee, February 7, 2009.
13. Ibid.
14. "Roy Rowan; Radio and TV Announcer for Lucille Ball Shows," *Los Angeles Times*, May 14, 1998, p. B14
15. Interview with Carl Lee, February 7, 2009.
16. Ibid.
17. "PRESIDENT FORMS TOP NEWS AGENCY; ELMER DAVIS CHIEF; Office of War Information Gets Control of Official Publicity but Not of Censorship OTHER SERVICES ABSORBED Director Will Decide on Policy for Matter to All World Except Latin America PRESIDENT FORMS TOP NEWS AGENCY," *The New York Times*, June 14, 1942,

p. 1; Records of the Office of War Information (OWI), The National
Archives. See: http://www.archives.gov/research/
guide-fed-records/groups/208.html (Accessed March 17, 2009).

18. Gerald Nachman, *Raised on Radio*, 401.
19. "President Forms Top News Agency; Elmer Davis Chief," *The New York Times*.
20. "Elmer Davis and the News" See: http://www.otr.com/davis.html (Accessed March 17, 2009).
21. Bernard Baruch, 1870–1965.
22. Paul Harvey, "From Here to Eternity," Address to Radio Television News Directors Association Meeting in San Antonio, TX, on September 26, 1992.
23. Ibid.
24. Ibid.
25. "Elmer Davis and the News."
26. Ibid.
27. "Who Bosses Paul Harvey? His wife 'Angel,'" Ibid.
28. Ewald, Dan, Kaline, Al, *On a Handshake*; and John Earl Fetzer: Biography, "Information on John Fetzer," http://reachinformation.com/define/John_Fetzer.aspx (Accessed March 17, 2009).
29. Ibid.
30. Interview with Carl Lee, February 7, 2009.
31. Ibid.
32. Ibid.
33. Ibid.
34. Marc Wilson, Associated Press, May 14, 1979.
35. "Gene Autry Sworn Into Army Air Corps," *This Day in History*: The History Channel. See: http://www.history.com/this-day-in-history.do?action=Article&id=3480 (Accessed March 17, 2009).
36. Susan Woolyhan Caine, "The First Lady in Radio."
37. Army Air Corps Military Personnel Record
38. Marc Wilson, Associated Press, May 14, 1979.
39. National Security Act of 1947. See: http://www.airforcehistory.hq.af.mil/PopTopics/natsecact.htm (Accessed March 17, 2009).

40. William Brashler, "Paul Harvey—The Rest of the Story," *Esquire*, November 9, 1978, p. 57.

41. Interview with Marc Wilson, March 23, 2009.

42. "A True Paul Harvey Story By a Journalist Who Knew Him," DCEXAMINER.COM, March 1, 2009. See: http://www.dcexaminer. com/opinion/blogs/TapscottsCopyDesk/A-true-Paul-Harvey-story- by-a-journalist-who-knew-him-40507942.html (Accessed March 17, 2009).

43. Army Air Corps Military Personnel Record.

44. Paul Harvey, *Remember These Things*, 167.

45. Ibid.

CHAPTER 12: HELLO, CHICAGO!

1. Dale Carnegie, *How to Win Friends and Influence People* (New York: Simon & Schuster, 1936).

2. Pseudonyms of Famous People. See: http://homepages.shu.ac.uk/~acsdry/quizes/pseudonym.htm (Accessed March 18, 2009).

3. Paul Harvey, "Freedom Has Four Wheels," *The Reporter*, September 13, 1994, p. 4.

4. Susan Woolyhan Caine, "The First Lady of Radio."

5. Lori Rotenberk, "Paul Harvey's Guardian Angel," *Chicago Sun-Times*, December 1, 1997, p. 31.

6. "Paul Harvey Sr.", *Daily Herald*, November 5, 1977, p. 47.

7. Steve Johnson, "The Golden Age of Radio," *Chicago Tribune*. See: http://www.latimes.com/news/nationworld/ world/mideastemail/chi-chicagodays-radio-story,0,387912.story (Accessed March 18, 2009).

8. Nina Burleigh Interview with Paul Harvey, "It Has Been a 'Good Day' in Chicago for 50 years," *Chicago Tribune*, 19 January 1992, p. C10.

9. Ibid.

10. Lori Rotenberk, "Paul Harvey's Guardian Angel."

11. "Paul Harvey Sr.," *Daily Herald*.

12. Ibid.

13. Paul Harvey, "Paul Harvey News," *The Pocono Record*, April 7, 1976, p. 27.

14. "Paul Harvey Sr.," *Daily Herald*.

15. American Broadcasting Company, The Digital Deli Online. See: http://www.digitaldeliftp.com/LookAround/la_networkspot_abc.htm (Accessed March 18, 2009).
16. Ibid.
17. Rick Kogan, "Good Days For Paul Harvey."
18. Earl L. Douglass, "Strength for the Day," *The Post-Standard*, February 7, 1951, p. 6.
19. Paul Harvey, "The International Language," *Aiken Standard*, September 30, 1986, p. 4.
20. Review of Chicago Radio Logs, June–September 1944.
21. "Paul Harvey Sr.," *Daily Herald*.
22. Paul Harvey Promotional Speaking Brochure, Redpath Lecture Series. See: http://sdrc.lib.uiowa.edu/traveling-culture/chau1/pdf/harvey/4/brochure.pdf (Accessed March 18, 2009).
23. Radio Log, Wisconsin State Journal, September 24, 1945, p. 9.
24. Paul Harvey, "Tulsa Once Known Isn't There," *Kerrville Times*, April 5, 1994, p. 4.
25. Adam C. Buckman, "The Rags-to-Riches Paul Harvey Story," *Electronic Media*, September 19, 1988, p. 1.
26. Joe Howard, "Paul Harvey: A Legend Looks Back," *Radio Ink Magazine*, November 2, 2006.
27. Paul Harvey, *Remember These Things*, 57.
28. Paul Harvey, "From Here to Eternity."
29. Interview with John Gambling, November 18, 2008.
30. "Mike Thomas, "Paul Harvey," Salon.com, September 25, 2001 and Interview with Carl Lee, Ibid."
31. "A. McFadden, Cotton Man, Killed by Snow Avalanche in Colorado; VICTIM OF AVALANCHE IN COLORADO," *The New York Times*, February 16, 1948.
32. Aspen Skiing Company. See: http://www.fundinguniverse.com/company-histories/Aspen-Skiing-Company-Company-History.html (Accessed March 18, 2009).
33. "Pacific Northwest Lashed with Storm," *The New York Times*, February 16, 1948, p. 1.
34. "3 Bind Maid, Steal $39,000 in Jewels," *The New York Times*, February 16, 1948, p. 40.
35. Paul Harvey, *Remember These Things*, 168.
36. Ibid.
37. Ibid.

38. Ibid., 166.
39. Paul Harvey, *Autumn of Liberty*, 183.

CHAPTER 13: FROM SEA TO SHINING SEA

1. "Old Joe Would be Proud," Forbes, July 23, 1979, p. 59.
2. Merchandise Mart Building Details, Archiplanet. See: http://www.archiplanet.org/wiki/Merchandise_Mart,_Chicago,_Illin ois (Accessed March 18, 2009); and Merchandise Mart Properties, "History/About MMPI," See: http://www.mmart.com/officeretail/ about.html (Accessed March 18, 2009).
3. Rich Samuel, "NBC Expands in Chicago," *Broadcasting in Chicago*, 1921–1989. See: http://www.richsamuels.com/nbcmm/x5.html (Accessed March 18, 2009).
4. Ibid.
5. Kermitt Slobb, "The Nineteenth Floor," *Broadcasting in Chicago*, 1921–1989. See: http://www.richsamuels.com/nbcmm/ slobb/floor.html (Accessed March 18, 2009).
6. "It Has Been a 'Good Day' in Chicago for 50 Years," *Chicago Tribune*, January 19, 1992, p. C10.
7. Fred W.S. Craig, British Electoral Facts: 1832–1987 (Aldershot, Hants., England : Parliamentary Research Services, Dartmouth ; Brookfield, Vt., USA : Gower, 1989).
8. Jack Beary, "Paul Harvey: Superman of the Airwaves: 'The Most Powerful Newsman since Clark Kent,'" *United Press International*, September 30, 1980.
9. Paul Harvey, *Remember These Things*. Personal notes from meeting/interview with Paul Harvey, June 7, 2000.
10. Paul Harvey, Paul Harvey News, *Jefferson City Post-Tribune*, December 27, 1968, p. 4.
11. Paul Harvey, Paul Harvey News, *The Brazosport Facts*, November 7, 1956, p. 1. Fabian policy is based upon the philosophy of Fabius Maximus, who attempted to avoid open conflict with Hannibal by marching, harassing, and otherwise delaying decisions. See: http://www. thefreedictionary.com/Fabian 1 policy (Accessed March 18, 2009).
12. Paul Harvey, *Remember These Things*, 11.
13. Ibid., 9.
14. Stephen E. Ambrose, *Ike's Spies* (New York: Doubleday, 1981).

15. Don S. Kirschner, *Cold War Exile: The Unclosed Case of Maurice Halperin*. (MO: University of Missouri Press, 1995); and Victor S. Navasky, *Naming Names* (New York: Hill and Wang, 2003).

16. Robert Montgomery Biography. See: http://www.earlofhollywood. com/RMbio.html (Accessed March 18, 2009); Frank Manchel, *Film Study* (New York: Fairleigh Dickinson University Press, 1990).

17. Radio News, Associated Press, June 8, 1950.

18. Robert Montgomery Biography.

19. "Radio and Television; Sammy Kaye's 'So You Want to Lead a Band' Going on N.B.C. Video This Sunday," *The New York Times*, June 8, 1950, p. 43.

20. Barbara Gamarekian, "Washington Talk: The Media; TV Coaches: Success Is Appearing to Be in Charge," *The New York Times*, August 25, 1988, p. A22.

21. Paul Harvey, "A Happy Visit to the Harvey Home," *The Lima News*, December 26, 1956, p. 20.

22. Ibid.

23. Ibid.

24. Ibid.

25. Paul Harvey, *Autumn of Liberty*, 49.

26. "Who Bosses Paul Harvey? His Wife 'Angel.'"

27. Paul Harvey, *Remember These Things*.

28. Nina Burleigh, "It Has Been a 'Good Day' in Chicago for 50 Years," *Chicago Tribune*, p. C10.

CHAPTER 14: BRITCHES ON BARBED WIRE

1. Interview with Art Hellyer, Chicago Radio Veteran, February 14, 2009.

2. "Cardinals Upset Bears, 20 to 10 In Fourth-Period Drive at Chicago," *The New York Times*, December 4, 1950, p. 42.

3. Paul Harvey, *Remember These Things*, 87.

4. Ibid., 91.

5. Ibid.

6. "Paul Harvey News," Transcript of December 3, 1950 Broadcast.

7. Ibid.

8. Ibid.

9. Comments based upon conversations with friends of Paul Harvey at the time of his on-air debut.

10. "Paul Harvey News", Transcript of December 3, 1950 Broadcast.
11. Ann Oldenburg, "This is Paul Harvey," *USA Today*, May 16, 1994, p.1D.
12. Paul Harvey, "Inventions and Necessity," *The Daily Times,* March 5, 1968, p. 29.
13. Mark Lawrence Ragan, "Profile, Paul Harvey: Stand By for … This Quirky Newsman," *Insight*, August 5, 1991.
14. Art Hellyer, *The Hellyer Say* (Lulu Publishing, 2008), 136.
15. Ibid., 244.
16. Speaker Brochure, Redpath Bureau. See: http://sdrc.lib.uiowa.edu/ traveling-culture/chau1/pdf/harvey/4/brochure.pdf (Accessed March 19, 2009).
17. Patrick Stout, "Around Town: Two to Remember," *The Macomb Journal*, March 2, 2009.
18. Paul Harvey, "Is Joe DiMaggio Finished?" *Man's World*, February 1951.
19. "Paul Harvey Column Will Start in Winona Daily News on Monday," *Winona Daily News*, December 29, 1954, p. 3.
20. Benjamin Rush, 1745–1813.
21. Holl, Jack, Richard, G. Hewlett, Harris, Ruth R. Hewlett, *Argonne National Laboratory, 1946-96* (IL: University of Illinois Press, 1997).
22. "Argonne Highlights," Argonne National Laboratory. See: http://www.anl.gov/Science_and_Technology/History/forties.html (Accessed March 19, 2009).
23. June Markey, "Atom Lab an 'Idea Factory,'" *Blue-Island Sun-Standard*, August 30, 1951, p. 18; "RADIO REPORTER DETAINED; Paul Harvey, Caught in Grounds of Laboratory, Released," *The New York Times*, February 7, 1951, p. 30; and "Suspect is on Trial in Atomic Prowling," *The New York Times*, March 20, 1951, p. 3.
24. Ibid.
25. "Radio Reporter Detained," *The New York Times*.
26. "Radio Commentator Seized as 'Intruder' by Atom Guard," *The Rhinelander Daily News*, February 7, 1951, p. 1.
27. "Suspect is on Trial in Atomic Prowling," 3.
28. "COMMENTATOR CLEARED; Grand Jury Votes Not to Indict for Atom Laboratory Entry," *The New York Times*, April 5, 1951, p. 12.
29. John M. McGuire, "The Rest of Their Story," *St. Louis Post-Dispatch*, May 10, 1998, p. C1.
30. F. N. Alessio, "Broadcaster Not Slowing Down at 70," Associated Press, September 22, 1988.

CHAPTER 15: BIRTH OF A SALESMAN

1. Jeffrey Zaslow, "The Sunny Side is Always Up for Paul Harvey," *Chicago Sun-Times*, May 15, 1994, p. 3.
2. Ibid.
3. Will Rogers, 1879–1935.
4. Ross Kaminsky, "Paul Harvey, Radio Legend, Dies at 90," *Human Events Online*, March 1, 2009.
5. Mike Thomas, "Paul Harvey," Salon.com, September 25, 2001.
6. Dale Carnegie, *How to Win Friends and Influence People*.
7. Ibid.
8. Don M. Green, "Lasting Advice from 'Mr. Positive Mental Attitude' W. Clement Stone," Financial Services Advisor, January/February 2003.
9. Napoleon Hill, *The Law of Success* (New York: Penguin, 2008); and Napoleon Hill, *Think and Grow Rich* (CA: Wilshire Book Company, 1966).
10. "Clement Stone," *The Times* of London, September 12, 2002, 38.
11. Paul Harvey, "W. Clement Stone Led a Social Revolution," *Seguin Gazette*, May 13, 1982, p. 11.
12. Larry King, "On the Air With Paul Harvey," *Larry King Live*, CNN, August 16, 1991.
13. Ibid.
14. Ibid.
15. Bankers Life and Casualty Company History. See: http://www.bankers.com/web/aboutus-timeline.aspx (Accessed March 19, 2009).
16. "Paul Harvey Holds Longest Continuing Sponsorship in Broadcast History; Sponsors Know He's the Voice of America," PR Newswire, January 8, 2004. See: http://goliath.ecnext.com/coms2/gi_0199-1262872/Paul-Harvey-Holds-Longest-Continuing.html (Accessed March 19, 2009).
17. Tom Sabulis, "Paul Harvey: One of the Last of a Dying Breed," *Syracuse Herald Journal*, December 2, 1990, p. 18.
18. Anne Keegan, "Harvey is Biggest 1-Man News Network in World," *Des Moines Register*, October 20, 1974.
19. Mark Lawrence Ragan, "Profile, Paul Harvey: Stand By for … This Quirky Newsman."

20. Philip Gulley, "The Day I Met Paul Harvey," *Heartlight Magazine*. See: http://www.heartlight.org/home/toh_991124_paulharvey.html (Accessed March 19, 2009).

21. Interview with Win Schuler, February 16, 2009.

22. Robert A. Peterson, Michael P. Cannito, and Steven P. Brown, "An Exploratory Investigation of Voice Characteristics and Selling Effectiveness," *Journal of Personal Selling & Sales Management*, Winter 1995, pp. 1–15.

23. Ibid.

24. Interview with John McConnell, November 20, 2008.

25. Interview with Tom Langmyer, January 2009.

26. ABC Sales Promotional Materials, "The Voice of America Belongs to … Paul Harvey!" Paul Harvey, *News and Comment*, "The Rest of the Story," 2000.

27. Ibid.

28. Ibid.

29. Citadel Broadcasting Corporation Reports 2008 Third Quarter Operating Results, November 6, 2008; Q3 2008 Citadel Broadcasting Corporation Earnings Conference Call, November 6, 2008; Citadel Broadcasting Corporation Reports 2008 Second Quarter Operating Results, August 7, 2008; Q2 2008 Citadel Broadcasting Corporation Earnings Conference Call, August 7, 2008.

30. Council on American-Islamic Relations Statement, December 3, 2003.

31. Ron Strom, "GE Returns to Paul Harvey Show," *World Net Daily*, December 29, 2003. See: http://www.worldnetdaily.com/news/article.asp?ARTICLE_ID=36364 (Accessed March 20, 2009).

32. Craig Harris, "FTC Fines Hi-Health $450,000 Over Ads," *The Arizona Republic*, August 24, 2005.

33. Kimberly S. Johnson, "Colorado AG, General Steel Settle Lawsuit," *Denver Post*, March 14, 2007, p. C1.

34. Paul Harvey, "A Message of Freedom with Responsibility."

35. Thomas Jefferson, 1743–1826.

36. Charles Revson, 1906–1975.

37. Interview with Al Peterson, December 10, 2008.

CHAPTER 16: DRIVE IT OR PARK IT

1. "Not New Frontier," *Newsweek*, December 24, 1962, p. 42.
2. Ibid.
3. Oklahoma Historical Society's Encyclopedia of Oklahoma History and Culture, "Paul Harvey, 1918-2009." See: http://digital.library.okstate.edu/encyclopedia/entries/H/HA044.html (Accessed March 20, 2009).
4. Biographical Sketch, prepared by the "Paul Harvey News" Office, 1970.
5. Paul Harvey, *The Testing Time* (Waco, Texas, Word Records, Inc.)
6. Paul Harvey, *The Uncommon Man* (Waco, Texas, Word Records, Inc.)
7. Biographical Sketch, "Paul Harvey News" Office, 1970.
8. Jon Anderson, "Standing By After 50-Years, Paul Harvey Still Comes in Loud and Clear," *Chicago Tribune*, September 15, 1998, p. C1.
9. Paul Harvey, *News and Comment* Broadcast of May 1, 1970.
10. Paul Harvey, "So the Communists Resorted to Torture," *The Lima News*, July 16, 1962, p. 14.
11. Paul Harvey, "The Crisis Atmosphere," *The Kokomo Morning Times*, August 13, 1964, p. 4.
12. Paul Harvey, "Is Vietnam Worth One American Life?" *The Kokomo Morning Times*, September 3, 1964, p. 4.
13. Ibid.
14. Paul Harvey, "The Dead End War," *Oshkosh Daily Northwestern*, November 21, 1964, p. 27.
15. Paul Harvey, "Man's Extremity," *The News Tribune*, February 23, 1965.
16. Ibid.
17. Transcript of Speech in Dayton, Ohio, April 18, 1969.
18. Paul Harvey, "'Best Dressed' Men Have Tribulations," *The Ada Evening News*, April 1, 1965, p. 16.
19. Seth S. King, "Paul Harvey, 'Voice of the Silent Majority,' Opposes Nixon's Cambodia Move," *The New York Times*, June 1, 1970, p. 25.
20. Paul Harvey, "There is No Humane War," *San Mateo Times*, September 19, 1966, p. 22.
21. Ibid.

22. Paul Harvey, "Learning from the Vietnam War," *Jefferson-City Post Tribune*, May 23, 1968, p. 4.
23. George Washington, "America and the World," Farewell Address, 1796.
24. Paul Harvey, *The Testing Time*.
25. Paul Harvey, Speech In Dayton, Ohio, April 18, 1969.
26. Ibid.
27. Wayne S. Cole, *America First: The Battle against Intervention, 1940-41* (Madison: University of Wisconsin Press, 1953).
28. F. N. D'alessio, "Broadcaster Not Slowing Down at 70," Associated Press, September 21, 1988.
29. Paul Harvey, "Does TV Worsen Street Rioting?" *The Lima News*, August 4, 1965, p. 21.
30. Ibid.
31. Paul Harvey, "Jungle Drums Prod Primate Passions," *Anderson Herald*, April 16, 1968, p. 4.
32. Paul Harvey, "Tele-Funeral a Study in Morbidity," *The Daily Times*, June 16, 1968, p. 34.
33. Megan Rosenfeld and Robert Wilson, "Success UNLIMITED; Selling It to the Masses—With a Dose Of Profits, Patriotism and Religion Thrown In," *The Washington Post*, June 17, 1978, p. B1.
34. Ibid.
35. Ibid.
36. Ibid.
37. President Richard M. Nixon, Address to the Nation on the Situation in Southeast Asia, April 30, 1970.
38. Ibid.
39. Paul Harvey, *News and Comment*, May 1, 1970.
40. Seth S. King, "Paul Harvey, 'Voice of the Silent Majority,' Opposes Nixon's Cambodia Move," *The New York Times*, June 1, 1970, p. 1.
41. Paul Harvey, Interview with Larry King, CNN *Larry King Live!* September 22, 2003.

CHAPTER 17: THE REST OF THE STORY

1. George Eliot, 1819–1890.
2. Rick Kogan, "Good days for Paul Harvey," *Chicago Tribune*.
3. Ibid.

4. Paul Harvey, "Interview with Paul Harvey," CNN's *Larry King Live!* June 22, 2003.
5. Megan Rosenfeld and Robert Wilson, "Success UNLIMITED; Selling It to the Masses—With a Dose Of Profits, Patriotism and Religion Thrown In."
6. Jim Daly, personal correspondence with Paul Harvey.
7. Marc Fisher, "Still Going," *American Journalism Review*, October 1998, 31.
8. A recording of Paul Harvey's daily routine was compiled by consulting with various written accounts through the years in addition to the author's interview with the commentator in June 2000.
9. Paul Harvey, "On the Air with Paul Harvey," CNN's *Larry King Live!* August 16, 1991.
10. Paul Harvey, *Paul Harvey's The Rest of the Story* (New York: Doubleday, 1977).
11. Johanna Steinmetz, "Paul Harvey—Short on Objectivity—Big with Listeners," *The New York Times*, June 6, 1976, p. 91.
12. "Young Paul is Not Quite Ready to Follow in His Father's Footsteps," *Daily Herald*, November 5, 1977, p. 46.
13. Ibid.
14. Ibid.
15. Ibid.
16. "Paul Aurandt at 19th Century Club," *News Journal*, November 12, 1975, p. 1.
17. "Young Paul is Not Quite Ready to Follow in His Father's Footsteps," *Daily Herald*.
18. Ibid.
19. Jean Guarino, "Showcase House Tells Family Story," *News Journal*, September 14, 1977.
20. Kathy O'Malley & Hanke Gratteau, *Chicago Tribune*, February 21, 1990, p. C20; Kathy O'Malley and Hanke Gratteau, *Chicago Tribune*, March 9, 1989, p. C26; Kathy O'Malley and Hanke Gratteau, Chicago Tribune, October 8, 1989, p. C5; Kathy O'Malley and Hanke Gratteau, *Chicago Tribune*, October 17, 1989, p. C22; and Bill Grady, Merrill Goozner and John O'Brien, "Prosecuters Here Not Into Numbers," *Chicago Tribune*, October 31, 1989, p. C3.
21. Kathy O'Malley & Hanke Gratteau, *Chicago Tribune*, February 21, 1990, p. C20;

22. Adrian McCoy, *Pittsburgh Post-Gazette*, May 9, 2001, p. E5.
23. Ken Tucker, "The Story Behind 'The Rest of the Story,'" *Billboard Radio Monitor*, May 26, 2006.
24. Ibid.
25. Ibid.
26. Ibid.
27. Paul Harvey, "Interview with Paul Harvey," CNN's *Larry King Live!* June 22, 2003.
28. "Brokaw Keynotes RTNDA's Murrow Awards," *Broadcasting and Cable*, October 4, 2004, p. 16.
29. Ken Tucker, "The Story Behind 'The Rest of the Story.'"
30. Ibid.
31. Ibid.
32. Ibid.
33. Ibid.

CHAPTER 18: GIVE ME SOME OF THAT OLD TIME RELIGION

1. Marc Fisher, "Still Going," *American Journalism Review*, October 1998, p. 31.
2. Paul Harvey, "Interview with Larry King," CNN's *Larry King Live!* June 22, 2003.
3. Paul Harvey, "America Needs Spiritual Revival," *Jefferson City-Post Tribune*, June 13, 1968, p. 4.
4. Paul Harvey, *Remember These Things*, 18
5. Paul Harvey, *Autumn of Liberty*, 188.
6. Ibid., 191.
7. Ibid., 192.
8. Billy Graham, *Just as I Am* (CA: Harper San Francisco, 1997).
9. Ibid.
10. "Ruth Graham was Husband's Anchor, But Shined on Her Own," *The Asheville Citizen-Times*, June 15, 2007, p. B4.
11. Paul Harvey, 1918–2009; "About the Game," Golfsilver.com, see: http://www.golfsilver.com/CRStage.cfm?Page=Ecom%20Shop&Active=Public&UID=0U812&Category=Golf%20Swing%20software&SubPass=False (Accessed March 22, 2009).
12. David Briggs, "Church Has Stiff Sunday Competition: The Grass is Greener on the Fairways," *Constitution Tribune*, May 12, 1994, p. 2.

13. Bill Williams, "Paul Harvey Like to 'Play Down the Middle,'" *Gastonia Gazette*, September 27, 1967, p. 25.
14. Ibid.
15. Ibid.
16. Ibid.
17. Ibid.
18. Kathleen Carroll, Associated Press, September 16, 1979.
19. Paul Harvey, "Kidnapping Ends with Joys and Tears," *Aiken Standard*, August 28, 1990, p. 4.
20. Ansel Oliver, "American Radio Legend Harvey's Death Ends Unique Era of Radio News," Adventist News Network, March 5, 2009.
21. George E. Vandeman, *Planet in Rebellion* (Nashville: Southern Pub Association, 1960).
22. Paul Harvey, *News and Comment*, November 7, 2000.
23. Ibid.
24. Paul Harvey, Speech in Dayton, Ohio, April 18, 1969.
25. Paul Harvey, "The Uncommon Man."
26. Clive Staples Lewis, *The Screwtape Letters* (London, 1944).
27. Paul Harvey, *The Testing Time*.
28. Ibid.
29. Seth King, "Paul Harvey, 'Voice of the Silent Majority,' Opposes Nixon's Cambodia Move," *The New York Times*, June 1, 1970.
30. Paul Harvey, "Paul Harvey Finds More Satisfaction in Life After Baptism," *Tulsa Daily World*, March 29, 1973, p. E6.
31. Ibid.
32. Ibid.
33. Ibid.
34. John 3:16 (King James Version).
35. Paul Harvey, "Paul Harvey Finds More Satisfaction in Life After Baptism," *Tulsa Daily World*.
36. Paul Harvey, "Interview with Paul Harvey," CNN's *Larry King Live!* September 22, 2003.
37. Paul Harvey, "Paul Harvey Finds More Satisfaction in Life After Baptism," *Tulsa Daily World*.
38. Ibid.
39. Ibid.

40. Paul Harvey, "Interview with Paul Harvey," CNN's *Larry King Live!* September 22, 2003.

41. Paul Harvey, *News and Comment*, Broadcast, April 9, 2004.

42. Ibid.

43. Paul Harvey, "The Man and the Birds," Our Lives, Our Fortunes, Our Sacred Honor (Waco, TX, Word Records, 1975).

44. Paul Harvey, "Interview with Paul Harvey," CNN's *Larry King Live!* September 22, 2003.

45. Paul Harvey, "Paul Harvey Finds More Satisfaction in Life After Baptism," *Tulsa Daily World.*

46. Paul Harvey, *News and Comment*, Broadcast, December 4, 2003.

47. "Muslims Demand Apology From Paul Harvey," Worldnet-daily.com, December 6, 2003. See: http://www.wnd.com/news/article.asp?ARTICLE_ID=35982 (Accessed March 22, 2009).

48. Doug Limerick as quoted on Paul Harvey, *News and Comment* Broadcast, December 9, 2003.

CHAPTER 19: SPEECHLESS

1. Julia Boorstin, "The Rest of the Story from Paul Harvey," *Fortune*, December 18, 2000, p. 52.

2. "New Deal Could Earn Harvey $100 Million," *Chicago Sun-Times*, November 2, 2000, p. 49.

3. Rick Kogan, "Good Days for Paul Harvey."

4. Ibid.

5. Ibid.

6. Julia Boorstin, "The Rest of the Story from Paul Harvey."

7. "New Deal Could Earn Harvey $100 Million."

8. Paul Harvey, "Interview with Paul Harvey," CNN's *Larry King Live!* September 22, 2003.

9. Jay Grelen, "Sweet Tea The Man to Replace Mr. Dan," *Arkansas Democrat-Gazette*, March 1, 2005.

10. Various Mentions on Paul Harvey, *News and Comment* Programs.

11. Pernell Watson, "Paul Harvey's Famous Voice Needs a Rest," *Daily Press*, July 15, 2001, p. H8.

12. Bob Betcher, "Quality All Around as A&E Delivered the Goods on 'Fourth!'" *The Stuart News/Port St. Lucie News*, July 6, 2001, p. C8.

13. Robert Feder, "Harvey to Have Surgery on Weakened Vocal Cord," *Chicago Sun-Times*, July 11, 2001, 65.

14. Bob Greene, "Commentary: Paul Harvey, Behind the Voice,"
    CNN.com, March 2, 2009. See:
    http://www.cnn.com/2009/SHOWBIZ/03/02/greene.harvey/
    (Accessed March 22, 2009).
15. Paul Harvey, "Interview with Paul Harvey," CNN's *Larry King Live!*
    September 22, 2003.
16. Bastian Voice Institute, "Medialization laryngoplasty," Glossary.
    See: http://www.bastianvoice.com/m.htm (Accessed March 22,
    2009).
17. Paul Harvey, "Interview with Paul Harvey, CNN's *Larry King Live!*
    September 22, 2003.
18. Jim Paul, "Paul Harvey Returns to Airwaves After Three-Month
    Loss of Voice," Associated Press, August 20, 2001.
19. Ibid.
20. Ibid.
21. Interview with Dr. Robert W. Bastian, March 20, 2009.
22. Paul Harvey, "A Message of Freedom with Responsibility."
23. Robert Feder, "New Owner Fox Putting Its Mark on Channel 50,"
    Chicago Sun-Times, October 3, 2002.
24. Rudolph Unger, "For Paul Harvey, It Truly Is A Good Day!"
    Chicago Tribune, November 16, 1988, p. C8.
25. Ibid.
26. First Friday Club of Chicago, October 4, 2002. Julia Boorstin, "The
    Rest of the Story from Paul Harvey."
27. "Remarks on Presenting the Presidential Medal of Freedom," Pub-
    lic Papers of the Presidents, November 14, 2005.
28. Edward Walsh, "This Is Paul Harvey . . .; The Mellow Voice of
    Mom, God, Apple Pie and Radio," *The Washington Post*, July 7,
    1995, p. F1.
29. Paul Harvey, *News and Comment*, Broadcast, November 11, 2005.
30. Johanna Steinmetz, "Paul Harvey—Short on Objectivity, Big With
    Listeners," *The New York Times*, June 6, 1976, p. 91.
31. Ibid.
32. Ibid.
33. Paul Harvey, "A Message of Freedom with Responsibility."
34. Ibid.
35. Robert P. Laurence, "Paul Harvey: Your Basic American With a
    Twist," *The San Diego Union-Tribune*, April 27, 1985, p. D19.
36. Ibid.

37. Domestic News, United Press International, April 30, 1982.

38. Ibid.

39. Ibid.

40. Phyllis Schlafly, "Equal Rights Redux: The ERA: Still a Bad Idea," *Los Angeles Times*, April 8, 2007, p. M3.

41. Mike Feinsilber, "Phyllis Schlafly Hailed as Heroine in Victory Against ERA," Associated Press, July 1, 1982.

42. Ibid.

43. Remarks of President George W. Bush at the Presidential Medal of Freedom Ceremony, The White House, November 14, 2005.

44. Emily Dickenson, "Crumbling Is Not an Instant's Act," available at http://www.americanpoems.com/poets/emilydickinson/10949.

CHAPTER 20: AN ANGEL DEPARTS

1. Monifa Thomas, "Producer for Radio Legend Husband Dies; Hall of Fame Inductee Credited with Paul Harvey's Success, Created Prototype for Today's Talk Shows," *Chicago Tribune*, May 4, 2008, p. A5.

2. Ibid.

3. "Paul Harvey News" and Comment Broadcast, May 17, 2007.

4. "Remembering Angel Harvey," ABC Radio Network Statement. See: http://abcradionetworks.com/Article.asp?id=685686 (Accessed March 22, 2009).

5. "A Service of Witness to the Resurrection in the Celebration of the Life of Evelyn Cooper Harvey," The Fourth Presbyterian Church of Chicago, May 6, 2008; Brother James' Air, J. L. Macbeth Bain, 1915.

6. "All Creatures of Our God and King," Words by Francis of Assisi, circa 1225 (Cantico di fratre sole, Song of Brother Sun). He wrote this hymn shortly before his death, but it was not published for almost 400 years. Translated to English by William H. Draper for a children's Whitsuntide festival in Leeds, England; first appeared in the *Public School Hymn Book*, 1919.

7. "Fourth Presbyterian Church Architecture," Interior Details. See: http://www.fourthchurch.org/interior.html (Accessed March 22, 2009).

8. "In the Sweet By and By," words by Sanford F. Bennett, 1868.

9. "I'll See You Again," words by Noel Coward, 1929.

10. "Great is Thy Faithfulness," words by Thomas O. Chisholm, 1923. The hymn first appeared in *Songs of Salvation and Service*, 1923,

compiled by William M. Runyan. It is the unofficial "school hymn" of Moody Bible Institute in Chicago, with which Runyan was associated for a number of years.

11. Paul Harvey Aurandt Jr., "A Service of Witness to the Resurrection in the Celebration of the Life of Evelyn Cooper Harvey," The Fourth Presbyterian Church of Chicago, May 6, 2008.

12. Ibid.

13. Ibid.

14. Ibid.

15. Ibid.

16. Ibid.

17. Ibid.

18. Reverend Charles White, "A Service of Witness to the Resurrection in the Celebration of the Life of Evelyn Cooper Harvey," The Fourth Presbyterian Church of Chicago, May 6, 2008.

19. "Wife of Broadcaster, Dies," Associated Press, May 3, 2008.

20. Ibid.

21. Al Peterson's Aircheck, May 6, 2008.

22. Interview with Al Peterson, December 10, 2009.

23. Interview with Tom Langmyer, January 2009.

24. Ibid.

25. Interview with John McConnell, November 19, 2009.

26. Ibid.

27. M. F., "A Lifetime on the Radio," *American Journalism Review*, October 1998, p. 35.

28. Dan Jedlicka, "The Auto Scene Is His, Too; Paul Harvey On Cars Old and New," *Chicago Sun-Times*, October 23, 1995, p. 3.

29. Ibid.

30. William Shakespeare, *Hamlet*, 1603.

31. Robert Feder, "In the Dark; Paul Harvey's Radio Affiliates Still Await the Rest of His Story," *Chicago Sun-Times*, July17, 2008, 41; See: www.radio-info.com.

32. Robert Feder, "No Cigar; Dahl, Stern Again Fall Short in Radio Hall of Fame Voting," *Chicago Sun-Times*, July 18, 2008, p. 42.

CHAPTER 21: AMERICAN ORIGINAL

1. Paul Harvey Aurandt, "A Service of Witness to the Resurrection in the Celebration of the Life of Paul Harvey," The Fourth Presbyterian Church of Chicago, March 7, 2009.

2. Ibid.
3. Ibid.
4. Ibid.
5. Dick Stouffer, "On the Scene," *American Model Airplane*, May 1972.
6. Paul Harvey, *News and Comment*, ABC Radio Network, July 17, 2008.
7. Paul Harvey, "The Banana and I—or We," *Aiken Standard*, October 14, 1983, p. 13.
8. Paul Harvey, "Books," *The Titusville Herald*, May 19, 1988, p. 4.
9. "Farewell, Paul Harvey," WGN Tribute, February 28, 2009. See: http://www.wgnradio.com/index.php?option=com_content&task=blogcategory&id=27&Itemid=125 (Accessed March 13, 2009).
10. John M. Buchanan, "A Service of Witness to the Resurrection in the Celebration of the Life of Paul Harvey," The Fourth Presbyterian Church of Chicago, March 7, 2009.
11. Artemis Cooper, ed., *The Letters of Evelyn Waugh and Diana Cooper* (New York: Ticknor and Fields, 1992).
12. Adam C. Buckman, "The Rags-to-Riches Paul Harvey Story," Electronic Media, September 19, 1988, p. 1.
13. "A Service of Witness to the Resurrection in the Celebration of the Life of Paul Harvey," The Fourth Presbyterian Church of Chicago, March 7, 2009.
14. John Wooden, "On Growing Old." Unpublished. Reprinted with permission.
15. Paul Harvey Aurandt, "A Service of Witness to the Resurrection in the Celebration of the Life of Paul Harvey," The Fourth Presbyterian Church of Chicago, March 7, 2009.
16. Ibid.
17. Ibid.
18. Paul Harvey, *News and Comment*, ABC Radio Network, February 9, 2000.
19. Paul Harvey Aurandt, "A Service of Witness to the Resurrection in the Celebration of the Life of Paul Harvey," The Fourth Presbyterian Church of Chicago, March 7, 2009.
20. Paul Harvey, *Autumn of Liberty*, 191–92.
21. Memoirs of Lee. Eulogy on Washington, Deember 26, 1799.
22. Ibid.

Index